D0542559

THE HISTORY OF MYDDLE

The History of Myddle

by RICHARD GOUGH

CALIBAN BOOKS

This edition first published 1979
by Caliban Books
13 The Dock, Firle, Sussex BN8 6NY

ISBN 0 904573 14 1

Typesetting by
Eager Typesetting Company, 22a Westbourne Place, Hove, East Sussex

Printed in Great Britain by
Newhaven Press, 44 Meeching Road, Newhaven, East Sussex

Richard Gough was a small freeholder living within the hamlet of Newton-on-the-Hill in the parish of Myddle in 1700 when he started writing this book. He was a sixty-six-year-old widower, with four children, two of whom (daughters) were living with him. Most of the book was written in 1701, but additional material was added piecemeal until 1706. Gough died in 1723.

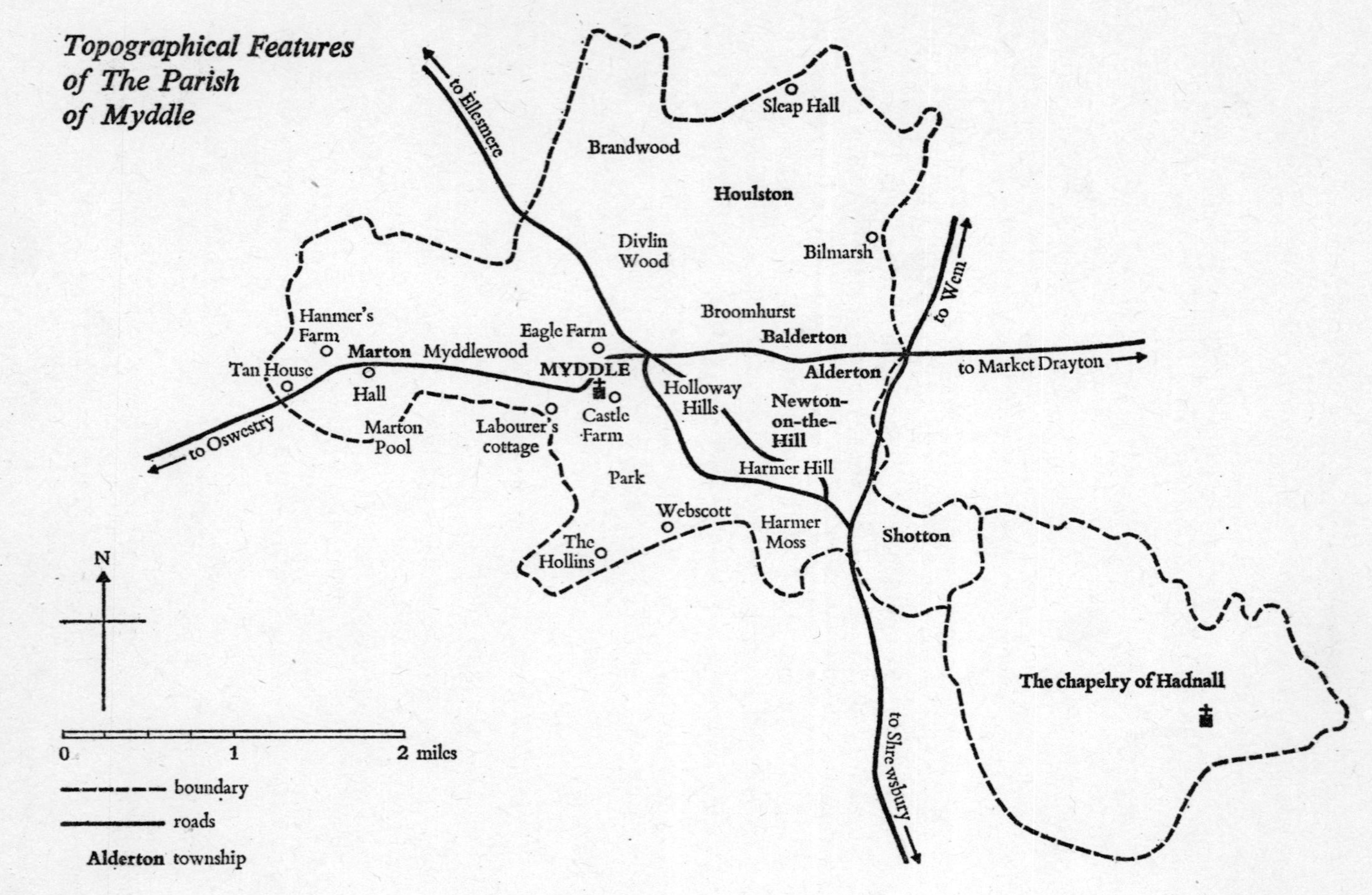

Topographical Features
of The Parish
of Myddle
to Ellesmere
Sleap Hall
Brandwood
Houlston
Divlin
Wood
Bilmarsh
to Wem
Broomhurst
Balderton
Hanmer's
Farm
Marton
Myddlewood
Eagle Farm
MYDDLE
Tan House
Hall
Alderton
to Market Drayton
Holloway
Hills
Newton-
on-the-
Hill
to Oswestry
Marton
Pool
Labourer's
cottage
Castle
Farm
Harmer Hill
Park
Webscott
Harmer
Moss
Shotton
The
Hollins
N
The chapelry of Hadnall
0
1
2 miles
to Shrewsbury
boundary
roads
Alderton township

CONTENTS

PREFACE

Professor Hoskins has written in the facsimile original edition of *The Antiquities and Memoirs of Myddle:*

> "Gough's *History of Myddle* . . . sounds like the narrowest kind of parish-pump history one could possibly imagine, of interest only to devoted local historians in Shropshire. It is in fact a unique book. It gives us a picture of seventeenth-century England in all its wonderful and varied detail such as no other book that I know even remotely approaches. If History is, as has once been said, the men and women of the past talking and we overhearing their conversations, then Gough's history of his native parish, written between the years 1700 and 1706, is History . . . A whole countryside, an entire society, comes alive in our minds, in a way that no historian, however skilled, can possibly evoke . . . this remarkable book is . . . one of the most entertaining books ever written in English, unique in our literature."[1]

Given the outstanding quality of Gough's work, why is the book not more widely known amongst historians and the general public? The answer lies probably in the nature of the original edition — not only is some of its content antiquarian in nature, but so is much of its style and lay-out. The aim of the present edition is to eliminate material of purely antiquarian interest, and to re-arrange presentation and style of the original — in particular spelling, which has been modernised throughout — so as to make it much more accessible to the modern reader. I have retained all biographical material, as it is the biographies which give the book its central fascination. No alterations have been made to Gough's language, for that is a part of the delight of his writing. Readers who wish to know more about the original are fortunate in having it readily available in the facsimile edition.

In my introduction I have sought to bring out the quality of Gough's writing — particularly the stories and anecdotes about his contemporaries — by quoting extensively from the text. I have discussed the book from the point of view of the social historian and historical sociologist, and have compiled a detailed subject index, so that anyone who wishes to know more about marriage, the family, the treatment of children, disease, violence, drunkenness, religion, love and a host of other topics in the seventeenth century, can turn to the index at the back of the book. But its main importance is Gough's unique history of a seventeenth century village community, bringing to life his contemporaries in such a vivid and entertaining fashion.

INTRODUCTION

Myddle is in Shropshire near the Welsh/English border, and had a population of about six hundred people at the end of the seventeenth century. It was situated in a woodland area and its economy was almost entirely agricultural, with a heavy emphasis on cattle-rearing; most of its population were small freeholders or tenant farmers, although by the time Gough wrote his book nearly a third of the men of the village had become labourers. Today Myddle is a quiet, peaceful place, a typical English country village. The idealisation of the countryside has led many to see this peacefulness as the dominant historical characteristic of village life, the title of one of Flora Thompson's books — *Still Glides the Stream* — perhaps epitomising this feeling. The romantic treatment of the English countryside has buttressed this image, and there is much in current ideology which points to a harmonious and serene traditional rural community, in order to condemn the perceived violence and disintegration of modern urban life. Gough's writing completely shatters this picture of a rural idyll, but in doing so, enriches our appreciation of the reality of our social history in a uniquely instructive way. Here is Gough on a sequence of events that occurred in Myddle and its neighbourhood:

> There was one Clarke, of Preston Gubballs, who had formerly been tenant to Sir Edward Kinaston, of a tenement in Welsh Hampton, and was indebted for arrears of rent, due to Sir Edward; whereupon he sued out a writ against this Clarke, and sent a bailiff to arrest him; and because Clarke had some lusty young men to his sons, therefore Sir Edward sent one of his servants to assist the bailiff, if need were. Clarke was cutting peat on Haremeare Mosse; Sir Edward's man stayed in the wood in Pimhill; the bailiff went towards Clarke, and being beaten back by Clarke's sons, Sir Edward's man came

with his sword drawn, and swore he would make hay with them. But one of Clarke's sons, with a turf spade, which they call a peat iron (a very keen thing) struck Sir Edward's man on the head, and cloave out his brains. The bailiff fled; Clarke was rescued; and his son fled, and escaped. The coroner was sent for and by appointment of Sir Humphry Lea, the inhabitants of Myddle paid the coroner's fees. Clarke's son escaped the hand of justice, but not the judgment of God, for he that spilled man's blood, by man shall his blood be spilt, for when all things were quiet, and this thing seemed forgotten, Clarke's son came into this country again, and lived at Welsh Hampton, where a quarrel happening between him and one Hopkin, his next neighbour, about their garden hayment, as they stood quarrelling, each man in his own garden, Hopkin cast a stone at Clarke, which struck him so directly on the head, that it killed him. How Hopkin escaped the law, I have not heard; but vengeance suffered him not long to live, for a quarrel happened between him and one Lyth, a neighbour of his, as they were in an alehouse in Ellesmere, in the night-time, which quarrel ended in words, and Hopkin went towards home; and not long after Lyth went thence. The next morning Hopkin was found dead in Oatley Park, having been knocked on the head with the foot of a washing stock which stood at Ellesmere meare, which foot was found not far from him. Lyth was apprehended, and committed to prison on suspicion of the murder . . .

Three men were killed, two of the killers themselves being murdered in turn. The first homicide occurred because of a dispute over non-payment of rent, the second because of a garden quarrel, and the third as a result of an alehouse brawl. All the disputes were in themselves trivial, and what is remarkable is that three such killings should be linked one to the other in such a small community. These were not isolated incidents however, as Gough mentions a total of ten homicides in the course of his narrative, and although these did not all occur in Myddle itself, it is inconceivable that such a level of violence could occur in a modern rural community or an urban area of equivalent size. But before I go on to discuss comparative homicide rates, I wish to illustrate the nature and type of violence in this seventeenth century rural area by further quoting from Gough's narrative. The following account of a murder of a young servant maid has tragic and comic qualities, and reminds us that Gough was both a contemporary of Pepys and lived near, both in space and time, to Shakespeare himself. The murderer's name was Hugh Elks, and

> he was an ill man — for he, knowing that a neighbour of his who lived in Eyton had a considerable sum of money in the house, this Elks and some other of his companions came to Eyton on the Lord's day at time of morning service, and having visors on their faces, they came into the house and found there only one servant maid who was making of a cheese, and this Elks stooping down to bind her she saw under his visor, and said, "Good Uncle Elks, do me no harm," and upon that he pulled out his knife and cut her throat. His companions being terrified at the act fled away to Baschurch Church, and Elks seeing his companions were gone fled likewise and took no money, and for haste shut the door after him and left his dog in the house, and came to Marton, but stayed not there, but ran to Petton to church whither he came sweating exceedingly a little before the end of service.
>
> When people came from church to Eyton, they found the girl dead, and Elks' dog in the house almost bursting with eating the cheese. They followed the dog, who brought them to Elks' house, and upon this, Elks was apprehended on suspicion.

We will see later in this introduction that theft was common in seventeenth century Myddle, although the above incident seems to have happened in the sixteenth century. "Good Uncle Elks" was presumably not a relative of the maid servant's, but the term was an adopted one (made familiar by anthropologists), i.e. was an expression of a particular kind of a close community relationship. This murder like the three previously discussed was a crime of passion, enacted in the heat of the moment out of spontaneous feelings of rage and aggression. The people of Myddle were capable however of much more deliberate, dispassionate and cold acts of murder, as is shown by an anecdote of Gough's about the attempt of three Myddle wives to rid themselves of their husbands through poisoning. A certain Thomas Hodden, husband of Elizabeth Hodden

> died, leaving his wife a young wanton widow, who soon after married with one Onslow, a quiet, peaceable man; but she soon grew into dislike of him, and was willing to be shot of him. There were other women in Myddle, at that time, that were weary of their husbands, and it was reported that this woman and two more made an agreement to poison their husbands all in one night; which (as it is said) was attempted by them all; but Onslow only died; the other two escaped very hardly. This wicked act was soon blazed abroad and Elizabeth Onslow fled into Wales, to her father's relations; but being pursued, she was found upon a holiday, dancing on the top of a hill amongst a company of young people.

In spite of this being a description of a murder, the reader cannot but be fascinated by the account of Elizabeth Onslow "dancing on the top of a hill amongst a company of young people" when apprehended. So even here where the quality of deliberateness is to be found, the spontaneity of her reactions in the aftermath has a very seventeenth century ring.

There was only one other murder of the total of ten that could be described as cold-blooded, and this involved another member of the Elks family.

> There was one Thomas Elks, of Knockin, who had an elder brother, who married and had one son, and soon after died and his wife also, and left the child very young.

> The grandmother was guardian to the child. This grandmother was mother unto Thomas Elks, and was so indulgent of him, that she loved him best of any of her children; and by supplying him with money to feed his extravagances, she undid him. But when she was gone poor, and could not supply him, he considered that this child stood in his way between him and the estate, and therefore contrived to remove him: and to that end he hired a poor boy, of Knockin, to entice the child into the corn fields to gather flowers. The corn was then at highest. Thomas Elks met the two children in the fields; sent the poor boy home, and took the child in his arms into the lower end of the field where he had provided a pail of water, and putting the child's head into the pail of water he stifled him to death, and left him in the corn.

But much more typical of homicide in Myddle was the following incident. A young maid was a

> servant to a gentleman who lived near Wellington, and as this young woman was holding water for her master to wash his hands in the kitchen, he cast a little water from off his finger into her face, which her mistress (who was present), seeing, and conceiving it too familiar an action, she in a rage took up the cleaver, and gave her such a blow on the head that she died.

This was the only other murder committed by a woman in Gough's account; like today, most murder and physical violence was committed by men. But the homicide rate was much higher for both men and women in the seventeenth century than it is today. It is impossible to calculate the rate for seventeenth century Myddle with any precision, as Gough does not always tell us when murders took place, and whether all the victims were living in Myddle at the time. According to recently published work, the homicide rate in thirteenth century England was in the range of 9 - 47 annual homicides per 100,000 population,[2] while other research indicates a rate for the sixteenth/seventeenth century period of 5 - 18 per 100,000.[3]

The rate for Myddle appears to have been as high as that found for the thirteenth century, but whatever the precise levels of homicide, it is clear that they were very much higher in all these periods than they are today. The homicide rate in Great Britain during the period 1930 - 59 was 0.4 per 100,000, and there has been little change in recent years.[4] Thus homicide in pre-industrial England — the thirteenth to the seventeenth century — was at least ten times as great as it is today, and may have even been a *hundred* times at particular periods. Certainly the number of violent murders described by Gough for his small rural community confirms the findings of research based on more statistical techniques.

Violence did not of course always result in death, and Gough describes a number of aggressive incidents of a non-fatal kind. He often mentions them in passing as if they were fairly commonplace, and almost murderous attacks were treated as if they were merely everyday incidents. An example of this occurred when Robert Morrall met his father-in-law William Tyler:

> Old William Tyler was his utter enemy, and often threatened to be his death, but Morrall was too hard for him. They met accidentally at a stile in Houlston, and discoursing friendly, they sat down on each side of the stile; but Tyler having a halter in his hand, cast it about Morrall's neck and drew him over the stile, and was likely to have hanged him: but Morrall by his strength and agility freed himself, and did not forbear to beat Tyler severely.

Tyler was obviously a very violent man who was capable of the most extreme acts of aggression, although he never actually murdered anyone as far as we know. But this violence was not limited to a few individuals, but was culturally sanctioned and at times could explode so as to almost engulf and involve the whole community. Gough was fascinated by

Tyler's personality and gave several pages to his exploits and personal history; the following incident described at length illustrates the communal nature of violence. Tyler owed money to a Mr. Bradocke, who had unsuccessfully attempted to serve a warrant on him.

> Afterwards Mr. Bradocke sent his tenant, William Byron (a little man, but stout of his hands), to serve Tyler with another warrant. Byron came (upon Sunday) to Myddle Church to morning prayer (for in those days all writs and processes might be served on the Lord's day). William Tyler came to church with a good backsword by his side, which then was not usual. After service, Byron stood at the church stile; and as soon as Tyler was gone over the stile, Byron leapt on his back, and cast him down. Many of Tyler's companions, and some women of his relations, came to rescue Tyler; but the high constable, Mr. Hatchett, a bold and discreet man, was present, some say on purpose, and he quieted the people. Roger Sandford, of Newton (who married Mary Bradocke, aunt to Mr. Bradocke), was there, with his servants and friends, to assist Byron; and one William Hussey, servant to Roger Sandford, came to assist Byron; and Tyler got Hussey's thumb in his mouth, and worried all the flesh to the bare bone: but Hugh Suker, a weaver, standing by with a pike-staff in his hand, put the pikes into Tyler's mouth and wrenched open his teeth, and released Hussey. At last Tyler was set on horseback, and Byron leapt up behind him to hold him there, and William Hussey led the horse, and thus Tyler went toward the jail. But the consternation and lamentation of Tyler's friends, especially the women, was such as I cannot easily demonstrate . . .
>
> All the company followed William Tyler out of town; and at the town's end there, upon a bank near the pinfold, stood John Gossage and several others of Tyler's drunken companions, with a pailful of ale. Gossage cried, "Ah, Will! art going to the jail?" Tyler said, "It is too true." Then says Gossage, "Come, boys; fall on!" but Tyler cried, "Hold, hold. It is to no purpose;" so they took him away. When they came a little below the Lea Hall, the miller of the windmill met them, carrying a sword on his shoulder, with the hilt behind him; Tyler

> put his hand in the hilt of the sword and drew it out, and struck at Hussey; but Byron soon pitched him beside the horse, and took the sword from him. Byron would not give the sword to the miller; and Hussey carried the naked sword in his hand, and led the horse; and so Tyler was brought to jail.

The story speaks for itself and is so rich in detail, that we can only touch on some of its sociological implications. The explosion of violence was contained by the presence of the high constable, although Tyler himself stopped his friends from using violence on his behalf after he had been arrested. We are in a different cultural world to that of today; Gough's world is that of Shakespeare's, a world that has not yet been "civilised", a world in which the Englishman of today — polite, tolerant and non-violent — would find very frightening. But Gough's social world is one of blood and roses — violence, but also of lamentation, loyalty, sadness and love — social intensities which English communities of today certainly lack. With Gough we are not in Freud's world of civilization and its discontents, but are in an era of passionate acting out of impulse and feeling. The language is rich in colour and feeling, and there are passages in Gough's writing which could be mistaken for the work of Shakespeare.

Freud believed that the acting out of intense feelings of violence was associated with a relative absence of neurosis, in particular freedom from clinical states of depression and melancholy.[5] This is based on the theoretical assumption that aggression not expressed outwardly is invariably turned inwards against the self, and that feelings of depression are the result of self-punishment and self-hatred. Several sociologists — including Durkheim — have pointed to the inverse correlation between homicide and suicide rates, i.e. the more murder, the less suicide, and vice versa.[6] This conclusion has come in for a certain amount of criticism in recent years, mainly on the grounds that such an inverse correlation does not hold in some societies studied.[7] However, most of the exceptions are for non-European societies in which additional cultural factors appear to be acting to complicate the analysis. In European societies Freud's theory seems to fit rather well, and in particular, Catholic countries have (at least until very recently) high homicide but low suicide rates, and Protestant countries the reverse. Seventeenth century England was still "Catholic" from this point of view, and certainly much of Gough's book could easily be mistaken for a description of Ireland and its historical culture until very recently. There were only two definite cases of suicide in Myddle as described Gough, although there was a third ambiguous case of a man who was suffering from grief due to his brother's death, who was soon afterward found dead in a well in his garden. Even if we count this as a case of suicide, the rate seems to have been very low compared to modern experience. Suicide rates were quite low generally in England in the pre-industrial period — varying between 0.6 and 4.0 annual suicides per 100,000 population,[8] compared to about 9.0 per 100,000 today. Whereas suicide is about ten times as common as homicide today, in Myddle homicide was about four times as common as suicide, and this was probably fairly typical of the country as a whole.

The suicide that did occur in Myddle seems to have been linked with violence, as is seen in the following case, which was one of the two unambiguous cases. A certain Clarke was son in law to Richard Wolph, and Clarke's wife having died he,

> by fair and flattering speeches, persuaded the old man to deliver all his estate to him, on condition of being maintained while he lived. Clarke having now got an estate, followed his old way of drinking; and when he came home drunk, he would so abuse the old man, that he made him a weary of his life; and, therefore, in a

> melancholic fit of grief, he went on foot to Wem, and bought poison, which he eat up as he came homeward; and when he came home he was extremely sick, and vomited exceedingly: he told what he had done, and would fain have lived; but no antidote could immediately be had, so he died. The coroner's inquest found him a *felo de se;* and he was buried on Myddle Hill, at that crossway where the roadway from Ellesmere to Shrewsbury, called the Lower-way, goes over cross the way that goes from Myddle toward the Red Bull, but was removed next night: and some say he was interred in a rye field of his own, which is over against John Benion's, in that corner of the piece next the place where Penbrook's gate stood.

The traditional practice of burying a suicide at the crossroads was followed in this instance, although the corpse was reburied privately the following day.

Why was there so much violence in Myddle and other seventeenth century English communities? One answer perhaps can be found in the sanctioning of violence by the government of the day and the relevant local authorities; hanging was of course practised and two of the ten persons responsible for the homicides mentioned by Gough were dealt with in this way. The possible deterrent effect of hanging must have been weakened by the frequency with which murderers escaped this form of punishment: two of the ten escaped detection, three successfully pleaded benefit of clergy — which in effect was a privilege of the rich — one languished in prison until released by the parliamentary authorities during the Civil War, and the fate of two is unknown. There is little evidence anyway that hanging or capital punishment has any deterrent effect, and the violence sanctioned by the authorities is more likely to have increased homicide. Several hangings are mentioned by Gough, but they are usually for quite trivial offences such as horse stealing, theft, and in one particularly pathetic case, a boy was hung for helping in a prison escape. Institutions such as the pillory helped encourage violence; this can be illustrated by the treatment of one Clarke, a Roman Catholic, who had been heard to utter threatening statements about the Church of England. After having been put in the pillory

> The people, by pelting him with eggs, turnips, carrots, stones and dirt, used him so hardly, that the under-sheriff took him down, for fear he should be killed outright. The people followed him to the jail door, and pelted him all the way. He lay some while sick and sore at Shrewsbury, and after he was brought to Ellesmere and there put to stand on the pillory, where he found the like favour from the under-sheriff, and the like hard usage, or worse, from the people; and hereupon the high sheriff wrote a letter to the judge, and acquainted him what he had done, and with all told him, that he could promise to put Clarke upon the pillory at Oswestry, but could not promise to bring him alive from amongst the enraged Welshmen; and thereupon the rest of the punishment was remitted.

Another factor in the high level of violence was almost certainly the amount of drunkenness and general consumption of alcohol. At least three of the ten homicides involved very heavy drinking, and we have seen how violent incidents of the kind associated with William Tyler and his friends were linked with drunkenness. Gough's pages are full of accounts of drunkenness and alcoholic drinking, the first alone having twenty-three entries in the subject index. Mentions of alehouses and inns proliferate, and a common theme is the economic ruin of families and individuals through debt on account of drink. Drinking was not confined to men, and there are several references to women going to the local alehouses, some obviously on a day-to-day basis (women appeared to have been free of some of the social constraints imposed on them in the later Victorian period — Gough himself admired women of "masculine spirit"). He moralizes on occasions about the evils of drink, but was capable of great sympathy for certain individuals partly ruined in this way. The following story shows him at his best, weaving a delightful mix of the comic and tragic, revealing at the same time a central feature of seventeenth century social life.

> Thomas Hayward the second was a handsome gentleman, a good country scholar and a pretty clerk. He was a person well reputed in his country and of a general acquaintance. He was just and faithful in affirming or denying any matter in controversy, so that less credit was given to some men's oath than to his bare word. He was well skilled in the art of good husbandry. His father left him a farm of thirty pounds (fee simple) in Newton-on-the-Hill and the lease of this farm in Balderton. He had eight pounds (land in fee simple) left him by an uncle in Whixhall. He married with Alice, the daughter of Mr. Wihen, high school master, in Shrewsbury. He had a good fortune with her in money, besides houses in town of considerable yearly value. She was a comely woman, but highly bred and unfit for a country life, besides she was shrewd with tongue, so that they lived unquietly and uncomfortably, and their estate consumed insensibly.
>
> He had little quietness at home which caused him to frequent public houses merely for his natural sustenance, and there meeting with company and being generally well beloved he stayed often too long. His intimate friend was Mr. Hotchkins of Webscott, and indeed there seemed to be a natural sympathy between them for they were both of them very just honest persons and well beloved — but their deportment when they were in drink was very different for Mr. Hodgkins could go but not speak, and Mr. Hayward could speak as well and seemed to be more acute and witty in his drink then at other times but could not go.
>
> This Thomas Hayward sold and consumed all his estate and was afterwards maintained on charity by his eldest son.

Addiction to drink and the local ale-house was not confined to the poor and the culturally rough; in fact the distinction between a respectable middle class and a rough working class did not properly emerge until the nineteenth century.[9] The segregation of social classes also probably did not arise until the same period, and the easy relationship between people of different social statuses was partly a function of cultural spontaneity (including drinking) mentioned earlier. An example of this lies in the relationship between Thomas Jukes and Sir Humphrey Lea.

> Thomas Jukes was a bawling, bold, confident person; he often kept company with his betters, but showed them no more respect than if they had been his equals or inferiors. He was a great bowler, and often bowled with Sir Humphrey Lea at a bowling green on Haremeare Heath, near the end of the Lea Lane; where he would make no more account of Sir Humphrey, than if he had been a plough-boy. He would ordinarily tell him he lied, and sometimes throw the ball at his head, and then they parted in wrath. But within few days, Sir Humphrey would ride to Newton, and take Jukes with him to the bowls; and if they did not fall out, would take him home and make him drunk.

The familiar mixture of aggression, drunkenness and sociability is to be found in this anecdote. It also illustrates the relative social openness of a community like Myddle, and this may have been partly a function of it having been in a woodland area. Contemporaries believed that woodland communities were particularly prone to violence; for example, Norden wrote that "the people bred amongst woods are naturally more stubborn and uncivil than in the champion counties", and Aubrey saw the woodlanders as "mean people (who) live lawless (with) nobody to govern them, they care for nobody, having no dependence on anybody."[10] This was because settlements were scattered in woodland areas — there was a total of seven townships (hamlets) within the parish of Myddle, plus the chapelry of Hadnall — and they tended to have a large number of freeholders and independent small farmers; this can be contrasted with champion villages, where the population tended to be concentrated into a single nucleated village under the control of the local squire.

An additional factor in the case of Myddle was that it was a marcher lordship, created to deal with border violence between the Welsh and the English. The marcher lord was given certain summary legal and military powers, including the power of immediate execution of Welsh raiders and criminals transgressing local laws. This institution was no longer in being when Gough was writing, but it may have left a tradition of violence in its wake. An instance of this was the heriot custom in lordship marches; the heriot on entering the lease of a farm was "the best weapon" — and the availability of personal weapons was associated with many of the incidents of violence described by Gough.

But the use of personal weapons in violence was not confined to border areas and they were worn almost universally at about this time. At the end of the sixteenth century William Harrison wrote:

> ". . . seldom shall you see any of my countrymen above eighteen or twenty years old to go without a dagger at least at his back or by his side . . . Our nobility wear commonly swords or rapiers with their daggers, as doth every common servingman also that followeth his lord and master."[11]

Little is known about the history of personal weapons — as far as I know virtually no research has been done on this important social historical subject — but it is probable that the wearing of such weapons declined mainly in the eighteenth century. This appears to have coincided with a dramatic fall in the homicide rate,[12] and both probably began to decline at the very beginning of the eighteenth century after Gough had completed his work. I suspect it is no accident that this was the period when the industrial revolution was getting underway, although what was cause and what was consequence is difficult to disentangle. Such a major topic is clearly beyond the scope of this introduction, although we might notice in passing that the decline of homicide and the outward expression of aggression occurred at the same time as the growth of puritanism (in particular Methodism), which Weber saw as instrumental to the development of capitalism.[13]

One special factor in the creation of violence during Gough's lifetime was of course the Civil War. Gough gives a number of accounts of incidents in the Civil War, some of which were based on personal experience, and it is this personal flavour which brings to life so vividly his narrative. An example of this was when he witnessed Robert More trying to recruit men for the king's army:

> I was then a youth of about eight or nine years of age, and I went to see this great show. And there I saw a multitude of men, and upon the highest bank of the hill I saw this Robert More standing, with a paper in his hand, and three or four soldier's pikes, stuck upright in the ground by him; and there he made a proclamation, that if any person would serve the king, as a soldier in the wars, he should have fourteen groats a week for his pay.

It is often because Gough knew the participants — or at least knew of them — that he was able to bring out the human side of a war which has often been treated in an abstract fashion. Listen to the following description of an incident between royalist and parliamentary forces; a certain Scoggan was made governor of a garrison placed at Abright Hussey:

> I remember the soldiers fetched bedding from Newton for the use of the soldiers there. They took only one

> coarse bed hilling from my father. A party of horse, of the parliament side, came on a Sunday, in the afternoon, and faced this garrison, and Scoggan, standing in a window, in an upper room, cried aloud, that the others heard him say, "Let such a number go to such a place, and so many to such a place; and let twenty come with me:" (but he had but eight in all in the house). And Scoggan, seeing one Phillip Bunny among the enemies, who was a tailor, born in Hadnall, he took a fowling gun, and called to Bunny, and said, "Bunny, have at thee!" and shot him through the leg, and killed his horse. The parliament soldiers took up Bunny, and departed.

Gough certainly makes us question some of our preconceptions about the Civil War period. The association between puritanism and parliamentarianism comes in for a shaking by the following story:

> Mr. Mackworth made Captain Hill (a prodigal drunken fellow, who before the wars was a pitiful barber in this town) lieutenant of the castle. But the townsmen and garrison soldiers hated him; and therefore as soon as there was a prospect of the return of King Charles II they conspired against him; and one of the townsmen sent for him out of the castle to drink with him at the Loggerheads, an alehouse hard by; and as soon as he was gone out of the castle, the soldiers shut the gate and cast his clothes and boots over the wall, and immediately the town was in an uproar; and Hill for fear of his life fled away that night and I never heard more of him.

A drunken barber made the lieutenant of a parliamentary garrison, and ejected on the advent of the return of the king — it is this type of evidence which leads to the re-writing of history books. But how reliable is Gough as an informant? Where it has been possible to check him against other sources, he has been found to be highly accurate.[14] He had the habit of repeating himself without realising it, and this allows us to check on his internal consistency; most of the repetitions are trivial and have been eliminated from the edited text, but in order to let the reader compare one duplicated story for himself, I give the following important passage which will be found in alternative form on page 118.

> Robert Hayward the eldest son of Thomas Hayward and Alice his wife, was set apprentice to a refiner of silver in London. (I have heard him say that his father gave only the price of an old cow with him.) His master was a dissenter and was one of that sect which are called millenarians, or fifth monarchy men. After the restoration of King Charles II, the men of this sect were persuaded or rather deluded by their teachers and ringleaders, that now the time was come that Christ's Kingdom was to begin on earth, that they must provide themselves of arms and fight for their Lord and King against Antichrist; that they need not fear, although they were but few, for one of them should chase a 100, and 100 should chase 10,000, and by such persuasions these poor deluded people made an insurrection in the city, which being showed to his majesty and his council, the king commanded that his life guard and the city militia should be sent to suppress them. I heard it reported that in the streets of the city they fought very desperately, and some were killed but many wounded on both sides. At last the city militia got some behind them, and some came upon them through cross streets, so that being encompassed about on all sides they were forced to lay down their arms and cry quarter; the prisons in London were filled with them. Robert Hayward was one of the prisoners. Some of the ringleaders were executed and some of the rest were fined, and those that had nothing were set at liberty.

Although both accounts give more-or-less the same version of the uprising, the above is more detailed on the degree of resistance and the tenacity of the rebellion. In the text account "they were all pardoned except their ringleader who I think was hanged", whereas in above "some of the ringleaders were executed". Gough was probably at his least reliable when he had no direct personal experience of the event described, and fortunately for us, most of his stories relate to the arena of his own personal life, i.e. the community of Myddle.

I mentioned at an earlier point the prevalence of theft in Myddle — thirteen pages in the text mention the subject — and not surprisingly most of the goods stolen were agricultural produce. I quote the following story at length as it illuminates a number of sociological themes in the one passage. A certain Reece Wenlocke

> was descended of good parentage, who were tenants of a good farm, called Whottall, in Ellesmere Lordship. But the father of this Reece was a bad husband, and a pilfering, thievish person, and this son, Reece, and another son, named John, who lived at Bald Meadow, in this parish, were as bad as their father. They never stole any considerable goods, but were night walkers, and robbed orchards and gardens, and stole hay out of meadows, and corn when it was cut in the fields, and any small things that persons by carelessness had left out of doors. Reece had a cow, which was stolen away, and it is reported that he went to a woman, whom they called the wise woman of Montgomery, to know what had become of his cow; and as he went, he put a stone in his pocket, and told a neighbour of his that was with him that he would know whether she were a wise woman or not, and whether she knew that he had a stone in his pocket. And it is said, that when he came to her, she said, thou hast a stone in thy pocket, but it is not so big as that stone wherewith thou didst knock out such a neighbour's harrow tines. But the greatest diskindness that he did to his neighbours was, by tearing their hedges. And it is reported, that he had made a new oven; and, according to the manner of such things, it was at first to be well burnt, to make it fit for use, and this he intended to do in the night. At that time William Higginson dwelt at Webscot, and he had a servant, named Richard Mercer, a very waggish fellow. This Mercer did imagine that Reece would tear his master's hedges to burn the oven; and as he walked by a hedge, which was near Reece's house, he saw there a great dry stick of wood, and took it home with him, and bored a hole in the end of it with

> an auger, and put a good quantity of powder in it, and a peg after it, and put it again into the hedge. And it happened, that Reece Wenlocke, among other hedgewood, took this stick to burn in his oven; and when he cast it into the fire in the oven, it blew up the top of it, and set fire on the end of the house. Reece went out and made hideous crying, fire! fire! William Higginson, being the next neighbour, heard him, and called Mercer, but he said I know what is the matter; however, they went both down to the Meare House, but Reece had put out the fire that was in the end of the house, and the oven was broken to pieces.

The combination of theft, humour and violence makes compelling reading, although it is easy to forget the ruthlessness involved in blowing up someone's house as a part of a practical joke. The theft which took place seemed fairly indiscriminate, and if we are worried today about the level of burglary and theft, we can take historical comfort in how much more our ancestors were prone to this particular problem. Gough's mention of the wise woman of Montgomery is his only reference to a contemporary belief in magic, although various beliefs which we would now consider superstitious (for example, the linking of pigeons with disease) are referred to. Some social historians have stressed the importance of witchcraft beliefs, but this is for other areas of the country and for an earlier period of the seventeenth century.[15] Its complete absence in Myddle is somewhat surprising nonetheless, particularly when it is remembered that Gough was capable of taking his history back a hundred years or more to before when he was born (the practise of oral history was obviously very strong in the village).

Ruthlessness was not confined to acts of personal violence, but could extend to personal relationships within the family. A certain Samuel Downton had contracted a great deal of debt, mainly through drink, and had come to run an alehouse.

> After some years this Samuel Downton and his wife (having sold some of their household goods) got away from Cockshutt in the night-time and left all their children behind them — four of which were after maintained by the parish of Ellesmere. They went into Staffordshire and there he went a begging like an old decrepit person and she carried a box with pins and laces. But after awhile she got a new spark that travelled the country and went away with him, and then this Samuel came again to Alderton to his son Thomas who maintained him during his life.

The harsh treatment of children seems to have been rare going by the evidence provided by Gough; they were occasionally deserted as in the Downton family, and sometimes (as we have seen) violence was used against them. But there are as many references to indulgent treatment of children, and this perhaps explains in the main why so many children were prepared to maintain and take care of their aged parents (there are eight pages in the text in which this is mentioned). Gough does mention however hostile reactions of children towards their parents; for example, one of the disputes resulting in homicide started when Charles Hesketh used "very scurrilous, abusive, and undutiful language towards his parents."

Fairly frequent mention is made of desertion and separation between marriage partners, such as occurred between Samuel Downton and his wife. Flight was a common response to unresolvable situations (Ireland was frequently mentioned as a place that people ran to in difficulty) such as a marriage breakdown; the other common reason for running away was in order to avoid responsibility for an illegitimate child. Illegitimacy appears frequently in Gough's pages (sixteen pages in the text include references to it), and the following gives a flavour of his treatment of the subject. William and Margaret Challoner had

> three daughters, two of which are as impudent whores as any in this country; one of them has two bastards, and she being run out of the country, they are both maintained by the parish. The other is now (Jan. 20, 1701) great with a bastard, and at Christmas last was sent by order into Wem parish, where her last service and settlement was. She has fathered it on Stephen Formeston, her uncle's son, and he has fled.

According to the local parish register, only about one per cent of all baptisms in the sixteenth and seventeenth centuries were of illegitimate children,[16] but this figure is very unreliable when set against Gough's evidence. Probably many illegitimate children were never baptised, and this should make one very wary of using these statistics uncritically.[17] Gough himself did not mention all examples of illicit sexuality in Myddle; the Anglican ecclesiastical court charged Arthur Davies and Jane Morris in 1699 and 1700 with "living together in open fornication",[18] and although Gough refers to them after they were married, there is no mention of any sexual impropriety.

Not surprisingly, venereal disease appears more than once in Gough — there are three pages of the text which mention it. Disease and illness were very common in Myddle at this time, and although there is no systematic treatment, we do get an invaluable insight into the subject. The symptoms of rickets and scurvy are described, and the presence of these illnesses indicate that inadequacies of diet were present. Both diseases were however extremely rare, and other evidence in Gough's book suggests that most people were adequately fed — meat appearing to be a central part of the staple diet. (The over-consumption of meat may have been a reason for the case of scurvy.) The most serious disease at this time appears to have been "fever", and there was at least one damaging epidemic outbreak in Gough's time (the exact cause of this fever is unknown — it was probably typhus). Plague had appeared in Shrewsbury, and Gough mentions certain individuals catching and dying from it in London — but by this period it was mainly an urban disease, on the point of disappearance. There are three mentions of smallpox, and although it was very widespread at this time, it was still a relatively benign disease — its virulence only really increased at the beginning of the eighteenth century. There is a frequent mention of childlessness and this may have been because of the prevalence of diseases like smallpox, because even in mild form it is capable of producing infertility. Lameness appears fairly frequently, often due to the accidents which were a common hazard in seventeenth century Myddle. Illness was treated by doctors and apothecaries, although probably only the wealthy used their services to any extent; much more common was the practice of amateur medicine, and women seemed to have played a significant role in this, particularly in surgical operations (this may have been associated with their roles of midwives). Gough does give an example of what we might call magical medicine; one woman tried to cure her illness through the "King's Touch" — this was the practice of people being touched by the king when he was touring the countryside, in the belief that he had charismatic powers of cure — sadly with the lady in question, the cure was unsuccessful.

If Gough is at all a reliable guide, mental illness was extremely rare at this time; there was only one case of what might be called a psychotic illness, and one other case of what we would now call mental defectiveness — although Gough describes the sufferer much more evocatively, in calling him an "innocent". Of course there were people displaying neurotic symptoms, but these seemed to have been less frequent than they are today. Melancholy is mentioned on four pages, but given the number of people mentioned in the book, this does not appear to have been a common complaint. This is consistent with the relatively low suicide rate, and it would therefore seem that people living in this seventeenth century community were less afflicted by the various forms of mental illness. This may have been due partly to their ability to express openly their most intense feelings — including those of aggression — in an open social context. Another factor might have been to the close-knit nature of the community; this is most strikingly illustrated by Gough's own knowledge of the people in the village — who today could know so much about so many people in the community in which they live?

We should not exaggerate however the absence of personal problems at this time; there are frequent mentions of unhappy marriages, quarrels and violence. One major problem that many people had to face was poverty and destitution. Gough mentions in passing the practice of paupers being made to wear a paupers' badge — a P sewn onto their clothing — which reminds us of the harshness of seventeenth century life, particularly in the treatment of the poor. Admittedly, Gough tells us that there were virtually no parish poor in his father's time — the payment of the poor-rate was virtually non-existent — but there were clearly people in great destitution, with mentions of begging and children being forced to maintain their aged relatives. Bankruptcy and debt were very common, often as we have seen on account of drink, but also due to the vagaries of trade and commerce. Many merchants and tradesmen are said to have gone bankrupt — Gough tells us that they "broke" — and this was frequently because of a chain reaction of bankruptcies. This subject is most often mentioned in connection with people living in Shrewsbury and other local towns, but in this connection London looms surprisingly large in the lives of the people of this small rural community. But London was the centre of prosperity as well as bankruptcy, and a number of poor people are said by Gough to have made their fortune by emigrating to that place.

The rise and fall in prosperity of tradesmen and merchants is a theme which is mirrored in the surprisingly large amount of social mobility. Nine pages in the text mention cases of upward mobility, and ten downward — with an additional seven pages giving cases of general social mobility — a total of twenty-six pages. This may have been the result of the relatively open nature of the social structure of the community discussed earlier. Education was also much more common in Myddle than might be expected, with frequent mentions of schools and the teaching of both reading and writing. Myddle in this respect was a "civilized" community, and we must set this aspect of social life against the violence and drunkenness discussed earlier in the introduction. The latter emphasis could be misleading if we did not balance it out against descriptions of contrary behaviour given to us by Gough. Many people are described as peaceable, honest, just, charitable, pious, hospitable and hard-working. Most good stories tend to involve the vices rather than the virtues, and Gough himself sometimes admits that he has little to say about a particular person because of their quiet peaceableness (there are ten pages of the text with an entry in the index under the heading of "peaceable"). The conclusions we come to about the nature and quality of life in seventeenth century must ultimately be personal and based on our own values; but as happy endings are best, I will conclude by quoting at length from Gough's account of a man who he considered to have lived a virtuous and happy life. Thomas Ash

> was a proper, comely person; his father gave him good country education, which, with the benefit of a good natural wit, a strong memory, a courteous and mild behaviour, a smooth and affable way of discourse, an honest and religious disposition, made him a complete and hopeful young man, insomuch as Mr. Edward Hanmer, of Marton, was easily induced to give him his

daughter Elizabeth to wife. This was a very suitable match, for she was a lovely, proper gentlewoman, and so like to her husband in disposition, that it should seem there was a sympathy in nature between them, and therefore they lived a loving and comfortable life together. This Thomas Ash was not so much blamed for being too nice in observing the canons, as he called them, of the first counsel of the apostles at Jerusalem, in abstaining from blood and things strangled, as he was commended for avoiding that abominable sin of profane swearing. For this Thomas Ash was much in debt; but how it was contracted I cannot say, unless he was charged with the payment of portions to his sisters, and I doubt he had but little portion with his wife; however he bore an honest mind, and was willing to pay every man, and to that end he set his tenement to Edward Payne of Meriton, for raising of money to pay debts; and to shelter himself from the fatigue of duns, he listed himself soldier in the king's service in the wars, tempore Car. I, and continued a soldier until the king's forces were utterly dispersed, but never attained to any higher post than a corporal of foot. At his return, he brought nothing home but a crazy body and many scars, the symptoms of the dangerous service which he had performed, and besides, he fould little of his debts paid, for the payment of taxes and charges of repairs had taken up most part of the rent; but he being minded that none should lose by him, sold his lease to William Formeston. He had some money to spare when he had satisfied his debts, and with that he took a lease off Mr. Crosse of Yorton, of several pieces of ground near Yorton Heath, and there he built a little warm house, made a neat little garden, planted a pretty orchard, built several outhouses, and made everything very handsome and convenient, and there he and his loving wife spent their old age, though not in a plentiful, yet in a peaceable and contented condition.

REFERENCES

1. Richard Gough, *Human Nature Displayed in the History of Myddle* (Centaur Press, 1968), pp. 1, 7. I would like to thank Centaur Press for allowing me to use this quote.
2. J. B. Given, *Society and Homicide in Thirteenth Century England* (1977), p. 36.

3. P. E. H. Hair, "Homicide, Infanticide, and Child Assault in Late Tudor Middlesex", *Local Population Studies*, No. 9 (Autumn 1972), p. 44; J. M. Beattie, "The Pattern of Crime in England 1660-1800", *Past and Present*, 62 (1974), p. 61; J. S. Cockburn (Ed), *Crime in England 1550-1800* (1977), p. 55.
4. Given, *op. cit.*, p. 39. The homicide rate in England and Wales was 0.9 per 100,000 in 1973.
5. S. Freud, "Mourning and Melancholia", *Standard Edition*, 14.
6. Emile Durkheim, *Suicide* (Routledge, 1968), pp. 338-360; A. F. Henry and J. F. Short, *Suicide and Homicide* (1964).
7. See for example, P. Bohannan, *African Homicide and Suicide* (1960). But recent WHO statistics seem to confirm the inverse relationship between homicide and suicide. In particular, traditional pre-industrial societies have high homicide but low suicide rates, whereas modern industrial societies —including Japan, Singapore and Hong Kong — have low homicide but high suicide rates. See *WHO Statistics Annual 1973-76 — Vital Statistics, Causes Of Death.*
8. P. E. H. Hair, "A Note on the Incidence of Tudor Suicide", *Local Population Studies*, No. 5 (Autumn 1970).
9. See for example, Mary Thale (Ed), *The Autobiography of Francis Place* (1972).
10. Quoted in David G. Hey, *An English Rural Community: Myddle Under the Tudors and Stuarts* (1974), p. 7. I have relied on Hey's excellent study for much of my background information on Myddle.
11. William Harrison, *The Description of England* (1968), p. 237.
12. Beattie, *op. cit.*, p. 61. Homicide rates in Surrey and Sussex fell from an average of about six per 100,000 in 1663-94 to just over two per 100,000 in 1722-24 and to lower figures thereafter.
13. Following Freud, puritanism can be seen as the turning of aggression inwards against the self, i.e. through the creation of a harsh, self-punishing super-ego.
14. Hey, *op. cit.*
15. See for example, A. D. J. Macfarlane, "Witchcraft in Tudor and Stuart Essex", in Cockburn, *op. cit.*
16. Hey, *op. cit.*, p. 224.
17. The treatment of illegitimacy in Peter Laslett's *Family Life and Illicit Love in Earlier Generations* (1977) is perhaps open to criticism on these grounds. It would be interesting to see how the new historical methodology of total reconstitution would stand up to independent assessment through the kind of information contained in Gough.
18. Hey, *op. cit.*, p. 225.

DR PETER RAZZELL

CHAPTER 1

Some Few Things That Have Happened Here In My Memory

King Charles I came to Shrewsbury

Mr. Camden (that famous antiquary) has discoursed at large of several memorable antiquities concerning this town: and therefore I shall only mention some few things that have happened here in my memory.

In the year of our Lord 1642, King Charles I came to Shrewsbury, and having gathered a strong army he departed thence about Michaelmas; and having observed that this town was a strong place both by nature and art, he sent Arthur Lord Capell to place a garrison here, who at his first coming found the castle so ruinous that it was neither fit for habitation nor defence. But he soon repaired it and made it exceedingly strong; he pulled down many houses without the wall near the castle, and near that gate of the town called the castle gates — he by a deep trench, brought the water of Severn up to this gate and made a drawbridge over it. There is a high bank at the end of that part of the suburbs which is called Frankewell or Frankeville, on which the Lord Capell built a strong fort to prevent an enemy from planting cannons there, which might have damaged a great part of the town. He placed many great cannons on the castle walls, and in this fort, and made a strong garrison. Soon after he was recalled and one Sir Michael Yarley was made governor, and one Captain Crowe was made lieutenant of the castle. At that time Colonel Mytton of Halston (an excellent soldier both for personal valour, policy, and conduct), was general of the parliament forces in this county, and governor of a small garrison at Wem. This bold and daring general had a great desire to reduce Shrewsbury, for which town he was then a burgess in parliament, and to that end he came on a Saturday afternoon when the townsmen were busy about their market and attacked the fort at Frankwell End, but was repulsed with some loss. On the Saturday next following in the night-time he with Major Braine, Captain Shipley, Captain Church, and Captain Sheinton (all valiant soldiers), and their forces, came to the Old Heath near Shrewsbury, intending to attack the town — but the night being very dark the horses mistook their way, and went towards Pimley and Atcham, and his forces could not be got together until the opportunity was lost. On the next Friday night General Mytton came with his forces to the Old Heath, and sent Colonel Rinken with the foot along Severn side until they came to the castle; and cutting down the pallisades that were between the castle and Severn, they went under the castle wall and got into the town at the place where the bowling alley now is, and came directly to the gate and the guard being fled away they threw open the gate and let in the horses. There was only two killed in this expedition, one of each side. On the parliament side was killed one Richard Wycherley, born in Clive; and on the king's side the captain of the main guard at the market-place. About one o'clock in the afternoon, the castle was delivered up, and Captain Crowe went down to Gloucester where he was hanged either for his cowardice or treachery. After this Colonel Mytton was made governor of Shrewsbury; but when he disliked the proceedings against the king, he laid down his commission, and Humphry Mackworth, the younger son of Judge Mackworth of Betton, was made governor. When King Charles II came out of Scotland and was at Drayton, in his march towards Worcester, he sent a letter to Mr. Mackworth, requiring him to surrender into his hands his town of Shrewsbury. Mr. Mackworth sent back a letter to the king — the direction was "To Charles Stewart, King of Scotland" — the contents to this purpose: — "I have received the government of Shrewsbury by commission from the parliament of England, and will surrender it to none but them upon any summons whatsoever, especially when only paper ones compel me."

Mr. Mackworth made Captain Hill (a prodigal drunken fellow, who before the wars was a pitiful barber in this town) lieutenant of the castle. But the townsmen and garrison soldiers hated him; and therefore as soon as there was a prospect of the return of King Charles II they conspired against him; and one of the townsmen sent for him out of the castle to drink with him at the Loggerheads, an alehouse hard by; and as soon as he was gone out of the castle, the soldiers shut the gate and cast his clothes and boots over the wall, and immediately the town was in an uproar; and Hill for fear of his life fled away that night and I never heard more of him. Soon after Colonel Hunt was made governor, and Mr. John Bromley an honest and substantial burgess, was made lieutenant of the castle. But when King Charles II was restored he made Richard Hosier, eldest son of Colonel Hosier, captain of the castle; and when the kingdom was wholly at peace this castle was by the king sold or given with the waste ground belonging to it, unto Francis Viscount Newport, now (1702) Earl of Bradford, who hath built two fair houses on the waste ground. In the time of King James II all the cannons and all the match of which there was several hundredweight, and many of the muskets that were in the castle, were by the king's order taken away and sent down water, I know not whither. Some of the townsmen secured part of the muskets in a private place of the castle, but I believe they are now unserviceable; for at that time the stocks of them were so rotten and worm-eaten that if a man did but handle them they would break and crumble to dust.

About the year 1649, it pleased God to visit this town with the plague. It broke out about the latter end of July, but was concealed by the townsmen till after Lambmas fair, and on the next day after the fair they fled out of town in whole shoals, so that there was no market kept there until Candlemas following. Howbeit, there was a small market kept on the Old Heath for things necessary for provision, and so at Monfords Bridge and in other places. There was frequent collections made in the parish churches for the relief of the poor of the town. The free school was removed to the school-house in Greensell; Mr. Challoner was then high school master, a learned and facetious man. The two chief and ablest ministers in Shrewsbury, viz. Mr. Thomas Blake, minister of St. Chads, and Mr. Fisher of St. Mary's removed to Myddle and dwelt both in Mr. Gittins's house at the higher well; they preached often at Myddle. Mr. Fisher was a man of middle stature and age, a fat plump body, a round visage, and black hair. Mr. Blake was a tall spare man, his hair sandy brown; he was somewhat aged a moderate, sober, grave, pious man; he wrote a learned treatise of the covenants, wherein he took some modest exceptions against some things mentioned by Mr. Baxter in his book of justification.

Oswestry is a market convenient for the inhabitants of some part of this parish. On the fourth of March is a good fair there for great oxen; on the first of May for cows and calves, and at St. Andrew's tide for fat swine. I will speak of some things that have happened here in my time. The governor of this town when it was a garrison for the king pulled down many houses that were without the wall lest they might shelter an enemy. The church also being without the wall was pulled down, and the top of the steeple unto that loft where the bell-frame stood. The bells were brought into the town and the organs were embezzled. After the town was well fortified, and the castle which was but small yet very strong, built by a Prince of Wales, Anno. 1111, General Mytton with his parliament forces came and beseiged it. He planted his cannons near that part of the steeple which was left; he battered the gate called the Church Gate in such sort that the garrison soldiers could not stay at it. General Mytton conceiving it was so but not being sure of it sent George Cranage, a bold and daring young man to see whether it were so; who took a hatchet in his hand and went to the drawbridge and found that the soldiers were gone and the gate was open, for the cannon had broken the doors, and this Cranage broke the chains of the drawbridge with his hatchet, and let it down so that the soldiers made haste to enter the town. But those that were within made like haste to meet them, which Cranage perceiving, and seeing a box of drakes standing within the gate ready charged, he turned the box of drakes towards those in the town, and one of Cranage's partners came with a firelock and gave fire to them which made such a slaughter among the garrison soldiers that they retreated and fled into the castle. Cranage was well rewarded and being well lined with sack was persuaded by the general to hang a buttar on the castle gate. Now a buttar is an iron shell as big as a pot; it was filled with powder and wild-fire balls, and had a handle with a hole in it by which it might be fastened with a nail to any place. Cranage takes this buttar with a cart-nail and a hammer, and got from house-to-house unto the house next the castle, and then stepping to the castle gate he fixed the buttar and stepping nimbly back again, escaped without any hurt; the buttar burst open the gate. I have been the longer in speaking of George Cranage, because that after the war was ended he came to live some while at the Red Bull, and afterwards at Newton on the Hill where he was tenant to Thomas Newans. He was a painful, laborious man in husbandry, and although he was a stout man of his hands, yet he was peaceable and a good neighbour. He went to live again at the Red Bull and there his wife died, and then he married Dorothy, the daughter of Rowland Plungen, and there he died.

Some Accidents which Happened in the Parish of Myddle in the Time of the Wars

King Charles I set up his standard at Nottingham, A.D. 1642, and because few there resorted to him, he removed thence to Shrewsbury about the latter end of summer 1642, in hopes that this country and Wales would soon furnish him with an army, and he was not disappointed in his expectation, for multitudes came to him daily. And out of these three towns, Myddle, Marton, and Newton, there went no less than twenty men, of which number thirteen were killed in the wars (vizt.)

First, Thomas Formeston, of Marton, a very hopeful young man, but at what place he was killed I cannot say.

Secondly, Nathaniell, the son of John Owen of Myddle, the father was hanged before the wars, and the son deserved it in the wars, for he was a Cataline to his own country. His common practice was to come by night with a party of horses to some neighbour's house and break open the doors, take what they pleased, and if the man of the house was found, they carried him to prison, from whence he could not be released without a ransom in money; so that no man here about was safe from him in his bed; and many did forsake their own houses. This Nat. Owen was mortally wounded by some of his own party, in an alehouse quarrel, near Bridgenorth, and was carried in a cart to Bridgenorth to be healed, but in the meantime the parliament party laid seige to Bridgenorth, and the garrison soldiers within the town set the town on fire, and fled into the castle, in which fire, this Owen (being unable to help himself), was burnt to death.

Thirdly, Richard Chaloner of Myddle, bastard son of Richard Chaloner, brother of Allen Chaloner, blacksmith. This bastard was partly maintained by the parish, and being a big lad, went to Shrewsbury, and was there listed, and went to Edgehill fight (which was October 23rd, 1642), and was never heard of afterwards in this country.

Fourthly, Reece Vaughan, he was brother to William Vaughan a weaver in Myddle, and brother to Margaret the wife of Francis Cleaton. He was killed at Hopton Castle in this county, where the garrison soldiers refusing fair quarter, when they might have had it, were afterward cut in pieces when the castle was taken by storm.

Fifthly, John Arthurs, a servant of my father's who was killed at the same castle.

Sixthly, Thomas Hayward, brother to Joseph Hayward the innkeeper then in Myddle was killed in the wars, but I cannot say where.

Seventhly, Thomas Taylor, son of Henry Taylor of Myddle, was killed, I think at Oswestry.

Eighthly and ninthly, William Preece of the cave (who was commonly called Scogan of the Goblin Hole), went for a soldier in the king's service and three of his sons (i.e.) Francis, Edward, and William, two of them viz. Francis and William were killed at High Ercall. The old man died in his bed, and Edward was hanged for stealing horses.

Tenthly and eleventhly, Richard Jukes and Thomas Jukes, sons of Roger Jukes, sometime innkeeper in Myddle.

Twelfthly, John Benion, a tailor, who lived in Newton in the house where Andrew Paine lives.

Thirteenthly, an idle fellow, who was a tailor and went from place to place to work in this parish, but had no habitation. These four last named went for soldiers, when the king was at Shrewsbury, and were heard of no more, so that it was supposed that they all died in the wars. And if so many died out of these three towns, we may reasonably guess that many thousands died in England in that war.

There were but few that went out of this parish to serve the parliament, and of them, there was none killed (as I know of) nor wounded except John Mould, son of Thomas Mould of Myddle Wood. He was a pretty little fellow, and a stout adventurous soldier. He was shot through the leg with a musket bullet, which broke the master bone of his leg and slew his horse under him. His leg was healed but was very crooked as long as he lived.

There happened no considerable act of hostility in this parish during the time of the wars, save only one small skirmage, in Myddle, part of which I saw, while I was a schoolboy at Myddle, under Mr. Richard Rodericke, who commanded us boys to come into the church, so that we could not see the whole action, but it was thus. There was one Cornet Collins, an Irishman, who was a garrison soldier for the king, at Shrawardine Castle. This Collins made his excursions very often into this parish, and took away cattle, provision, and bedding, and what he pleased. On the day before this conflict, he had been at Myddle taking away bedding, and when Margaret, the wife of Allen Chaloner, the smith, had brought out and showed him her best bed, he thinking it too coarse, cast it into the lake, before the door, and trod it under his horse feet. This cornet, on the day that this contest happened, came to Myddle and seven soldiers with him, and his horse having cast a shoe, he alighted at Allen Chaloner's shop to have a new one put on.

There was one Richard Maning, a garrison soldier at Morton Corbett, for the parliament. This Maning was brought up as a servant under Thomas Jukes, of Newton, with whom he lived many years, and finding that Nat. Owen (of whom I spoke before), did trouble this neighbourhood, he had a grudge against him, and came with seven more soldiers with him, hoping to find Owen at Myddle with his wife. This Maning and his companions came to Webscott, and so over Myddle Park, and came into Myddle at the gate by Mr. Gittin's house at what time the cornet's horse was a shoeing. The cornet hearing the gate clap, looked by the end of the shop and saw the soldiers coming, and thereupon he, and his men mounted their horses; and as the cornet came at the end of the shop, a brisk young fellow shot him through the body with a carbine shot, and he fell down in the lake at Allen Chaloner's door. His men fled, two were taken, and as Maning was pursuing them in Myddle Wood Field, which was then unenclosed, Maning having the best horse overtook them, while his partners were far behind, but one of the cornet's men shot Maning's horse which fell down dead under him, and Maning had been taken prisoner had not some of his men came to rescue him. He took the saddle under his arm, and the bridle in his hand, and went the next way to Wem, which was then a garrison for the parliament. The horse was killed on a bank near the further side of Myddle Field, where the widow Mansell has now a piece enclosed. The cornet was carried into Allen Chaloner's house, and laid on the floor; he desired to have a bed laid under him, but Margaret told him, she had none but that which he saw yesterday; he prayed her to forgive him, and lay that under him, which she did.

Mr. Rodericke was sent for to pray with him. I went with him, and saw the cornet lying on the bed, and much blood running along the floor. In the night following, a troop of horses came from Shrawardine, and pressed a team in Myddle, and so took the cornet to Shrawardine, where he died the next day.

Those two soldiers that were taken at Myddle, were Irishmen, and when they came to Wem were both hanged; for the parliament had made an ordinance, that all native Irish, that were found in actual armies in England should be hanged, upon which thirteen suffered; which thing, when Prince Rupert heard, he vowed, that the next thirteen that he took should be so served; which happened not long after, for Prince Rupert in the summer after, viz. 1644, came with a great army this way, and made his rendezvous on Holloway Hills (as he had done once before, and his brother Prince Maurice at another time), and took his quarters all night at Cockshutt, and the next day he made his rendezvous at Ellesmere. At which time, Mr. Mitton, of Halston, was general of the parliament forces in this county, and was a valiant and politic commander; and hearing the prince made only his rendezvous at Ellesmere and intended to go forward, the general hoping to find some stragglers in Ellesmere, that stayed behind the army, came with a troop of horses through byeways, but when he came to the gate that goes out of Oateley Park, he found that he had come too soon, for there was three or four troops of horses at Oateley Hall, which got between him and home; and therefore, when he and all his men had come through the gate they shot a horse dead up to the gate, to keep it from opening; but the others soon broke down two or three ranks of pales, and followed so close, that all the general's men before they came to Ellesmere were taken, except the general, and one George Higley (a little fellow). At last, one that had a good horse overtook the general, and laid his hand on his shoulder, and said, "you are my prisoner," but Higley struck the other in the face with his sword, which caused him to fall, and so the general and Higley turned down the dark lane that goes towards Birch Hall, and the others went straight into the town. But the general and Higley escaped, and when they came to Welsh Frankton there they made a stay and one other of his men came to them. The general had lost his hat, and being furnished again, he went to Oswestry, a garrison for the parliament.

The next day the prince caused these prisoners to be brought before him, and ordered thirteen of them to be hanged. They cast the dice on a drum-head to see who should die, and amongst them there was one Phillip Litleton, who had been servant and keeper of the park to my old master, Robert Corbett of Stanwardine, Esq. This Phillip saw Sir Vincent Corbett, of Morton Corbett, ride by, and said to some that stood by, "if Sir Vincent Corbett did know that I were here, he would save my life." Upon this a charitable soldier rode after Sir Vincent and told him what one of the prisoners said. He came back immediately, and seeing Phillip, he alighted from his horse and fell on his knees before the prince (who sat there on horseback to see the execution), and begged for the life of Phillip, which was readily granted on condition he would never bear arms against the king. Phillip promised and escaped, and afterwards no more Irish were hanged.

The Sword went through into his Body

I will mention later how Nathaniel Reve purchased off William Crosse the reversion of a lease of Billmarsh Farm for £20, which money Reve borrowed off Mr. Robert Finch, of Cockshutt, and pawned his lease for security of the money; and Reve being laid in jail, Mr. Finch entered upon the farm and became tenant to the Earl of Bridgewater. I will speak of his family: Robert Finch is descended of the ancient and substantial family of the Finches of Sheard Oake, in the township of Kenwicks Wood, in the parish of Ellesmere. His father's name was Francis Finch, who in my time was returned to serve the office of high constable, but he made his application to the justices at the general quarter sessions, and declared before the worshipful bench that the serving of that office had been very ominous to their family; for his grandfather and his father both died when they were high constables. The justices accepted of his apology and excused him. Howbeit, this Robert of whom I am speaking served the office of high constable, and no such accident befell him as his father seemed to fear.

Francis Finch has two sons Roger and Robert, and one daughter named Jane, who is married to Richard Payne of Weston Lullingfield. Roger enjoys his father's estate in Sheard Oake and Bagley. Robert married the widow of Francis Lloyd of Cockshutt; he is a good-humoured man and well-beloved, but for his wife . . .

His lease expired at Candlemas, 1704, and Samuel Newton of Broughton, took a lease for lives of Billmarsh Farm, and therefore I will say something of his family.

Thomas Newton (whom for distinction sake I must call Thomas Newton, the elder) had a fair estate in a place called Newtowne, in the parish of Wem, he married a sister of William Jenks of Cockshutt (who was cousin-german to my grandfather Richard Jenks), and had issue by her, two sons — John and Thomas. This Thomas, the younger, married Martha, the daughter of George Reve of Billmarsh. He lived some while at Albright Hussey, and held £140 per annum under Mr. Robert Corbett; and afterwards he removed to Broughton and held a farm under Richard Lyster, Esq., of about £100 per annum. He had many children of which this Samuel is one. He married a wife who was born about Melverley; she had some money and some land to her portion. The land was sold to raise money to take a lease of Billmarsh Farm.

John, the eldest son of Thomas Sewton the elder, married the sister of William Shaw of Tylley. He had issue by her, two sons — Thomas and John besides daughters. Thomas married the daughter of a rich widow who lived at Low Hill, near Wem. This widow's husband was dead long since and left her a good estate in money and two daughters. This Thomas Newton married the eldest, and Arthur Noneley of Burleton, married the youngest. This Thomas Newton had no child and yet he got into debt, and after some while he sold up his stock, set his lands, and came to sojourn with his brother-in-law Arthur Noneley, in Burleton. This Thomas was apt to drink, and in his drink was somewhat rude, often fighting in the alehouse. This Thomas Newton delighted to be accounted valiant, when indeed he was only rude, quarrelsome, and foolhardy. It happened that while he was at Burleton, and after he had been most part of the day in the alehouse, he was walking in his brother's-in-law's garden in the evening; the garden joins to the road that leads from Shrewsbury towards Ellesmere; and there he saw Mr. Robert Hesketh of Kenwicke, and his wife riding along the road, and their son Charles Hesketh riding after them and using very scurrilous, abusive, and undutiful language towards his parents. Thomas Newton somewhat sharply reproved him for it; Charles answered him with that rude damning language which he had learned when he was a soldier; and either struck him or struck at him with his staff. Some more words passed and they appointed to meet in the street; Newton ran through the house and took a long pike-evell in his hand; Hesketh with his sword in his hand met Newton at the wicket that goes into the street, and as Newton opened the wicket, Hesketh pricked him in the breast with his sword, and it seems the sword went through into his body. Whether Newton perceived himself much wounded or not I know not; but he struck Hesketh many blows with the butt end of the pick-evell and broke Hesketh's sword; now when Hesketh's sword was broken he alighted from his horse, and Newton casting away the pike-evell ran to close with him, but before he came to him he fell down and died. This tumult had gathered many people together, but while they were taking up Newton, this Hesketh fled away on foot into Burleton Moores and escaped, but left his horse behind him. The people were amazed to see the man dead and saw no blood; but when they had opened his clothes they found some blood and a small orifice of a wound in his breast, and therefore they conceived that he bled inwardly and that killed him.

Charles Hesketh appeared at the next assizes and was

arraigned, found guilty of manslaughter, had the benefit of his clergy, and saved his life: I wish he would spend it better. After the decease of this Thomas Newton, the estate in Newtowne came to his wife for her life, paying £10 per annum to her father-in-law John Newton, who is yet (1706) living; but the reversion belonged to John Newton, brother to Thomas Newton that was killed. This John loves drink as well or more than his brother Thomas: and conceiving that it would be a great while ere any profit came to him from this land, he first mortgaged it and then married the daughter of Peter Spendlove, a minister, son of Roger Spendlove of Tylley: her portion was small and he soon spent it; and now as I hear, he has sold the reversion of his land for ever, and now is spending the money merrily.

A short account of what family Richard Evans, Esq. was descended, who was slain at the foot of Myddle Hill, the 10th November 1704, and of the manner of his death:

Roger Evans (descended of the ancient and worthy as well as wealthy family of the Evanses of Trevloch, near Oswestry, in this county), was a younger brother, and was set an apprentice in London; and when the wars broke out, in the reign of King Charles I, between the king and parliament, this Roger Evans enlisted himself a soldier in the parliament army; and being a proper and strong man, and a person of good courage, he was first made a captain, and afterwards a colonel. He had a cut with a sword over his face, just between the end of his nose and his mouth, which left a scar of about a finger long, which continued as long as he lived, which was all that he got by the wars. His elder brother died in the time of the wars, and the paternal estate in Trevloch descended to this Roger Evans, who after the wars, was made a justice of peace, and was also high sheriff of the county. He demeaned himself with such wisdom and moderation in all things, that he was well respected by the best men in the county.

He married Dorothy Griffiths, who was daughter-in-law to my uncle William Gough of Sweeney, who paid the marriage portion. My uncle had purchased a farm in Trevloch, and this he gave to Mrs. Dorothy Evans and her heirs for ever, chargeable with the payment of £5 per annum to the parish of Oswestry, and £5 per annum to the parish of Myddle, for setting out of apprentices; he made Mr. Roger Evans, trustee for Oswestry parish, as he did me for Myddle, but of this I have spoken before.

Roger Evans had issue by his wife Dorothy — Richard Evans, who was a proper comely person. He was a kind and good-humoured man, but too much given to drinking, and being a stout man of his hands, he would not take an affront especially when he was in drink which caused him to be engaged in many frivolous affrays and quarrels in which he commonly had the better. But the pitcher that goes often to the well comes home broken at last.

Mr. Roger Evans, when he died left his son Richard in debt, which he (not without the help of his mother) quickly increased to such a rate, that they were forced to sell a considerable part of the estate, and then she died. Richard Evans was never married, and I think he had no inclination that way, but lived as if he designed to be his own heir, but did not forecast to keep anything to maintain him if he happened to live unto old age. But when he had plunged his estate in as much as it was worth, he sold all to Thomas Hunt, of Boreatton, Esq.; and among the rest, the land charged with the annuities aforesaid. Some say the purchase money was not all paid when he died.

In the beginning of November 1704, Richard Evans intending a journey to London, came to Boreatton, and being furnished with money came forward to Myddle, in company with one Price, a sort of a crack brain fellow, who in the summer before, had been a prisoner in Shrewsbury jail for debt; at which time Thomas Moore of Myddle, was there on the like account; and he called to see his jail fellow, Thomas Moore, who invited them to the alehouse, where they had two or three pints of ale at the door; and because the afternoon was far spent, they set forward again. But when they came to the lower end of Myddle town, Mr. Evans by all means would call and take his leave of his host, John Benion who lived at the foot of Myddle Hill. Now it happened that John Benion had been so busy with the cup that day, that he was not able to do anything but sleep, and could not go to bed to do that, and therefore his wife was helping him to bed when Mr. Evans came. There was also in the house one Laurence Bassnett, a shoemaker, who was descended of good parentage in Baschurch parish, but was a drunken fellow. There was likewise one Mathew Hinton, a weaver, descended of a substantial family in the parish of Wem; but he was an idle, drunken, rude fellow as any in this country.

When Mr. Evans called and Bassnett opened the door, and when Mr. Evans saw him, he said, Dam ye thou art not mine host. What provoking words Bassnett gave I know not, but Mr. Evans drew his sword, and Bassnett shut the door and talked with him through the window. What passionate words passed I cannot tell, but I have cause to think they were such as is too usual amongst drunken persons. Bassnett stepped out at the back door and Hinton with him, and coming to the oven on the back side Bassnett took a peel with which they put bread into the oven, and Hinton took a pole which they call an oven poker. They leaped over the hedge and meeting with Mr. Evans as he was going from the house Bassnett struck him with the peel which broke at the first blow, and Hinton coming behind Mr. Evans gave him a blow with the pole on the hinder part of his head which made him crouch down to the horse's neck, and with a second blow he struck him off his horse; some say he gave him several blows when he had fallen. They went again into the house and made fast the door and left Mr. Evans wallowing in his blood in the highway. The people of the house did not come out nor call the neighbours, but Price who was his companion came into the town and enquired for the constable, and sent him and several of the neighbours to him. It was half-an-hour, some say an hour before anyone came to him; and when they came they found there was life in him, but neither sense nor motion. The neighbours desired Mary Benion to open her door that they might bring him in and lay him on a bed but she refused. But when Bassnett and Hinton were fled out at the back door and the constable threatened to break the door, she opened it.

Mr. Evans was carried into the house and laid on a bed, and they found he had several wounds in his head, and that the hinder part of his scull was broken all to pieces; about eight o'clock that night he died. The neighbours apprehended Bassnett and put him under the constable's hands, and immediately pursued after Hinton, but by the benefit of a dark night he escaped. The inhabitants of Myddle and several other neighbouring towns made search several days all over the country for Hinton but he was never taken. Mr. Evans's friends were sent for in all haste; and when they came they caused the coroner's inquest to pass on him, and the jury, some say by persuasion of the coroner found it wilful murder, and that Laurence Bassnett and Mathew Hinton were guilty of it. The coroner committed Bassnett to jail and bound John Benion and Mary his wife to appear at the next assizes. On the Lord's day following Mr. Evans' friends and neighbours and several persons of quality took the corpse in a fair coffin on a coach draught and brought him to Oswestry where he was that afternoon solemnly buried amongst his ancestors. Laurence Bassnett was arraigned at the next assizes, and by the jury was found guilty of manslaughter; had the benefit of his clergy and saved his life. But soon after was taken for a soldier and is now, 1706, in the queen's service in Ireland.

CHAPTER 2

The Gallows Stood . . . Upon A Bank

The Situation of the Parish of Myddle

MYDDLE PARISH is wholly in the hundred of Pimhill, in the county of Shropshire. Nevertheless part of the said parish is in the allotment of Myddle and Loppington, and part of it is in the liberties of Shrewsbury. That part of the parish which is in the allotment of Myddle and Loppington contains Myddle Lordship, and the town and township of Balderton, and is commonly called this side of the parish. (Now the lordship of Myddle contains the towns and townships of Myddle, Marton, Newton on the Hill, and Houlston.) That part of the parish which lies in the liberties of Shrewsbury, contains Hadnalls Ease, the town and township of Alderton and Shotton Farm, and is called the further side of the parish. Hadnalls Ease contains the towns and townships of Hadnall, Haston, Smethcott and Hardwick Farm . . .

Brooks that Divide the Parish from other Parishes

There is a small brook on the east side of the parish, which has its rise head at a certain old marl pit, called Dunstall Pit, in Newton on the Hill; this brook passing awhile through land in Newton, turns south east, and for a short space parts the lands belonging to Newton from the township of Alderton, and afterwards it parts Myddle parish and Broughton parish (leaving Myddle parish on the westward), and passing over the lane called the Old Field Lane, it has there got the name of the brook in the Old Field Lane . . .

There is another brook which takes its rise head at a little pond or moat in Preston Gubballs, and passing thence to Haremear, it goes through the middle of it, and leaves it at a place called the Meare House, and passing still northward it goes over the lane or roadway that leads from Ellesmere to Shrewsbury; it there runs under a stone bridge, built about sixty years past at the parish charge, and at the instigation of Robert More, brother, and farmer, of Mr. Thomas More, then Rector of Myddle. This bridge is called Bristle Bridge, the reason of this name was thus: there is a certain cave in the rock near this bridge, this cave was formerly a hole in the rock, and was called the Goblin Hole, and afterwards was made into a habitation, and a stone chimney built up to it by one Fardo, after whose death one William Preece, son of Griffith ap Reece of Newton on the Hill (a wealthy tenant there holding the lands of Mr. Corbett, Esq., in Newton), dwelt in it. This William Preece was set an apprentice by his father to a goldsmith in London, but he soon out went his master, and went for a soldier (in Queen Elizabeth's time) into the Low Countries. At his return he married the daughter of Chetwall of Peplow, in the parish of Hodnett, and came to live in this cave. After his return from the wars he told so many romantic stories, of his strange adventures, that people gave him the name of Scoggan, by which name (at last) he was better known than by the name of William Preece. But amongst the rest of the stories that were told of him, or by him, one was, that he had killed a monstrous boar, of so large a size that the bristles on his back were as big as pike-eval grains. This story being fresh among the neighbours and the workmen that were building the said bridge, they gave it the name of Bristle Bridge, which name still continues . . .

Rectors of Myddle

I have heard of one Foster, or Forester, formerly rector here. But because he lived here before the reformation (as I believe), we have nothing memorable of him; I will therefore begin with Mr. Thomas Wilton, a reverend divine, and the first (as I conceive) after the reformation. He continued rector of this place many years. He was careful to reform those things, that through negligence, were grown into disorder, and to settle things in such a way as might conduce to the future peace and benefit of the parishioners . . .

About forty years ago, a certain reverend grave divine came to Myddle and sojourned with Mr. Joshua Richardson, then rector. They called him Dr. Richardson. I suppose he was outed of some benefice by the parliament party. He preached sometimes at Myddle, he wore always (yea, even when he was preaching) a dagger at his girdle under his upper garment. He died at Myddle and was buried under Mr. Wilton's gravestone. I saw the bottom of Mr. Wilton's coffin taken up; it was a plank of about two or three inches thick, and was not consumed although Mr. Wilton had been buried above fifty years.

Next to Mr. Wilton, was Mr. Ralph Kinaston who was well descended, deriving his pedigree (though by many descents) from the ancient and worthy family of the Kinastons of Hordley.

He was a person of bold and undaunted spirit, which appears in that he adventured the lists in a great suit at law (about the bounds of the parish in some part of Hardwick Farm) with Sir Humphrey Lea, of Lea Hall, who was a person brought up to the law, but when his eldest brother died without issue he cast off his bar gown and entered upon his paternal estate. He was one of the first baronets that were created in Shropshire by King James I. This Sir Humphrey Lea was impropriator of the tithes of Greensell parish, and he then claimed and carried away the tithes of some pieces of land belonging to Hardwick which were then, and still are by some persons, reputed to be in the parish of Myddle . . .

This Mr. Kinaston kept good hospitality and was very charitable. An instance of the latter, I will briefly mention. There was a poor weaver, named Parks, who lived in Newton on the Hill, he had eleven children, all baptized by Mr. Kinaston; at the baptizing the tenth or eleventh, Mr. Kinaston said (merrily) "Now one child is due to the parson," to which Parks agreed, and Mr. Kinaston chose a girl, that was about the middle age among the rest, and brought her up at his own house, and she became his servant; and when she had served several years, he gave her in marriage with thirty, some say sixty pounds' portion to one Cartwright, who lived beyond Ellesmere, and had an estate to balance such a portion . . .

Mr. Kinaston was succeeded (but not exceeded) by Mr. Thomas More, a Yorkshireman, the first rector that was presented by the Earl of Bridgewater. This Mr. More was Rector of Myddle, and Vicar of Ellesmere. His residence was at Ellesmere. He kept a curate at Myddle and let out the whole tithes to his brother, Robert More, at a dearer value than ever they have been since set for. He had his rent paid weekly, not daring to adventure his brother too far. He was much commended for an excellent preacher and as much blamed for his too much parsimony, or covetousness, and want of charity. He came constantly once a month to officiate at Myddle. He would ride to the church stile, go straight into the church, and after the service and sermon ended, he would take horse at the church stile and ride back to Ellesmere. He regarded not the repair of the parsonage-house and buildings, one large barn whereof went to ruin in his time. The riches and money that he had got together, he lived to see most of them spent by his children. He was a loyal subject to King Charles I, and therefore to avoid the troubles that the parliament forces did put him to, he left his places, and fled to London. During his absence, his places were slenderly and seldom served. About the year 1646, or soon after, the parliament (having gained the upper hand of the king's forces), began to displace all scandalous and insufficient ministers, and all malignants (for so they called all such as had adhered to the king), whereupon Mr. More came into the country seeking to retain his places. He was entertained by Robert Corbett Esq., who had a great respect for him, upon the account of his excellent preaching. During his stay, he preached every Lord's day in Cockshutt chapel. But notwithstanding Mr. Corbett's and his own endeavours, he was outed of both his places, and preaching his farewell sermon in the said chapel (because he could not be admitted into either of his parish churches), he went back again to London, and never returned again into this country.

The same power that displaced Mr. More did, in his stead, place in Myddle Mr. Joshua Richardson, M.A., son of Joshua Richardson, of Broughton, upon condition that he would allow the tithes of Hadnall's Ease, or pay a salary much what equivalent to the value thereof to a preaching minister, to be constantly resident in Hadnall's Ease.

This Mr. Richardson was an able and laborious minister. His whole employment was about the concerns of his ministry; his wife being a prudent and careful woman, managed the rest of his affairs with great diligence and discretion. After the death of Mr. More, the Right Hon. John Earle of Bridgewater (knowing that Mr. Richardson was well beloved in his parish), by a certain kind of state amnesty, permitted him to continue minister on the same terms and conditions that he was put in by the parliament. This Mr. Richardson built that part of the parsonage house which is the kitchen and the rooms below it, in which he made use of so much of the timber as was left of the barn that fell down in Mr. More's time.

After the restoration of King Charles II, when the act for conformity came out, Mr. Richardson refusing to subscribe the declaration inserted in the act concerning the solemn league and covenant, lost his place; and with him fell the minister of Hadnall's Ease. I had so much intimate acquaintance with Mr. Richardson, that he would willingly have conformed to the discipline and constitution of the Church of England, but he told me he could not with a safe conscience subscribe to the declaration against the covenant. He received the tithes due before Bartholomew-tide, according to the act of parliament, at which time all the rye and the wheat was got in, and some oats. He removed to Broughton, where he lived one year with his brother, Captain Richardson, and afterwards went to a farm called Ditches, near Wem, but when the act of parliament came forth that no outed minister should live within five miles of the place where he had formerly officiated, he removed to Alkinton, near Whitchurch (the place from whence his father came, when he had purchased his lands in Broughton, of Mr. Ottey). Here Mr. Richardson lived a private, peaceable, and pious life; exercising himself in religious duties, and instructing and teaching his own and some of his relations children in good literature.

He died at Alkinton, and was buried at Whitchurch. Dr. Fowler preached his funeral sermon, and there gave him a deserved commendation. He bequeathed a certain number of bibles, and of those books of Mr. Baxter entitled, "A Call to the Unconverted," to be given to certain poor people in the parish of Myddle, after his decease, which legacy was faithfully performed by his prudent widow and executrix.

He was succeeded by Mr. William Hollway, M.A., some time student of Christ Church, in Oxford. The transactions and occurrences of his time are fresh in memory, and, therefore, I shall only say, that he was a man short-sighted, but of a discerning spirit to discover the nature and dispositions of persons. He was naturally addicted to passion, which he vented in some hasty expressions, not suffering it to gangreen into malice. He was easily persuaded to forgive injuries but wisely suspicious (for the future) of any one that had once done him a diskindness.

He died about midsummer, A.D. 1689, and lies buried in Myddle chancel, within the communion rails, under an old plain gravestone, over the middle of the communion table.

Parish Clerks

The first that I remember was Will. Hunt, a person very fit for the place, as to his reading and singing with a clear and audible voice, but for his writing I can say nothing. He commonly kept a petty school in Myddle. There was a custom in his time, that upon Christmas Day, in the afternoon after divine service, and when the minister was gone out of the church, the clerk should sing a Christmas carol in the church, which I have heard this Will. Hunt do, being assisted by old Mr. Richard Gitting, who bore a base exceeding well. This Will. Hunt lived in that tenement in the lower end of Myddle, which is called Hunt's Tenement.

The next was Richard Ralphs, a person in all respects well qualified for that office. In his time there was an ordinance of parliament that there should be a parish registrar sworn in every parish. His office was to publish the banns of marriage, and to give certificates thereof; and also to register the time of all births (not christenings), weddings, and burials. This Richard Ralphs was sworn registrar of this parish by Robert Corbett, of Stanwardine in the Wood, Esq., then justice of the peace and quorum, and custos rotulorum of this county. Not long after the restoration of King Charles II, the young people of Myddle, and some drunken fellows, were about setting up a maypole near the church stile in Myddle, and this Richard Ralphs spoke some words against them; upon which he was brought before Francis Thornes, of Shelvocke, Esq., then justice of the peace, and there it was deposed on oath, against him, that he said it was as great a sin to set up a maypole, as it was to cut off the king's head. (These words he denied, even to his dying day.) Upon this, he was bound over to the assizes, and there indicted for these treasonable words, and fined in five marks; and an order was made that he should lose his place.

Mr. Hollway, in the room of Ralphs, chose Thomas Highway, a person altogether unfit for such an employment. He can read but little; he can sing but one tune of the psalms. He can scarse write his own name, or read any written hand, but because he continued all Mr. Hollway's time, and has now got an able assistant (viz) John Hewitt, Jnr., a person in all points well qualified for the place, therefore Mr. Dale is pleased to continue him although he is now little more then a sexton . . .

Myddle Lordship

This lordship was formerly a lordship marcher, because this and others, were the bounds and borders (which they called marches) of Wales; and to prevent the out roads, pilfering, and plundering of the Welsh, there were made barons of the marches, and lords marchers, of whom the lord of this manor was one. There were several privileges which belonged to these lordships, as that the lords had the administration of laws to the inhabitants in their courts, that the king's writs, in some cases, shall not here take place, and that the lord marcher had power of life and death in criminal causes.

We have by tradition that there was such enmity between the Britains and Saxons, that the Welshmen accounted all for a lawful prize which they stole from the English. And we have a tradition, that the inhabitants of these neighbouring towns, had in every town, a piece of ground adjoining to their houses, which was moated about with a large ditch, and fenced with a strong ditch fence and pale, wherein they kept their cattle every night, with persons to watch them; and that there was a light-horseman maintained in every town with a good horse, sword, and spear, who was always ready, upon the least notice to ride straight to the Platt Bridge, there to meet his companions; and if they found any Welshman on this side of the Platt Bridge, and the river of Perry, if they could apprehend him he was sure to be put to death: but if the Welshmen had got over the bridge with stolen cattle, then we have an ancient saying that they would cry, "*Ptroove* mine own," for the horsemen durst not follow any further; if they were taken beyond the bridge they were straightaway hanged.

The place of execution, or gallows, in this lordship was on Myddle Hill, in that field formerly called the Gallowtree-field, and now the Hill field. I have often heard that stile on Myddle Hill (near John Williams's cottage) called the Gallowtree-stile. Richard Wolph, of Myddle, a very old man (who died in my time) would promise to show the very place where the gallows stood, which he said, was upon a bank, in the higher end of that piece of land wherein John Bennion's house now stands . . .

Inhabitants of Myddle Castle

We have a tradition that the Lord Strange, whilst he was Lord of Myddle, did live part of the year at Myddle Castle, and part of the year at Knockin Castle. But after these lordships descended to the Darbys, then there was a constable, or castle keeper of this castle. The first that I read of in ancient deeds was Will. Dod, constable of the castle of Myddle, after him Sir Roger Kinaston, of *Hordley,* was, by commission, made castle keeper of Myddle Castle and Knockin. After his decease, his younger son, Humphry Kinaston (who for his dissolute and riotous living was called the wild Humphry), was tenant of this castle. He had two wives, but both of so mean birth, that they could not lay claim to any coat of arms, as appears by the card of Kinaston's arms, which Mr. Edward Kinaston of Oateley, showed me not long before his death. I have not heard of any children which wild Humphry had but I have heard of much debt that he had contracted; and being outlawed in debt, he left Myddle Castle (which he had suffered to grow ruinous, for want of repair); and went and sheltered himself in a cave near to Nescliffe; which, to this day, is called Kinaston's Cave, and of him the people tell almost as many romantic stories, as of the great outlaw Robin Hood. Yet one thing I must remember that on a time when he was got over Monford's Bridge, and was on that side Severn which is next to Shrewsbury, and must needs return over that bridge, the under sheriff came with a considerable company of men to the bridge (which then was made with stone pillars and wooden planks) and having taken up several planks, and made such a breadth as they thought no horse was able to leap over, they laid themselves in ambush; and when wild Humphry returned, and was about to enter upon the bridge, they rose up to apprehend him, which he perceiving, put spurs to his horse, and riding full speed, leaped clearly over the breadth. The measure of this leap was afterwards marked out upon Knockin Heath, upon a green plot by the wayside that leads from Knockin towards Nescliffe, with an H and a K cut in the ground at the ends of the leap. The letters were about an elne long, and were a spade graff broad and a spade graff deep. These letters were usually repaired yearly by Mr. Kinaston, of Ruyton. I confess I have seen the letters, but did not take the measure of the distance. After wild Humphry's time, this castle was never inhabited, but went utterly to ruin . . .

Meares and Pooles

The inhabitants of Myddle Castle were plentifully furnished with fresh fish out of the waters within the lordship. And first Haremeare yielded great plenty of silver-coloured eels, beside an abundance of other fish. When Myddle Castle was gone to ruin, so that it was unhabitable, the meare was leased by Will. Earle of Darby, unto Sir Andrew Corbett, of Morton Corbett, and to Mr. Kelton, of Withyford.

Haremeare Mosse was encompassed round with the water of this meare; howbeit, the neighbours did get some *turfs* upon it, which they carried over the water in boats; but Sir Andrew Corbett caused a large causey, or bank, to be raised through the water, so that teams and carts might easily pass from Haremeare Heath to the Mosse, and the turfs (which before were had freely) were sold at 8d. a yard, that is, 80 square yards, to cut and lay upon, which yielded a load for the best team that was.

Afterward, Sir Andrew Corbett and Mr. Kelton caused this meare to be loosed and made dry, and converted it to meadow and pasture. After their lease was expired, my father, and Richard

Jukes, of Newton, took a lease for 21 years of Haremeare, the Mosse, and Haremeare Warren. They took a lease of the warren at the request of the neighbours, as I will show hereafter. After this lease, I took a lease of Haremeare and the Mosse for twenty-one years, which expired about three years ago, and now Mr. William Watkins, of Shotton, has a lease of it. Haremeare and the Mosse are in the township of Myddle but yet they pay leawans in Newton. That it is in Myddle will appear by a tragical story that I shall relate, concerning the death of a servant of Sir Edward Kinaston's of Oateley, which thus happened. There was one Clarke, of Preston Gubballs, who had formerly been tenant to Sir Edward Kinaston, of a tenement in Welsh Hampton, and was indebted for arrears of rent, due to Sir Edward; whereupon he sued out a writ against this Clarke, and sent a bailiff to arrest him; and because Clarke had some lusty young men to his sons, therefore Sir Edward sent one of his servants to assist the bailiff, if need were. Clarke was cutting peat on Haremeare Mosse; Sir Edward's man stayed in the wood in Pimhill; the bailiff went towards Clarke, and being beaten back by Clarke's sons, Sir Edward's man came with his sword drawn, and swore he would make hay with them. But one of Clarke's sons, with a turf spade, which they call a peat iron (a very keen thing) struck Sir Edward's man on the head, and cloave out his brains. The bailiff fled; Clarke was rescued; and his son fled, and escaped. The coroner was sent for and by appointment of Sir Humphry Lea, the inhabitants of Myddle paid the coroner's fees. Clarke's son escaped the hand of justice, but not the judgment of God, for he that spilled man's blood, by man shall his blood be spilt, for when all things were quiet, and this thing seemed forgotten, Clarke's son came into this country again, and lived at Welsh Hampton, where a quarrel happening between him and one Hopkin, his next neighbour, about their garden hayment, as they stood quarrelling, each man in his own garden, Hopkin cast a stone at Clarke, which struck him so directly on the head, that it killed him. How Hopkin escaped the law, I have not heard; but vengeance suffered him not long to live, for a quarrel happened between him and one Lyth, a neighbour of his, as they were in an alehouse in Ellesmere, in the night time, which quarrel ended in words, and Hopkin went towards home; and not long after Lyth went thence. The next morning Hopkin was found dead in Oatley Park, having been knocked on the head with the foot of a washing stock which stood at Ellesmere meare, which foot was found not far from him. Lyth was apprehended, and committed to prison on suspicion of the murder, and lay there several years, for it was in the heat of the wars, and no assizes or gaol delivery was then held. But when the parliament forces had taken Shrewsbury, they set at liberty all prisoners, as well criminal as debtors, and this Lyth among the rest. I have written this story for the strangeness of it, though it be beside the matter . . .

Haremeare Warren

This has been a warren of no long continuance, for although there might be some connies among these rocks, in the times of the Lords Strange and the Earles of Derby, yet there was no warren until the Lord Keeper Egerton had purchased this manor, and then he procured a charter for a free warren on Haremeare Heath, Holloway Hills, Myddle Hill, and the rocky grounds (where the plough cannot go) in those pieces called the Hill Leasows, which lie between Holloway Hills, and Myddle Hill. After the obtaining of this charter, the warren was leased to one Twiford, a man that had been well educated, but whence he came I know not, unless he were that Twiford who sold lands in Marton to Richard Acherley. This Twiford built the lodge or warren house, on Haremeare Heath, and more buildings adjoining to it, which are now gone to ruin. He lived in good repute, he taught neighbours' children to read, and his wife taught young women to sew, and make needleworks; he had a daughter named Sarah, she married one Francis Jones, *alias* Reece, and lived in a small tenement of Crosses near Yorton Heath. After the death of Twiford, Mr. Thomas Hoskins of Webscott, took a lease of the warren for his life. He was a habituated drunkard, and kept one Reynold Sherry for his warrener, as bad a drunkard as himself; and after him one Francis Trevor, the worst drunkard, but craftiest of the three. He sold ale in the lodge, and would often brag that Prince Rupert was once his guest and commended his ale; for it happened that as the prince came that way with his army, he called and asked Francis whether he kept ale, and Francis answered "yes". The prince called for a flagon, drunk part of it, and said it was good ale, and thereupon alighted and came into the lodge and wrote a letter there and sent it away. He gave Francis sixpence for his ale, and gave a charge to the soldiers that none should drink his ale without paying but they observed it not . . .

Commons

Haremeare Heath; this common belongs wholly to the inhabitants of Newton on the Hill . . .

Upon this common there is great store of free stone, very useful for building. The inhabitants within the manor pay to the lord one shilling for every hundred (that is six score) foot of stone, but foreigners pay one shilling and sixpence. Upon this common there is found a sort of blue stone, which they say is copper mine. In the summer before King Charles I came to Shrewsbury, to raise his army in the beginning of the wars (which was, I conceive, about the year 1643), certain miners got a great quantity of this stone, which was brought in carts to the warren house, and there laid up to the house wall, and proclamation made in Myddle Church, that it was treason for anyone to take away without orders. But when the king came to Shrewsbury the miners went all for soldiers . . .

Highways in that part of this Parish which lies without the Liberties of Shrewsbury

The Church way from Newton on the Hill to Myddle, comes into . . . the middle of the space between Myddle Hill and Haremeare Heath; and that place (being a sort of a cross way) was, by ancient people, called the Setts, because in the time of popery, the people, when they went that way with a corpse to be buried, they did there set down the corpse, and kneeling round about it did mumble over some prayers, either for the soul of the deceased, or for themselves. This usage is now forelet in this country; but is still observed (as I have seen) in some parts of Wales . . .

And . . . because I have often used the name of Divlin Wood and Divlin Lane, and because the name seems strange, and is not now used, but only found in ancient writings, I will give the signification of the word, and first, I find that dive, dep, depen, and dup, are the same with what we term deep; and . . . secondly, I find that lin, lene, and laune, do signify a plain place amongst wood (vide. Co. on Litt. p.6) and therefore it is plain that this word signifies a deep plain amongst woods. And if you take notice of the situation of the place, you will find it more unlevel with banks and deep slades, than any other low grounds in the lordship. This may confute that idle conceit that the superstitious monks and friars did formerly persuade ignorant people that there were fairies (or furies) and hob-goblins. And this wood being a thick, dark, and dismal place, was haunted by some aerial spirits, and, therefore called Divlin Wood. But truth and knowledge have, in these days, dispersed such clouds of ignorance and error.

OBSERVATIONS CONCERNING THE SEATS IN MYDDLE AND THE FAMILIES TO WHICH THEY BELONG WRITTEN BY RICHARD GOUGH, AGED 67, 1701

CHAPTER 3

A Bawling, Bold, Confident Person

The Church

A pew is a certain place in church encompassed with wainscot, or some other thing, for several persons to sit in together. A seat or kneeling (for in this case they are the same) in such a part of a pew, as belongs to one family or person. And a pew may belong wholly to one family or it may belong to two or three families or more. The disposal of seats in the body of the church does belong to the ordinary, and no man can claim a right to a seat without prescription or some other good reason (Boothby v. Bailey). A pew or seat does not belong to a person or to land, but to a house, therefore if a man remove from a house to dwell in another, he shall not retain the seat belonging to the first house . . .

I hope no man will blame me for not naming every person according to that which he conceives is his right and superiority in the seats in church, because it is a thing impossible for any man to know; and therefore, I have not endeavoured to do it, but have written the names according as they came to my memory; but if anyone be minded to give a guess in this matter, let him first take notice of every man's church *leawan,* and then look over what I have written concerning the descent and pedigree of all, or most part of the families in this side of the parish, and then he may give some probable conjecture in this matter. If any man shall blame me for that I have declared the vicious lives or actions of their ancestors, let him take care to avoid such evil courses, that he leave not a blemish on his name when he is dead, and let him know that I have written nothing out of malice. I doubt not but some persons will think that many things that I have written are altogether useless; but I do believe that there is nothing herein mentioned which may not by chance at one time or other happen to be needful to some person or other . . .

1. The first seat on the north side of the north isle belongs to Mr. Hanmer's farm in Marton . . .

Mr. Hanmer's farm did formerly belong to the manor of Walford. The family of the Hords were lords of it and of the manor of Stanwardine in the Wood, and (issue male of Hord failing), one of the Kinastons of Hordley married the daughter of Hord, and so became Lord of Walford, etc. The last (save one) of the Kinastons of Walford, was Phillip Kinaston, who had three sons — Thomas, to whom he gave Walford and Stanwardine and several other lands; Richard, to whom he gave a farm in Eyton (which is now Tomkins' farm, Richard died without issue, and this farm reverted again to Walford); Edward, to whom he gave this farm in Marton, which I call Mr. Hanmer's farm. Thomas Kinaston of Walford had two legitimate daughters and a bastard son. He left (as I conceive), Sir Vincent Corbett of Moreton Corbett, guardian to his two daughters. This Sir Vincent Corbett was a very eminent person in this county. In his time he had the sons of esquires and worthy gentlemen to wait on him as his servants. He married the two daughters of Kinaston to two of his servants, viz. Dorothy the eldest, who was an easy, mild-natured gentlewoman, he married to Ralph Clive a branch of that worthy family of the Clives of Stits or Stich, who had issue by her, Edward Clive. This Edward married the daughter and heirs of Richard Lloyd of Kayhowell, and by that means added the farm of Kayhowell, and seven tenements in Edgerley to his other estate which was Walford, Wooderton, Eyton farm, and some part of Boreatton. Edward had issue, George Clive, a very bad husband; he sold Kayhowell, and the seven tenements. He sold Wooderton and what he had of Boreatton; he sold all, save what was so settled at marriage that he could not sell it. He lay long a prisoner for debt; but whether he died a prisoner I cannot say. He married Judith, the daughter of — Hanmer of Marton, and had issued by her, Thomas Clive, who was a colonel in the parliament army, in the wars, *temp.* Car. I. He married the daughter of Mr. Wareing of Woodcott, and had issue by her, George Clive, who married Elizabeth, daughter of Robert Corbett of Stanwardine, Esq., and had issue by her, Thomas Clive, now (1701) living.

Jane, the second daughter of Thomas Kinaston, was married to Robert Corbett, son of Roger Corbett of Shawbury, Esq., descended from the right worship family of the Corbetts of Moreton Corbett. He had with her Stanwardine in the Wood and several lands in Hampton Wood, Sugdon, Burleton, Wikey Marton, and Newton of the Hill. He built Stanwardine Hall that now is. The hall formerly stood in a place not far distant, which was moated about. It is now converted into a garden, and still retains the name of the old hall. This Robert Corbett had issue, Thomas and Richard, and a daughter, who has married to Phillip Young of Keinton, Esq. Richard was a barrister at law, and sometime steward to the right honourable Earl of Arundel; he died without issue. Thomas, the eldest son, enlarged Stanwardine Park, and purchased lands in Wicherley and Bagley. He married Elizabeth, the youngest daughter of Sir Vincent Corbett, of Moreton Corbett, and had issue by her, Robert and Mary, and then died. His widow afterward married Sir Thomas Scriven; she lived to a good old age, and I have seen her read a letter without spectacles when she was above eighty years old. Mary, the daughter of Thomas Corbett, married — Reve, Esq. steward to the Marquesse of Winchester, immediately before Daniel Wicherley of Clive Esq. Robert, the only son of Thomas Corbett, was a very eminent person in this county, in his time; he was a justice of the peace and quorum custos rotulorum of this county, and a master in chancery. Under him I had my education for many years, and served him as his clerk; he was once chosen a knight for the shire, and served in parliament, where they presented the protector with twenty-four acts; he was willing to sign some of them, but not all, but the parliament had voted that all should be signed or none. The protector took time to consider until next day, and then he came to the parliament house with a frowning countenance, and with many appropriate terms, dissolved them, and gave them the character of a pack of stubborn knaves. This Robert married Elizabeth, the daughter of Sir Henry Ludlow of Clarington Park, in Wiltshire, and had issue by her, Thomas, and four daughters. Thomas Corbett married Mary Gerard, of Stroton in the West. They are both living in the county of Worcester, for Stanwardine is sold to Sir John Win, of Watstay, so-called from Wat or Walter stopping here.

I should now return to Marton, but because many marriages of persons in this parish of Myddle have been made with persons of Cayhowell, I will say something of that farm. I have before mentioned, that Edward Clive had this farm by the marriage of the daughter and heiress of Richard Lloyd, and that he had issue by her, George Clive. This George Clive sold it to Sir Thomas Harris (one of the first baronets which King James I created in this county, and a great lawyer). But when this Sir Thomas Harris had purchased Boreatton and the manor of Baschurch of Sir William Onslow, he sold this farm to Thomas Bradocke a citizen of London, who came down and lived at Kayhowell. Roger Sandford, of Newton on the Hill, married Mary, the sister of this Thomas Bradocke. His son, Thomas Bradocke, married Elizabeth, the daughter of Rowland Hill, of Hawkston, Esq. Richard Tyler, of Balderton, married Mary, the sister of this Thomas Bradocke; and Andrew, the son of this Thomas Bradocke, married Dorothy, my only sister, and dying a few years after, left one son and one daughter behind him, both which died without issue, and the inheritance descended to the two daughters of Frances (the sister of Andrew), which she had by Mr. Bourey, then minister of Holt, in the county of Denbigh. The eldest of these daughters married one Mede, a proctor in the consistory court of Dublin, in Ireland. The younger married one Fennyhurst, a mercer in the city of West Chester. These four joining together, sold the inheritance to Mr. Simon Hanmer of Duffrid; but my sister being yet alive, retains her jointure out of it.

There is a wonderful thing observable concerning this farm, of which I may say, in the words of Du Bartas —

"Strange to be told, and though believed of few,
Yet is not so incredible as true."

It is observed that if the chief person of the family that inhabits this farm do fall sick, if his sickness be to death, there comes a pair of pigeons to the house about a fortnight or a week before the person's death, and continue there until the person's death, and then go away. This I have known them do three several times. First, old Mr. Bradocke, fell sick about a quarter of a year after my sister was married, and the pair of pigeons came thither, which I saw. They did every night roost under the shelter of the roof of the kitchen at the end, and did sit upon the ends of the side raisers. In the daytime they fled about the gardens and yards. I have seen them pecking on the hemp but as if they did feed, and for ought I know they did feed. They were pretty large pigeons; the feathers on their tails were white, and the long feathers of their wings, their breasts, and bellies, white, and a large white ring about their necks; but the tops of their heads, their backs, and their wings (except the long feathers), were of a light-brown or nutmeg colour. (My brother-in-law Andrew Bradocke, told me that he feared his mother would die, for there came such a pair of pigeons before his father's death, and he had heard they did so before the death of his grandfather.) After the death of Mrs. Bradocke, the pigeons went away. Secondly, about three-quarters of a year after the death of Mrs. Bradocke, my father going to give a visit to them at Kayhowell, fell sick there and lay sick about nine or ten weeks. About a fortnight before his death, the pigeons came; and when he was dead, went away. Thirdly, about a year after his death, my brother-in-law, Andrew Bradocke, fell sick, the pigeons came, and he died; they seemed to me to be the same pigeons at all these three times. When I went to pay Mr. Smalman, then minister of Kynerley the burial fee for Andrew Bradocke, which was in April, Mr. Smalman said, this is the fiftieth corpse which I have interred here since candlemas last, and God knows who is next, which happened to be himself. Andrew Bradocke died of a sort of a rambling feverish distemper, which raged in that country, and my sister soon after his decease fell sick, but she recovered, and during her sickness, the pigeons came not, which I observed, for I went thither every day, and returned at night. Afterwards my sister set out her farm to John Owen a substantial tenant, who about three years after, fell sick; and my sister coming to Newton, told me that she feared her tenant would be dead, for he was sick, and the pigeons came; and he died then. You may read a parallel story to this in Mr. Camden, who speaking of the worshipful family of the Brereton's in Cheshire, says, that before the death of any heir of that family, of Breretons there be seen in a pool adjoining, bodies of trees swimming for certain days together. He there likewise gives his opinion how these things come to pass; but I leave it to those who are better learned than I am in the secrets of philosophy. But now I return to Marton.

Mr. Kinaston had issue four daughters; the first was married unto Roger Hanmer a younger brother of that right worshipful family of the Hanmers, of Hanmer in Flintshire. The second was married to one Onslow, of the family of Boreatton. The third to one Partridge of Aderley. The fourth was married to some person thereabout whose name I have not heard. The two younger sisters sold their parts to Mr. Hanmer; but Onslow had a fourth part of the lands appointed out for him, and built a house upon it, which is that house in Marton which stands next to this end of the lane that leads from Marton to Weston Lullingfield. Roger Hanmer had issue, Edward and Judith. This Judith was married to George Clive of Wallford, as I said before. Edward Hanmer had issue — Humphrey, and Elizabeth, who was married to Thomas Ash of Marton. Humphrey had issue, William, who married the daughter of one Baker of Marton, a tenant to the Corbetts of Stanwardine, and had issue by her, William, the second of that name. His father was wanting in giving him good learning; but he had good natural parts, and for comely lineaments of body, and for a nimble strength and activity of body none in the parish exceeded him. He married Elizabeth, the daughter of Edward

Tomkins of Grafton, in the parish of Baschurch, and had issue by her, Humphrey Hanmer, who married Elizabeth the youngest daughter of John Groom, of Sleape, and had issue by her, Humphrey and Elizabeth, who both died when they were almost come to their maturity. His wife died about the same time: and after he married Mary, the daughter of Edward Thornes of Treginvor, and had several children by her, and, dying, left them very young.

There is a kneeling in this pew, which belongs to that chief house in Marton which Thomas Acherley purchased of Lloyd Peirce, Esq.; it is not that house wherein Andrew Acherley now dwells but the house which stands on the right hand as we go from the street to Andrew Acherley's dwelling-house, and is now made use of for malting rooms and corn chambers; and the barn that stands on the west side of it is all the building that belongs to it. I can give no account of the family of Lloyd Peirce, neither is it necessary; but I shall give an account of the Acherleyes, since they had any estate in this parish.

There was one Richard Acherley, a younger brother of that ancient and substantial family of the Acherleyes of Stanwardine in the Fields. He was a tanner, and had his tan-house in Stanwardine in the field, but he lived (as a tenant) at Wicherley Hall. He purchased lands in Marton of David Owen, and one Twiford. I suppose these two had married two co-heiresses, for I find no mention of but one house of the lands, and that stood on a sandy bank on this side of Mr. Acherley's new barns. Richard Acherley had issue, Thomas Acherley, to whom he gave these lands in Marton. This Thomas was a tanner and dwelt in Marton, and held Mr. Lloyd Peirce's house there, and dwelt in it, and suffered the other to go to decay. He built a tan-house, which is now standing by the old mill brook. He had two sons — Thomas, the second of that name, and Richard — he had also two daughters. After the death of his first wife he married the widow of Nicholas Gough of Wolverley, a very wealthy widow. He went to live with her at Wolverley, and gave his lands in Marton to his eldest son Thomas, who married Elleanor, the sister of Roger Griffiths, an eminent alderman in Shrewsbury; and this Roger Griffiths likewise married Mary the oldest sister of this Thomas Acherley. The younger daughter was married to one Simcocks, a mercer in Whitchurch. Richard, the younger son, was married at Wolverley, and died about middle age. Thomas Acherley, the second, was a tanner. He was at first tenant to Lloyd Peirce, Esq., and had his house burnt; but Lloyd Peirce caused him to rebuild it, but he, having a lease, built a house as large as the old one, and employed it for a malt house, and built a fair house near it for his habitation upon the lands which his grandfather purchased of Owen and Twiford, and afterward purchased Lloyd Peirce's lands. He also purchased Onslow's tenement in Marton, the tithes of Weston Lullingfield and several lands there, on which he built a fair house and buildings, lands in Montgomeryshire, and took several leases. He was a great dealer in timber, and bought Myddle park, and a wood in Petton, called the Rowelands. He had three sons — Thomas, who was set apprentice to a draper in Shrewsbury served his time, and soon after died unmarried; Andrew, who he married to a wealthy farmer's daughter in Montgomeryshire, and gave him the lands that were in that county; Richard married the daughter of Mr. Rowland Hill of Hawkstone, and to him Thomas Acherley gave all his lands in Marton, his leases, his tithes, and lands in Weston Lullingfield. For this Thomas Acherley was blamed by many persons, who said, that this was a disinheriting of the elder son, and that such things do seldom prosper, of which they gave many examples, as in Mr. Lockett's estate in Wollerton, Mr. Jennings' estate in Muckleton, etc. Richard Acherley died, and left his wife priviment insent of a daughter, which was born after the father's decease, and is yet living (1701). The widow married Mr. Thomas Harwood, a rich grocer, in Shrewsbury. Upon the death of Richard without issue male, the ancient inheritance in Marton, and the lands purchased of Peirce Lloyd, reverted to Andrew Acherley, and his heirs. Mr. Harwood, in right of his wife, and as guardian to Margaret, daughter of Richard Acherley, has the tithes and lands in Weston Lullingfield, Onslow's tenement in Marton, and a lease of a small tenement in Marton, called Edge's tenement. Thomas Acherley, the second, had four daughters. 1. Anne, who married Clutton, a Cheshire gentleman, and had issue by him, now living (1701); but he is long since dead, and she is married to another. 2. Elinor, who married Nathaniel, the son of Mr. Ralph Kinaston, of Lansaintfraid, and after his decease married Mr. Lloyd, minister of Lansaintfraid, who is likewise dead. She is a widow, and has no child. 3. Jane, who married Cole, of Shrewsbury, Esq., and has no issue. 4. Mary, who married Mr. Charles Chambre of Burleton, and had issue by him, two sons, both comely and hopeful youths. This Thomas Acherley, the second, did serve many offices with much care and faithfulness. He was three times high constable of the hundred of Pimhill; he was often churchwarden of this parish. He bequeathed 24s. per annum to the poor of this parish. His wife, Elinor, survived him, and she left £10, the interest to be given yearly at all-hallow-tide.

Sleape Hall; Alias Lytte Sleape

There is a part of this pew belonging to Sleape Hall, the estate of the Manwarings, of esquire's degree, in Cheshire. This farm has usually been set to tenants. The family of the Groomes were tenants here (by several leases) for many generations. They had likewise a good estate in lands in Sleape town; and when the eldest son was married, he had the estate in Sleape town, and the father lived, as a lease tenant, at Sleape Hall. My grandmother was born in this hall, and was daughter of John Groome, and sister to William Groome, of Sleape town, great grandfather of Thomas Groome, now (1701) of Sleape town. The last of the Groomes that was tenant of this farm was John Groome, brother, by a second venter, to my grandmother. He married a daughter out of that ancient family of the Lovekins of Tylley. He was a bad husband; and, having wasted most part of his stock, he parted with this farm, and took a less place. After him, one George Reve, a Cheshire dairyman, came to be tenant of it. He was a bragging, boasting, vain-glorious person, and having the benefit of some fruitful years, he got some money beforehand, but could not fare well, but he must cry "Roast," which his landlord hearing of, packed him off, and came to live there himself. His name was George Manwaring; he repaired and beautified the house, and made a new ground cellar under the parlour.

In the time that this Mr. Manwaring dwelt at Sleape Hall, he complained to my old master, Robert Corbett, Esq., and Thomas Hunt, Esq., justices of the peace at their monthly meeting held for this hundred of Pimhill, that Billmarsh Lane, which was his churchway, was out of repair, and desired an order for the inhabitants of Myddle, or the parish of Myddle to repair it. But the justices being acquainted by the parish officers that it was no roadway, they refused to make such order, and told him if it was his churchway, he must make it fair for his own benefit. After some years, Mr. Manwaring removed again into Cheshire, and Rowland Plungin became tenant to this farm; he had Arthur and John. This Arthur displeased his father by marrying the widow of Thomas Tyler of Balderton, who had many small children, so that he gave them little or nothing; but his mother was kind to him. John married Margaret, the daughter of Richard Jukes, of Newton; and (as is reported), had £50 portion with her. After the decease of Rowland, his son John (to whom he had given most part of his stock and household goods) became a bad husband, wasted his stock, and went behind hand with his rent, and, therefore, the landlord, making him a considerable abatement of his arrears, turned him away. He went afterward to Balderton Hall, where he spent the rest of his stock, and now lives in a cottage in Myddle where he maintains himself by day labour.

After John Plungin, William Cooke, a Cheshire man, came to be tenant there and lives there now, in good repute. All the time that Mr. Manwaring dwelt at Sleape Hall, he sat uppermost in this seat; but when tenants are there Mr. Acherley sits above them. The church leawan for Sleape Hall is 4s.; for Hanmer tenement, 2s. 8d. What Mr. Acherley pays for Lloyd Peirce's land, I know not; for the leawan of his ancient inheritance and this land, are joined together, and are 2s. 10d.

The second pew on the north side of the north aisle

This seat belongs wholly to the farm called the Hollins, whose leawan is 1s. 6d. This farm is the Earl of Bridgewater's land; and it is reported that the house was a dairy house belonging to Myddle Castle. I can give no account of any tenant of this farm, further than Humphrey Reynolds who was churchwarden of this parish when the register was transcribed in Mr. Wilton's time. One William Cleaton married a daughter of this Reynolds, and so became tenant of this farm, and had a lease for the lives of himself, his wife, and Francis, his eldest son. He lived in good repute, and served several offices in this parish. He had four sons. 1. Francis, who displeased his father in marrying with Margaret Vaughan, a Welsh woman, sometime servant to Mr. Kinaston, Rector of Myddle, and therefore he gave him little or nothing during his life. 2. Isaac, who married a daughter of one White, of Meriton, and had a good portion with her. The widow Lloyd, of Leaton, who is very rich in land and money, is a daughter of this Isaac. 3. Samuel, who married Susan, the daughter of Thomas Jukes, of Newton on the Hill, and lived a tenant to Mr. Hunt, in Baschurch. 4. Richard, an untowardly person. He married Annie, the daughter of William Tyler, a woman as infamous as himself. The parents on both sides were displeased (or seemed so), with this match, and therefore allowed the new married couple no maintenance. Richard Cleaton soon out-run his wife, and left his wife big with child. She had a daughter, which was brought up by Allen Challoner (the smith) of Myddle; for his wife was related to William Tyler. This daughter came to be a comely and handsome woman. She went to live in service towards Berrinton, beyond Shrewsbury, but I have not heard of her lately.

Richard Cleaton went into the further part of this county; and below Bridgenorth he got another wife, and had several children by her. At last, Anne Tyler, his first wife, caused him to be apprehended, and indicted him at an assizes at Bridgenorth upon the statute of poligamy. She proved that she was married to him, but could not prove that he was married to the other woman, but only that he lived with her, and had children by her. The other woman denied that she was married to him; and thereupon the judge said "Then thou art a whore." To which she answered "the worse luck mine my lord." Cleaton was acquitted, and went out of the country with the other woman, and I never heard more of him.

William Cleaton, by his last will, bequeathed his lease of this farm to his eldest son Francis, and his second son Isaac, equally between them. It was divided accordingly; Isaac had the dwelling-house; and Francis built for himself a little house and out-houses on his part. Some while after the death of William Cleaton, the Earl of Bridgewater's officers gave notice to the tenants that any person that had a life, or lives, in a lease, might have them exchanged, but no more lives put into the lease. Upon this, Isaac Cleaton desired his brother Francis, that he might exchange Francis' life and put in another, which was agreed upon; and Isaac took a new lease, and put in his son William's life and gave security that Francis should hold the one-half during his life. But it happened that Isaac died, and his son William proved a bad husband, and spent most of his estate and then died; so that the lease was expired. The security given to Francis had become poor and not responsible. Francis was still living, and lost all. His son William took the farm on the rack rent; and during his father's life, which was many years, he paid rent, and now, his father being lately dead, he holds the farm.

The third pew on the north side of the north aisle belongs wholly to Sleape Hall

The fourth pew on the north side of the north aisle

This belongs to Mr. Hanmer, of Marton, and to that house in Marton which Mr. Acherley purchased off Mr. Onslow. I have showed before, that this land, and Mr. Hanmer's, did both belong to Mr. Kinaston, of Walford, and that he gave it to his son, Edward, who had four daughters, and co-heirs; and that Onslow married the second daughter, and had a fourth part of the land assigned to him, and built a house upon it; and so came to sit in this pew. Mr. Thomas Acherley the second, bought this house and land off one of the Onslows. Thomas Manning was then in possession of it and had a lease of it for his wife's life. She was a sickly woman for many years, and no one conceived that she could live a twelve-month to an end; yet Thomas Acherley gave seven years purchase for Manning's lease. Manning removed to Welsh Hampton, and lived a tenant under my master Robert Corbett, Esq. The woman recovered her health, and lived many years. Thomas Acherley gave this house and land to his son Richard; and now Mr. Harwood, who married the widow of Richard, hath it in right of his wife, but Mr. Andrew Acherley holds it on a rent, and his daughters sit in the seat.

The fifth pew on the north side of the north aisle

This pew belongs wholly to Mr. Lloyd's house in Myddle; which house stands over against the north door of the church. The family of the Lloyds is very ancient, if not the ancientest family in this part of the parish, as appears by ancient deeds; yet I can give no account, further than Thomas Lloyd, grandfather of Richard now owner of this house and lands, and of a tenement in Houlston, which also is the ancient inheritance of the Lloyds. This Thomas Lloyd lived at Emstrey; where he had a lease of a considerable farm, or tenement. His brother, Roger Lloyd, was tenant to him at Myddle, and was a rich man.

Thomas Lloyd, of Emstrey, had issue, Thomas, who lived sometime at Emstrey, and married . . . Afterward he sold his lease at Emstrey, and came to Myddle. He purchased a small tenement at English Frankton, and some lands in Balderton, off Mr. Thomas Hall; and some meadows, in Newton called Bald Meadows (in ancient deeds, Borde Medues). He was a peaceable man, and well beloved. He had issue, two sons and one daughter. Richard, the eldest, he brought up to the study of divinity. He is now Rector of Petton. He married a gentlewoman of a good family: her maiden name was Dormer. He has no issue. Thomas, the other son, married the daughter of Thomas Freeman, of Marton, and has one son. To this Thomas the father gave all his purchased lands. His daughter was married to one William Vaughan, a freeholder in Kinton, and has several children. Thomas Lloyd, of Myddle, gave and bequeathed £5 to the poor of this side of the parish of Myddle; the interest to be distributed on St. Thomas's Day, yearly.

The sixth pew on the north side of the north aisle

This pew belongs to Edward Garland's house, in Newton on the Hill, and Balderton Hall, for their servants to sit in. I will speak of Balderton Hall when I come to the chief seat belonging to it; and at present, of this land of Edward Garland . . .

In the third year of Edward VI, Thomas Colfex gave his lands in Newton to Arthur Jukes, of Haston, in exchange for lands in Haston. There was a cottage in Newton, which was the lands of one Richard Knight, Esq. and was held by one Browne. This cottage was sold by Knight, in the fifth of Edward VI, for £7, to Robert Ireland, a draper in Shrewsbury. Knight covenanted that the cottage was worth 14s. per annum. In the fourteenth of Queen Elizabeth, this Robert Ireland sold the cottage to Arthur Jukes. Thus you have an account of the lands of Arthur Jukes in Newton; he had lands in Haston, of about £20 per annum, besides the lands which he gave in exchange to Colfex. This Arthur Jukes had (by Joan his wife), two sons, Thomas and John. He gave the lands in Newton to Thomas and the lands in Haston to John.

Thomas Jukes was a bawling, bold, confident person; he often kept company with his betters, but showed them no more respect than if they had been his equals or inferiors. He was a great bowler, and often bowled with Sir Humphrey Lea at a bowling green on Haremeare Heath, near the end of the Lea Lane; where he would make no more account of Sir Humphrey, than if he had been a plough-boy. He would ordinarily tell him he lied, and sometimes throw the ball at his head, and then they parted in wrath. But within few days, Sir Humphrey would ride to Newton, and take Jukes with him to the bowls; and if they did not fall out, would take him home and make him drunk. This Thomas Jukes married Margaret, the sister of James Wicherly, of Yorton, of an ancient and substantial family. He had issue by her, Thomas and Michael, whom he usually called Mim, and two daughters, Elizabeth and Alice. (I will here, and in other families, speak of the heir last of all.) Michael was set an apprentice in London, but for some misdemeanor, came to an untimely end. Elizabeth married one Moses Sharpe, who had a small tenement or cottage, on the side of Leaton Heath; they were pretty rich, and had no issue. Alice married William Maddox, a weaver in Greensell, who held a small tenement there under the worshipful family of the Corbetts, of Moreton Corbett. Thomas Jukes, the second of that name, was a good ingenious person, well skilled in any country affairs. He was churchwarden when the steeple was built, and when the church was uniformed; at both which times, he managed those matters with much discretion. He married Margaret, the daughter of . . . Twisse of Hadnall, of a substantial family. He had issue by her, four sons, Richard, Thomas, John, and James — and six daughters, Mary, Elizabeth, Sarah, Susan, Jane and Margaret. Thomas, the second son, was set an apprentice in London, to a leather seller. He was set up, and being a bad husband, broke. He was killed on Tower Hill. The occasion of his death was thus: Soon after the restoration of King Charles II, there came an ambassador from Spain, and an ambassador from France, who both landed (much about the same time) in one day at Tower wharf, and were both lodged that night in the Tower; to the end, that the king's coach and other nobleman's coaches might the day following come thither to conduct them to Westminster, to the places appointed for their several lodgings. There was a report that there would be a difference between the ambassadors about precedency (*i.e.*) who should follow next after the king's coach, and this being known to the king, he caused proclamation to be made, that if any dissention happened between the ambassadors, none of the king's subjects, upon pain of his displeasure, should take part with either of them. Now there was in London at that time far more Frenchmen than Spaniards, and therefore, the Spaniard endeavoured to hire persons to assist him; amongst whom this Thomas Jukes was one, who had a Spanish suit given him, and had, or was to receive fifty shillings. That night, the Spanish ambassador caused all his coach harness to be made anew, and chains of iron to be put within the harness, but the French ambassador did not do so. On the next morning all the Spaniards and Frenchmen then in London, flocked together on Tower Hill. The Frenchmen marched in great companies along the street, with every man a white handkerchief tied about his arm. The apprentices cursed them, and would willingly have been doing with them, but their masters with great care restrained them. At last the king's coach came to Tower Hill, and both the ambassadors' coaches set out, and immediately the Frenchman's harness was cut his horses went away: the French ambassador in his coach stayed behind. The like was endeavoured to be done to the Spaniard, but they could not cut the chains. In this hurly burly, a Frenchman that came behind Tom Jukes ran him clear through the body with an halberd. He fell down dead by the side of the Spanish ambassador's coach, who took him into his coach, and brought him down to Durham Yard, where lodgings were appointed for that ambassador. He was at the charges of his funeral, and gave his widow five pounds. In Mr. Baker's chronicle it is said, that a Dawber was killed, and that this Tom Jukes after he was broke did work day labour, and perhaps at this calling, to get his living.

John, the third son, married the sister of Richard Nightingale, of Harlescott, and afterwards of Myddle. James, the youngest son, was a baker, and lived in Wem. He was a very ingenious person, and a very skilful cook. He had a courteous, obliging carriage, and had great custom to his house. He married first a daughter of Robert Higginsons of Tylley; secondly he married a daughter of one Hussey, of Aston, near Wem, a handsome woman, who hardly escaped the censures that are usually cast upon a fair hostess. And thirdly, he married a daughter of William Menlove, an innkeeper, that held the Raven in Wem. She out-lived him. He died of a dropsy, when he was about forty years of age. The two eldest daughters of Thomas Jukes, namely, Mary and Elizabeth, went to London, and were there married and lived happy. The third daughter, Sarah, was married to Samuel Davis, tenant of a farm called the Lea; it lies between Stanwardine in the wood, and Petton, and is in the township of Kenwick's Wood. Susan, the fourth daughter, was married to Samuel Cleaton; as I said before, Jane, the fifth daughter, married Thomas Hughes, and lived at Hadnall. After her decease he married a second wife. Margaret, the youngest daughter, married Robert Ames, whom they call, "little Robert Ames." She lived and died at Broughton.

Richard, the eldest son, and heir of Thomas, was a sort of a morose, lofty, imperious person, and was beloved of few. He married Elinor, the daughter of Roger Bird, who had some time an estate in Haston, but sold it, and took a lease of a farm in Harlescott, under Pelham Corbett, off Adbright Hussey, Esq. This Elinor was a comely proper woman, of a friendly and courteous disposition. He had issue by her, Richard, and Margaret who was married to John Plungin, as I said before. After the decease of Elleanor, he married Anne, the daughter of William Catchett, of Harlescott, and had with her sixty pounds portion, which was all given to a woman in Shrewsbury, whom he had wounded with an halberd in the belly, in one of his prodigal drunken humours at Battlefield fair. He had four or five children by her, and died somewhat past middle age, and left his children all young, except his eldest daughter Margaret. Richard Jukes, the second of that name, was about thirteen years of age at his father's death. He was left in no debt by his father, but, by his bad courses, he soon got far in debt. He married Mary, the daughter of one Pidgeon of Besford, who had fifty pounds to her portion in her own hands; when his wife's friends came to understand how much he was indebted, they conceived it was impossible for him to retrieve it without selling his land; and when it was set to sale I purchased it, and I intended it for my eldest son; but it pleased God that he died, and my other two sons were both set apprentices, and therefore, I sold the house, and some part of the land to Edward Garland; who, by this means, came to have this kneeling. This

Edward Garland was son of Roger Garland, of Sleape, who married Margaret, the daughter and heiress of George Tyler, a rich freeholder in Sleape, whose first wife was the daughter of Mr. Richardson, a wealthy farmer, of that large farm in Wem parish, called the Trench Farm, which is thought to be worth 300 l. per annum. This Richard Jukes died poor, and left many small children behind him.

The seventh pew on the north side of the north aisle

This belongs wholly to Mr. Andrew Acherley. I do believe it did belong to that house which Richard Acherley purchased of Owen and Twiford, but now it is made use of only for servants.

The eighth pew on the north side of the north aisle

	£	s.	d.
This pew belongs to Samuel Braine, whose leawan is ...	0	1	4
To John Eaton, whose leawan is	0	1	0
To Thomas Peirce, whose leawan is	0	0	8

Braine's family is very ancient in this parish. William Braine had three sons — William, Michael, and Samuel, who was first plough-boy, and after groom of the stable to Mr. Chambre, of Petton. William, the father, left a widow behind him, who married one Michael Almond. He built a little apartment at the end of Braine's house, next the street, and lived in it; and now one Judith Downton lives in it. William Braine, the second, married a wife, and had one son, named William; and soon after he and his wife both died, and left the son very young. Michael, the second brother, lived then as a servant with Mr. Barker, of Haughmond, and was brewer and baker there. Upon the death of his brother William, he came to Myddle, and entered on his brother's stock and living, and maintained the child. Whether Michael used this child well or not I will not say; but sure it is, that he did not put him to school, and that when he was grown up to be a pretty big boy, he broke several neighbours' houses, and took only meat; which, people that heard it, adjudged was done for want; and at last he was sent away, I know not whither. It is said, that Mary Groome, who now lives in Myddle, sent him away, and cannot tell whether he was ever heard of after; and yet (not long ago), there came a lusty man to the ale-house in Myddle; he was in good habit, and lay there all night, and pretended he was this William Braine; but whether he was or not, it was not known. I cannot say that Michael Braine and his wife, or either of them, did deal unkindly with this boy, for Michael did always behave himself as an honest man; and was as peaceable a man amongst his neighbours as any was in Myddle. This Michael Braine married Susan, the daughter of Roger Lloyd, of Myddle, which so displeased her father, that, although he had but that only child, yet he gave her nothing. But at his death, she having two daughters then born, he gave them 50 l. a piece, which they bestowed near home, for John Eaton of Myddle, married one. The other married Francis, the second son of Francis Cleaton, of Hollins. After the death of Roger Lloyd, this Michael Braine had by his wife, Susan, two sons, Michael and Samuel, and a daughter, whose name, I think, was Anne, who married one Robert Davis, of Hadnall. He was an honest and laborious person, and she, being a fashionable, modest woman, they were likely to live well; but he died of the smallpox, about his middle age, and left one son, which was set apprentice by the parish to William Watson, of Myddle Wood. The widow afterwards married Richard Rogers, of Petton, and soon after died. Michael, the eldest son of Michael Braine, displeased his father by marrying Jane, a bastard of one who went abroad a spinning for neighbours, and was called Black Nell. The reputed father of this Jane was Thomas Fardoe of Burleton. He fled to London, and there became very rich. It was thought that he was worth several thousands of pounds, in houses and timber, which he had in his timber yard in Southwark. But he broke, and was laid in prison, and died poor. This Michael, the son, died, and left many small children behind him, of which the eldest was set apprentice to one John Rogers, a shoemaker, in Cockshut. He soon packed up St. Hughe's bones and ran his country. Afterward he was set apprentice to Thomas Highway, Jnr., of Myddle. He is not yet gone, but stands on tiptoes. Samuel, the younger son, married Mary, the daughter of Thomas Baugh, of Clive, and now holds this tenement, and maintains Susan, who is of great age (1701).

John Eaton has a share in this pew. The tenement that he lives in is the Earl of Bridgewater's; and the family of the Gossages was formerly tenants of it. The last was John Gossage, a drunken, debauched person. He married a widow, who was mother to Allen Challoner, the smith in Myddle. He bedded with her one night; in the morning he curst her for a whore, and turned her off, and came near her no more. He was accused for uttering counterfeit money, and for keeping a tinker in his back house, who made money. I have heard my father say, that there was a sort of sixpences which they called Myddle sixpences, which seemed to be good silver, and went for current money. The back house stood in the further side of the yard, near to Myddle Park, and when, for want of repair, it fell down, some years past the ground was dug up to sow with beans, there was found in the earth a copper pot, made in the shape of a large earthern cup; it had a straight handle at it, of about a foot long, and was thought to have been a melting pot. It was much decayed with rust. This pot I saw. John Gossage was committed to prison: and (as some have said), by the assistance of Edward Meriton, then jailer, acquitted. He sold his lease to Mr. Meriton, and conditioned maintenance for his life. This Edward Meriton was a proper corpulent person, of a comely presence, and well beseeming the place of a jailer. This Edward Meriton for some while kept servants to manage this tenement; but they were such as had been acquitted of felony, and were continued in jail for non-payment of fees. When Owen, his son, was married, he came and lived in this tenement in Myddle. He lived very high, and kept a pack of beagles. He had a son born at Myddle, whose name was Edward, and was jailer after him. After the death of old Edward Meriton, his son, Owen, was made jailer, and then removed from Myddle to Shrewsbury, and sold the title of his lease to Mr. Thomas Price, who is now owner of Webscott. He first set, and after sold it to Richard Eaton, who was born at Losforde, in Hodnett parish. This Richard Eaton was a drunken, debauched person, a great and intimate companion of Mr. Hall, of Balderton, a good benefactor to the ale-sellers. This Eaton was somewhile bailiff of the manor of Myddle, but did not perform that office so faithfully as others had done before him. As often as he went to Shrewsbury, he would bestow ale of John Gossage, whom he called his lease, and would many times sit up drinking with him all night; but after some years, it happened that Richard Eaton was in town, and had bestowed pretty store of ale upon Gossage, but had occasion to go home that night, and told Gossage so; but Gossage did not believe, but conceited he told him this only on purpose to shirk him off, and in that drunken humour went and bought arsenic, and poisoned himself, and died before morning. Richard Eaton did come home that night, and before he was out of bed next morning, a messenger came and told him that John Gossage was dead, and he must come to take care for his burial. Thus Eaton's lease was ended, which was one of the last leases of the Earls of Derby in this manor, at which time there were only two more in being; viz., Wolph's lease, and the lease of Broomhurst farm. Richard Eaton took a new lease of this tenement, and John Eaton, his son, succeeded him. He married Alice, the daughter of Michael Braine, and is now tenant of it.

Thomas Peirce, of Myddle, has a share in this pew. His tenement is one of those which is called a half tenement, and is the land of the Earl of Bridgewater. The family of the Tylers were formerly tenants of it. The first that I read of was Thomas Tyler, who married Margery, daughter of William Braine, of Myddle; he was a tailor by trade. He had issue, Humphrey Tyler, who was likewise a tailor, and married Margaret, a servant of Baylie Morgan. Humphrey had issue, William Tyler, of Myddle, who married Anne, the daughter of Arthur Jukes, of Newton. He had two sons — Thomas (who married Margaret, daughter of John Formestone, of Marton), and William Tyler, who was a tailor, but altogether unseemly for such a calling, for he was a big, tall, corpulent person, but not so big in body as bad in conditions. He was a great comrade of John Gossage, of whom I have spoken before.

There was another William Tyler, in Balderton; and, therefore, for distinction sake, they called this Don John, or Dun John, by which name he was best known. He lived more by cheating than by his trade. If any person was brought from Hadnall's Ease to be buried at Myddle, this Dun John (as soon as the corpse was interred), would enquire who paid the ringers; and, if he were a ringer, would go to him and hold out his hand, and if he got the money, would straightaway go with it; and if the ringers came to him for it he would only say, leave Dun alone, leave Dun alone; but would give them not a penny. It were endless to tell of the cheats he used; but he could not cheat death, for he died of a fever at Allen Challoner's, the smith. When I was a schoolboy, at Myddle his distemper was so violent, that in a raging fit he leaped out of bed in the night, and ran (in his shirt) about the fields, in a frost and snow; but soon after he was brought back to his bed he died. After the death of Thomas Tyler, one Bartholomew Peirce came to be tenant of this tenement (but whether he married a daughter of Thomas Tyler for his first wife, I know not, and so came to be tenant). He married Susan, daughter of Thomas Formeston, of Marton. He was a tailor by trade, and was a cross, troublesome, litigious person amongst his neighbours. His wife was as bad in that behalf as he was. He had three sons — Bartholomew, Thomas, and Nicholas. He gave to Nicholas a lease of a cottage of the Earl of Bridgewater's, which is in Myddle township, but lies near Houlston, by the side of Houlston Lane. This is an ancient cottage, and there was a family of the Jukes who were tenants of it for many generations. The last of them was Thomas Jukes who married Elleanor, the daughter of Richard Hussey, of Balderton, and had issue by her,

Roger Jukes (who was never married) and two daughters. The eldest was married unto Roger Rodon, of Peplow, in the parish of Hodnett; the other daughter was married to William Formeston, weaver, third son of Thomas Formeston, of Marton. This William Formeston purchased Thomas Ashe's lease of this tenement in Marton, and sold his lease of this cottage to his brother-in-law, Bartholomew Peirce, who gave it to his son, Nicholas who married Mary, a servant of one Henry Cooke, of Balderton. Thomas, the second son, married Jane, the daughter of Rowland Plungin, of Sleap Hall, and is now tenant of this tenement. Bartholomew, the eldest son, was but a little man, but he was a quarrelsome, fighting fellow, and would fight the tallest man that was.

This Batt. Peirce listed himself a soldier in the protector's service, in the close of the wars, and was sent over into Flanders in one of those regiments which the protector lent to the French king, to assist him against the king of Spain . . . He was a garrison soldier at Dunkirk; and when Dunkirk was sold, he came with the rest into England, and was disbanded, and came down to Myddle; and soon after, by the assistance of his cousin, Thomas Formeston, then servant to Roger Kinaston, or Hordley, Esq., he was preferred in service to Mr. Mytton, of Hallston, who had married the daughter of Mr. Kinaston. But this Batt. Peirce was grown such a sad drunken fellow, and so accustomed to fighting, that his master, not able to indure his rudeness, cashiered him; whereupon, he returned to London, and was listed a soldier in the Tower, and afterwards, when a certain number of soldiers were picked out of every regiment, to be sent for garrison soldiers at Tangiers, this Batt. Peirce was one that was sent thither, where (being expert in arms), he was first made an officer, and afterwards a captain, and there he died.

The ninth pew on the north side of the north aisle

This was a supernumerary pew; for before the uniforming of the church with wainscot seats, there was but eight seats on this side of the north aisle, so that this was a void seat; and then those that lived in Meare House, and Clarke of Haremeare Heath, and those that lived in a cottage in Myddle (which belongs to the Castle Farm) wherein the widow Russell now dwelleth — these persons, I say (although none of them pays any church leawan but Clarke, which is but 2d.), got into this seat, and have ever since used it; and now (happily), they plead prescription.

The Meare House, at Haremeare, stood over cross the brook that issued out of Haremeare; but when the Meare was let dry, the house was removed, and set by the side of the brook, and one Spurstow dwelt in it, and was employed by Sir Andrew Corbett to look to the Heyment of Haremeare, and to tend the cattle that were in it, for when it was let dry, there were cattle put in it as a lay; and after, as it became dry and sound, it was divided into several pieces. After Spurstow, one Reece Wenlocke dwelt in it. He was descended of good parentage, who were tenants of a good farm, called Whottall, in Ellesmere Lordship. But the father of this Reece was a bad husband, and a pilfering, thievish person, and this son, Reece, and another son, named John, who lived at Bald Meadow, in this parish, were as bad as their father. They never stole any considerable goods, but were night walkers, and robbed orchards and gardens, and stole hay out of meadows, and corn when it was cut in the fields, and any small things that persons by carelessness had left out of doors. Reece had a cow, which was stolen away, and it is reported that he went to a woman, whom they called the wise woman of Montgomery, to know what had become of his cow; and as he went, he put a stone in his pocket, and told a neighbour of his that was with him that he would know whether she were a wise woman or not, and whether she knew that he had a stone in his pocket. And it is said, that when he came to her, she said, thou hast a stone in thy pocket, but it is not so big as that stone wherewith thou didst knock out such a neighbour's harrow tines. But the greatest diskindness that he did to his neighbours was, by tearing their hedges. And it is reported, that he had made a new oven; and, according to the manner of such things, it was at first to be well burnt, to make it fit for use, and this he intended to do in the night. At that time William Higginson dwelt at Webscot, and he had a servant, named Richard Mercer, a very waggish fellow. This Mercer did imagine that Reece would tear his master's hedges to burn the oven; and as he walked by a hedge, which was near Reece's house, he saw there a great dry stick of wood, and took it home with him, and bored a hole in the end of it with an auger, and put a good quantity of powder in it, and a peg after it, and put it again into the hedge. And it happened, that Reece Wenlocke, among other hedgewood, took this stick to burn in his oven; and when he cast it into the fire in the oven, it blew up the top of it, and set fire on the end of the house. Reece went out and made a hideous crying, fire! fire! William

Higginson, being the next neighbour, heard him, and called Mercer, but he said I know what is the matter; however, they went both down to the Meare House, but Reece had put out the fire that was in the end of the house, and the oven was broken to pieces. After Reece Wenlocke, one William Suker was tenant there many years, and after him, George Yeomans was tenant; and now John Harris, Jnr. is tenant of it. (It is now, 1706, pulled down.)

Richard Clarke, of Newton, used to sit in this pew. His tenement belongs to Mr. Thomas Gittins, Vicar of Loppington. The first of the Clarkes that came into this parish, was Walter Clarke, who came from Hadley, near Oaken Gates, in this county. He dwelt in a little cottage on Haremeare Hill, and had a little encroachment to it. He was a day labourer. His wife's name was Anne, by whom he had two sons, Morgan and John. This John was an innocent and went a begging in the parish. Morgan was a weaver. He built a house upon a butt's end of Mr. Gittin's land in Newton field, and had only a garden and hemp butt belonging to it. He left the cottage; and when Robert Moore took a lease of the Eagle Farm, in Myddle, he put this cottage and encroachment in his terror, and so had a lease of it, and put one Thomas Davis, a weaver, eldest son of Thomas Davis, of Marton, weaver, to dwell in it; and afterward Mr. Gittins had it, by exchange for lands in Myddle Field, near Draken Hill. The cottage was pulled down some years ago. Morgan Clarke married a wife, whose name was Cybell, and had issue by her, Thomas and Richard. This Richard married Anne, the daughter of Allen Chaloner, of Myddle, cooper, and built a house upon Myddle Wood, of which I shall have occasion to speak hereafter. Thomas married Mauld, a Welsh woman, servant to Mr. Kinaston, Rector of Myddle, and had by her two sons, Francis and Morgan, and a daughter named Joan. This Thomas Clarke took more land of Mr. Gittins, and joined it to his cottage, and made it a small tenement of about 50s. per annum. His daughter, Joan, was married to Charles, the eldest son of John Reve, of Fennimeare, and lived in a cottage on Myddle Wood. Morgan, his youngest son, was a blacksmith, and lived in the nearer part of Montgomeryshire. He has two sons, now living, lusty young men; Francis, the eldest son, married Elizabeth Kyffin, descended of a good, but a decaying family in Wales. There were three hall houses in Sweeney, and her brother was owner of one of them; but it is long since sold. Francis had but little portion with her but a sad drunken woman. He went to fetch her from the ale-house on a very dark night, but she, being unwilling to come, pretended it was so dark that she could not see to go; he told her he would lead her by the arm, and got her away almost half-way home, and then she pretended she had lost one of her shoes; and when he had loosed her arm, and was groping for the shoe, she ran back to the ale-house, and bolted him out, and would not come home that night. He had one son by her, named Richard, who is tenant of this tenement, and two daughters. One is married to Luke Roe, who came from Welsh Hampton; the other is married to John Primus, alias Davis. I know not whence he came, but now lives in a cottage on Haremeare Heath.

Widow Russell's cottage. This is the Earl of Bridgewater's land, and is in lease to William Gittins, as part of the Castle Farm. One John Hall, alias Dudleston, was formerly tenant of this cottage in Myddle. He was a weaver, and a common fiddler, who went abroad to wakes and merriments, but took care to spend what he had got before he came home.

This John Dudleston had a wife, whose name was Elizabeth, and by her he had two daughters, Elizabeth and Martha. The eldest married John Bennion, who died in the wars, and she died soon after him. Martha was married to a man that they called Welch Franke. He could speak neither good Welsh nor good English. When he came first out of Wales, he lived as a ploughboy with William Geslin, or Goslin, of Myddle, and people called him Franke Goslin; but when he was married he was called in the court, and when the steward asked him his name, he said Franke. And what else? says the steward. He said, Francis. Then the steward asked him his father's name, and he said it was David; so he got the name of Francis Davis. He had one daughter, named Mary, who, after her father and mother were dead, was married to one Robert Pitchford, of Preston Brockhurst, who soon spent that little that she had, and they then went both together to London, where he died, and I have heard that she maintained herself very well by her own labour.

John Huett succeeded Pitchford. His grandfather was John Huett, and came out of Wirrall, in Cheshire, and dwelt with Mr. Manwaring, of Sleape Hall. He was married there, and Mr. Manwaring built a house for him by the side of Sleape Hall Lane, which is now pulled down. There is only some appearance of the garden place or yard. This John Huett, the first, had three sons; Robert, who was a blacksmith, John, the second, who was a blacksmith, and Richard, a husbandman. (She that is now wife of William Fosbrooke, of Shropshire, is daughter to this Richard.) John the second had issue, John, the third, a blacksmith. He lived in this cottage, and married Margaret, daughter of John

Tydor, of Sleape, and had issue by her, John, the fourth, who is also a blacksmith, and married Elizabeth, the daughter of Thomas Lovett, and lives in Myddle, in the house over against the parson's barn. His father lives with him; and the widow of Solomon Russell lives in this cottage.

CHAPTER 4

Good Uncle Elks, Do Me No Harm

Seats in Myddle Church on the south side of the north aisle

The first pew belongs wholly to Shotton Farm. This farm did anciently belong to the Kinastons, of Leightaches. I do not find that the Kinastons came over into England with the Conqueror, and therefore it is possible that this farm did belong to the Kinastons before. It is thought that Smethcott did formerly belong to this farm, and that these two made one manor; and that therefore Smethcott was called Shotton Smethcott, for so I find it written. This farm, of Shotton, was given in marriage unto Banaster, of Hadnall, Esq., with a daughter of one of the Kinastons; but she dying without issue, it reverted to the family of the Kinastons. We have a tradition, that one Bishop Rowland was sometime tenant of this farm; that he was a lord marcher, and that the place of execution was on the bank between Shotton and Smethcott, which I have sometimes (though seldom) heard called the gallow-tree bank. I have shown before what the power of the lord marchers was.

Hugh Ridley was sometime a tenant of this farm, he was a rich farmer. He married a daughter (perhaps his only daughter) to Mr. Russell, of Sandsaw, a person of a good family, and a great estate. I have seen the settlement that was made at this marriage. It was written in old court hand, on a piece of parchment no bigger than a quarter of a sheet of paper, and yet had comprehensive and significant words sufficient to make it a good deed. The name Hugh, was written Hue. Afterward, this farm was given to a younger brother of the Kinastons for his portion. I think his name was Francis. He lived at Shotton, and had issue, Roger Kinaston, who had a son named Thomas. This Roger and Thomas (if I mistake not), sold this farm to Mr. William Watkins, son of Mr. Humphreys Watkins, of Whixall. This William Watkins was a person well educated, and fit for greater employment than that of a husbandman. He was once under shreive of this county: but his chief delight was in good husbandry, which is, indeed, a delightful calling.

He found this farm much overgrown with thorns, briars, and rubbish. He employed many day labourers (to whom he was a good benefactor), in clearing and ridding his land; and having the benefit of good marl, he much improved his land, built part of the dwelling-house, and joined a brewhouse to it, which he built of free stone. He built most part of the barns, and made beast houses of free stone, which is a good substantial piece of building. He was a cheerful, merry gentleman, and kept a plentiful table for his own family, and strangers, which brings to my mind that of Chaucer in his Franklin's Tale.

"His table dormant in his hall allway
Stood ready covered all the live long day;
Without baked meats was never his house,
Of fish, and flesh, and that so plenteous."

His wife's maiden name was Lee, a provident and prudent gentlewoman, and a very good housekeeper, and in all things very suitable for such a husband. He had issue by her four sons, Francis, George, Richard, and Thomas, and four daughters, Jane, Susan, Elizabeth, and Christabell. This Christabell was an exchange woman, as they call them in London. I have not heard that she was married. Elizabeth went to London, and married one Poole. She survived all the rest of her sisters and brothers. Susan married one Manning, of Great Berwicke, and Jane married one Poole, a draper of Welsh cloth, in Shrewsbury. Thomas, the youngest son, was a distiller of strong waters in London. He was a rich man, and never married. He grew into a melancholy distemper, and died. Richard was a goldsmith in London (I bought Mrs. Mary Corbett's wedding ring of him.) He had one daughter which I knew. She was a modest, comely gentlewoman, and was housekeeper to her uncle, Thomas. George was a tradesman in London, but I know nothing else of him, for I never saw him since I was his schoolfellow. Mr. Francis Watkins married Mrs. Mary Teague, of the parish of Pontesbury. The banns of matrimony were published between them by Mr. Richardson, then Rector of Myddle. This I note, because nowadays the proud foolish girls, though they have not money enough to pay for a licence, yet will scorn that ancient and commendable way of being asked in church. This Mr. Francis Watkins was a captain in the wars, and was on the parliament party; but I never heard of any company of soldiers that he had, or any service that he did in the wars, for there were several gentlemen in our neighbourhood that were forced to fly from their houses in the wars, and to shelter themselves in garrisons; and because they could have but little benefit from their lands towards maintaining them, therefore they had commissions to be captains, to the end they might receive a captain's pay to maintain them. Of this number was Captain Whitcomb of Hardwicke, Captain Richardson of Broughton, Captain Rea of Wicherley, Captain Swanwicke, and others. Howbeit, Captain Whitcomb had a company at last turned over to him, upon the death of a captain of the parliament party, and this Captain Whitcomb was commanded over into Anglesey, where, in the close of the wars, many of the king's forces were gathered together and kept in a body. In this expedition (it is reported), that Captain Whitcomb (his soldiers being old experienced soldiers), did good service for the parliament. But to return to Mr. Watkins:—

Mr. Francis Watkins was married after the wars in England. He was heir to his father's lands, and also to his art of good husbandry, in which his care, diligence, and skill, was not exceeded by any in this county. He marled several pieces, and got abundance of corn. He purchased lands in Tylley Park, and certainly, if he had lived, he had been an exceeding rich man. His wife was provident and sparing, even to a fault; and, therefore, he could not keep so good a house as his father did, which was no small trouble to him. He died and left five small children behind him; viz three sons and two daughters. His widow afterwards married with Mr. Charles Dimock, a younger brother of that ancient family, of the Dimocks of Willeton. He had no knowledge in husbandry, and his whole delight was in drinking; not as some drunkards plead, for company's sake, but for the sake of drink. He lived but few years with her before he died. She had no child by him, and she got nothing, but rather lost by this marriage. She married a third husband, his name was John Cotton, an ancient bachelor. He was son and heir of Richard Cotton, of Haston. She got well by this marriage, which was helpful to her children. She had no child by him, and he died before her. She was much to be commended for giving her children good education, and put every one of them in a good condition to live. Mary, the youngest daughter, was married to Mr. Roe, of Preece. He was a fair and good-humoured man. He died and left her a widow, and now she is married again, but I know not what his name is. Elizabeth, the eldest, was married to John Joyce, who lives at the lodge in Kenwicke Park. John, the youngest son, was set apprentice to a grocer or merchant in Bristol, and was set up but broke; and, after receiving a small supply from his mother, he set up at Wolverhampton, and there married, and after grew melancholy and died. Francis the second son, was a grocer in Shrewsbury, and was set up in a good condition. He married a daughter of Mr. Collins Woolrich, an apothecary, and one of the senior aldermen of Shrewsbury, and had a good fortune with her; but he (trusting out goods too rashly) broke. William, the eldest son, was put a covenanted servant unto Mr. John Edwards, one of the ablest attorneys at law in this county. At expiration of his term, he married Elizabeth, eldest daughter of Mr. John Edwards.

This Mr. William Watkins is now (1701) owner of this farm, and very happy in that it hath pleased God to give him such skill, care, and industry in good husbandry as his grandfather and father had, for he is not inferior to either of them therein. He is also happy in a prudent, provident and discreet wife who is every way suitable for such a husband. They live very lovingly together, very loving to their neighbours, and very well beloved by their neighbours, and they are both happy in that it hath pleased God in token of his love to them, and their mutual love one to another to bless them with many comely and witty children.

The second seat on the south side of the north aisle

This pew belongs to the Eagle Farm. It is the lands of the Earl of Bridgewater, and Thomas More is now tenant of it. The leawan is 1s. 4d. John More, father of this Thomas, knew not where he had any seat in church. The reason was this: Robert More was tenant of this farm before John More, and he was farmer of the tithes, and brother to Mr. More, the rector, and lived in the parsonage house, and sat in the rector's seat in the chancel, and so the seat belonging to this farm was lost; and, therefore, at a parish meeting, February 9th, 1658, John More was seated in this pew, which is the passage pew, but because there were many things ordered at that meeting, I will recite the order wholly when I come to the next seat, and in the meantime speak of the tenants of the Eagle Farm. One Richard Gittins, a wealthy tradesman's son in Shrewsbury, had a lease of this farm, and lived in it. His son, Richard Gittins, married Anne, the daughter and kinswoman of Morgan ap Probert, commonly called Baylie

Morgan; and so this Richard Gittins the second, came to be tenant to the Castle Farm in Myddle, and after the death of his father he set this Eagle Farm to Thomas Jukes, who was born in a cottage by the side of Houlston Lane, of which cottage and family I spoke when I mentioned the family of the Pierces, of Myddle. Thomas Jukes* married a wife, whose name was Lowry, of the Parish of Llanguedwin; she was a handsome woman but he might have had one as honest nearer home.

Thomas Jukes had three sons, and never a good one. Thomas, the youngest, did use to break his neighbour's houses, but had the fortune to be caught before he had done any mischief. At last, his father, in some drunken humour, set him apprentice to a juggler, a very hopeful employment. He only gave with him an old petticoat of his wife's, which was given to the juggler's wife. The second son, Richard, was a companion of John Owen, of Myddle, who was one of the falsest thieves in this country. I knew this Richard Jukes lie in Shrewsbury jail for stealing horses; he was discharged, and went for a soldier. Vincent, the eldest son, was an active, nimble man; he went to be a seaman, and was taken prisoner by the Turks, of Tangiers, and another Englishman, his companion. These two, after some time, changed their religion (if they had any before), and became Turks, and so got more favour and liberty than other slaves. After some time, these two were sent a roving in a small vessel, and only eight Turks in their company; and these two, watching an opportunity, when the Turks were all under deck, shut down the hatches, and kept them there, and hoisted up sail for England; and meeting with some English merchants, they got relief and so brought the little vessel to England, and put the Turks on shore, and sold the vessel. Vincent Jukes bought a new suit of cloths, and a good horse, and came down to Myddle, and was there at what time they were singing ballads abroad in market towns of this adventure. He went after to sea again, and was heard of no more. When the lease, made to the Gittinses (of this farm) was expired, Robert More, by the assistance of his brother, the rector, got a lease of this tenement. This Robert More was a busy person in raising forces for the king in the beginning of the wars. There was a commission granted by the king to several persons to raise what forces they could for his service. It was called the commission of array. Sir Paul Harris, of Boreatton, was a commissioner. He was a person not well loved by the ancient gentry of this

*This Thomas Jukes kept an inn, and put up the sign of The Eagle and Child; and by that means it came to be called the Eagle Farm.

county, for being (as they termed him) but a buck of the second head; yet, being a baronet, and a proud imperious person, he took place of those that were of ancient knight's degree. Neither was he beloved by the common people. His only favourites and confidants were this Robert More, and Mathew Bagley, of Bagley; and these two were accounted the veriest knaves in Pimhill hundred. Sir Paul Harris sent out warrants requiring or commanding all men, both householders with their sons, and servants, and sojourners, and others within the hundred of Pimhill that were between the age of sixteen and three score to appear on a certain day upon Myddle Hill. I was then a youth of about eight or nine years of age, and I went to see this great show. And there I saw a multitude of men, and upon the highest bank of the hill I saw this Robert More standing, with a paper in his hand, and three or four soldier's pikes, stuck upright in the ground by him; and there he made a proclamation, that if any person would serve the king, as a soldier in the wars, he should have fourteen groats a week for his pay. About that time, Sir William Breton, of Brereton in Cheshire, being a member of parliament, was sent down into Cheshire to raise forces for the parliament. He placed a garrison in Nantwich, and having intelligence given him that this More and some others were busy in raising forces for the king, there came a party of horses and apprehended Robert More, and brought him to Nantwich, where he soon after died a prisoner . . .

He left behind him two sons, Thomas and Robert, and one daughter named Sarah. His widow and children lived some time in this farm, and after sold the reversion of the lease to one John More, who was nothing kin to them, but was a stranger, and came to Shrewsbury in the war time, and there married a sister of Mr. Richard Taylor, an alderman of great account in Shrewsbury. This John More kept an inn in Myddle, and set up the Earl of Bridgewater's armies for his sign. His wife was a discreet, well-bred woman, and the inn was in great repute in their time. They died both at Myddle, and left behind, a son, Thomas, and two daughters, Judith and Sarah. This Sarah was married to Thomas Tomkins, and lives in Fenimeare. Judith was first married to Robert Merriton, of Shrewsbury, and kept an inn there of great custom. After his death, she was married to one Courtney, and went with him to London.

Thomas, the son, married Mary, the daughter of Samuel Formeston, of Brandwood. They are both yet (1701) living, and have two daughters. The widow of Robert More removed with her children into Yorkshire, and thus that family of the Mores ended in this parish.

The third pew on the south side of the north aisle

These two pews, which I have spoken of last before, were wholly taken up by the pulpit and reading pew, when the pulpit stood up to that arch where the table of benefactors hangs, and then this pew and that which is between it and the south aisle were the passage pews, and any person that would, did sit in them. My father, who was thick of hearing, did constantly sit in the seat that I am now speaking of. But after, when the pulpit and reading pew were removed, then the pew next above this was made the passage, and that at the end of it.

About that time there happened a difference between John Downton, of Alderton, and William Formeston, about the right of kneeling in the sixth pew on the south side of the north aisle, and John Downton put a lock on the pew door, but William Formeston, at Marton, who claimed a share in that seat, came on the Lord's day following, and giving the pew door a sudden pluck, broke off the lock. Upon this there was a parish meeting appointed (for then there were no ecclesiastical courts held in England) to decide this controversy, and to settle persons in vacant seats; for it was held a thing unseemly and indecent that a company of young boys, and of persons that paid no leawans, should sit (in those pews which had been the passage) above those of the best of the parish . . .

. . . The third pew on the south side of the north aisle . . . was settled and appointed to Mr. Hall, Thomas Acherley, John Downton, and Richard Jukes. Of these families, I have spoken of two of them already — of the other two I intend to speak when I come to their ancient seats, but it will be necessary that I show what title I have to a share in this seat, and therefore I say that I have as good a title as any man in Myddle has to any seat both by prescription and by this order. As for prescription, it is known that my father from the time of the uniforming of the church with wainscot pews, and which is about sixty-two years past, before this year 1701, did usually sit in this seat — after his time I did sit in it usually before I purchased any of these messuages to which this seat was granted by the third order — and as to my title by the order, I do say that Mr. Hall had two messuages in Newton; I bought one of them and most part of the lands belonging to both — and so I may claim a share by order. Afterward I purchased Jukes's messuage and lands wholly, and though I sold the house, and some of the ground to Edward Garland, yet I reserved the privilege in this seat wholly to myself as appears by the writings made between me and Edward Garland.

The fourth pew on the south side of the north aisle

This pew belongs to Richard Groome's tenement in Marton, this leawan is 2s. 8d. — to Mr. Mather's tenement in Balderton, the leawan is 2s. 0d. — to Billmarsh farm the leawan is 1s. 4d., and to Mr. Hayward's land in Newton whose leawan is 1s. I know not who ought to have the chief seat in this pew, for I have seen Richard Groome's mother-in-law, and after her decease, his wife, sit uppermost in this seat — I have seen Mr. Mather do the like — I have seen Mrs. Alice Hayward sit uppermost in their seat, and I have seen widow Reve of Billmarsh do the like. But I have placed their names here (but not in the platform of the seats) according to their leawans, and, in that order will speak of their families and predecessors.

Richard Groome's tenement or farm in Marton, is the lands of the Earl of Bridgewater; it was formerly held by the family of the Elkses, the last of which family (if I mistake not his name) was Hugh Elks, but whatever his name was, he was an ill man — for he, knowing that a neighbour of his who lived in Eyton had a considerable sum of money in the house, this Elks and some other of his companions came to Eyton on the Lord's day at time of morning service, and having visors on their faces, they came into the house and found there only one servant maid who was making of a cheese, and this Elks stooping down to bind her she saw under his visor, and said, "Good Uncle Elks, do me no harm," and upon that he pulled out his knife and cut her throat. His companions being terrified at the act fled away to Baschurch Church, and Elks seeing his companions were gone fled likewise and took no money, and for haste shut the door after him and left his dog in the house, and came to Marton, but stayed not there, but ran to Petton to church whither he came sweating exceedingly a little before the end of service.

When people came from church to Eyton, they found the girl dead, and Elks' dog in the house almost bursting with eating the cheese. They followed the dog, who brought them to Elks' house, and upon this, Elks was apprehended on suspicion. The next day the coroner summoned his inquest, and Elks stifly denied the fact, alleging that he was at Petton Church that morning; but a servant maid of John Ralphe's of Marton witnessed, that she heard the town field gate at Marton clap, and looking through the window out of her master's house, she saw Elks coming from that gate about the middle of service time. But Elks pretended that it was impossible to see the town field gate through any window in that house; and thereupon the whole jury came from Eyton to Marton, and then the maid showed them through the window the town field gate, and thereupon the jury found him guilty of the murder. He was after found guilty upon his trial at Shrewsbury, and was hanged. Thus ended the family of the Elks in this parish, and this was one of the first escheats, or forfeitures, which happened to the lord keeper Egerton, after his new purchases in this country. But because another happened about the same time, by a person of the same name, I will briefly relate it although it was done in another lordship.

There was one Thomas Elks, of Knockin, who had an elder brother, who married and had one son, and soon after died and his wife also, and left the child very young. The grandmother was guardian to the child. This grandmother was mother unto Thomas Elks, and was so indulgent of him, that she loved him best of any of her children; and by supplying him with money to feed his extravagances, she undid him. But when she was gone poor, and could not supply him, he considered that this child stood in his way between him and the estate, and therefore contrived to remove him: and to that end he hired a poor boy, of Knockin, to entice the child into the corn fields to gather flowers. The corn was then at highest. Thomas Elks met the two children in the fields; sent the poor boy home, and took the child in his arms into the lower end of the field where he had provided a pail of water, and putting the child's head into the pail of water he stifled him to death, and left him in the corn. At evening, the child was missing, and much inquiry made for him. The poor boy told how his uncle had hired him to entice the child into the corn fields, and there took him away in his arms. The people suspected that the child was murdered, and searched the corn field. They found the child, whether buried or not or whether he intended to bury him that night, I know not. Elks fled, and took the road directly for London. (I think he was a journeyman shoemaker.) The neighbours had intelligence which way he went, and sent two men to pursue him, who followed him almost to London; and as they were passing on the road near Mimmes, in Hertfordshire, they saw two ravens sit upon a cock of hay, pulling the hay with their beaks, and making a hideous and unusual noise. Upon this, the two men alighted from their horses and went over to see what the matter was, and there they found Tom Elks fast asleep in the cock of hay, and apprehended him, who being tormented with the horror of a guilty conscience, confessed that these two ravens had followed him continually from the time that he did the fact. He was brought back to Shrewsbury, and there tried, condemned, and hanged on a gibbet, on Knockin Heath.

But to return to Marton. When Elks' tenement there was forfeited to the lord of the manor one Clowes took a lease of it, and had a daughter who was married to Richard Groome, of Sleape Hall, brother by a second venter to my grandmother (on my mother's side). This Richard Groome had no son by Clowes' daughter, but had five daughters. The eldest was married to Thomas Freeman, a younger brother of the family of the Freemans of Isombridge, in this county. The second was married to Thomas Acherley Edge, of Wykey. The reason why he had three names was thus — he was a bastard child of one Edge's daughter, who lived in a tenement beyond Marton near the wood, called the Rowlands. It is called Edge's tenement to this day, and is now in lease to Mr. Thomas Harwood, who married Richard Acherley's widow. Edge's daughter, in her labour at child bearing fathered the child upon Thomas Atcherley, grandfather of Andrew Acherley, now living. At the baptising of the child, old Edge was one of the godfathers, and he named the child Thomas Atcherley. The minister paused awhile, as supposing it was a mistake, and after said again, name this child. To whom old Edge answered, "I am neither drunk nor mad; I say, Thomas Atcherley," and so he was named. The third daughter was married to William Gough, of Edgboulton, near Shawbury. He was my cousin german, (*i.e.*) my father's brother's son. The fourth daughter was married to Abraham Puller, of Edgboulton. He was a long time bailiff to my lady Corbett, of Acton Reyner, alias Acton Reynold. The youngest daughter was married to Richard Groome son of John Groome, of Sleape; they are both living, and proceeded both of the same common ancestor, John Groome, of Sleape Hall, who was great grandfather to this Richard Groome, and grandfather to his wife. This Richard Groome is now tenant of this farm.

Thomas Mather has a share in this pew for his farm or tenement in Balderton, which is a freehold estate, and is not in the manor of Myddle, but belongs to the manor of Lilshull, which formerly was a famous abbey in this county. The owners of this tenement do owe suit and service to the court held for the hundred of Pimhill, as it is a court leet; but they pay a yearly chief rent to the lord of the manor of Lilshull and a heriot at the decease of every principal tenant . . . By reason of the chief rent, they appear at the great court and court baron of the lords of the manor of Lilshull, which he holds for his manor of Hardwicke. This tenement did formerly belong to the family of the Husseys, which was of great antiquity and repute in this parish. It is likely that it was sold by the abbots of Lilshull before the dissolution of the abbeys, temp: Henry VIII. The last of the Husseys (save one) that was owner of this farm, was John Hussey (unless I mistake his name). He was guardian to a young woman whose name was Elleanor Buttry, or Butter. (I believe she was born near Drayton, which we call Drayton in Hales, or Market Drayton.) This Elleanor had one hundred pounds to her portion, and for covetousness of that money, old Hussey married her to his son, Richard Hussey, whilst they were under years of consent to marriage. Perhaps he was of the same mind as old January was, when he married the young lady May who said;

A yong thing a man may gy,
As warm hand do wax ply — *Chaucer.*

But he might rather have taken notice of our old English proverb, which says, that to marry children together, is the way to make whoremongers and whores; and so it happened, for she had no love for her husband, and told my aunt, Joan Gough, of Newton, that at the time of consent she would part, and take her portion and begone. My aunt approved of her design, and told her that he was such a worthless person that she did not conceive that she could ever live comfortably with him. But my uncle, Roger Gough, overhearing them, said, "Go, thou fool, thou wilt never come to such an estate with a hundred pounds portion, and if thou wilt be a careful, good wife, no doubt but he will be a painful, laborious husband, and you may live happy." She took the old man's counsel by the halves, for she consented to the marriage, but proved a bad wife, for she soon became too familiar with William Tyler, her next neighbour (a person of the most debauched morals of any that were then in the parish), that she got so bad a report as was not to be endured by her husband: and when he reproved her in friendly terms, she did not answer as May did in the like case, as Chaucer reports in his tale of the marriage between old January and Lady May:

I wish that never daw the day
That I ne starve as fowle as woman may,
If ever I doe my kin that shame
Or else that I impaire soe my name;
That I bee false, and if I doe that lacke,
Doe strip me and put me in a sacke,
And in the next river doe me drench:
I am a gentlewoman, and noe wench.

But this Elleanor upbraided her husband in such opprobrious terms, that, being not able to live in peace with her, he left her and went to Preston Gubballs, and there sojourned a while with Mr. Robert Mather, to whom he sold this tenement in Balderton. He gave his wife her £100 portion, and she went to Lytle Drayton, where she kept an ale-house, and William Tyler went often to visit her and at last had a child by her whom they called Nell Hussey.

Richard Hussey was preferred by Robert Mather to a knight's service in Kent. The knight's name was Conningham, and the said Richard Hussey died, and so ended the family of the Husseys in this parish and is utterly extinguished.

Robert Mather was a stranger in this country; he came hither to serve Sir Humphrey Lea, as his bailiff. He was a person very expert in buying and selling of cattle, and had a commission to be one of the king's purveyors, which was an office to buy fat beasts for the king's household. Some of these officers did wrong the country very much, for the purveyor would come to a fair or market with his long goad in his hand, and when he saw a pair of oxen that were for his purpose, he would lay his goad upon them, and if they were unsold, would mark them for the king's use, unless the owner gave him silver persuasions to forbear; but if the oxen were once marked, the owner durst not sell them to any other, and the purveyor would take care not to give too much. These purveyors were likewise drovers, who bought cattle in this country, and brought them into Kent to sell again. If the king had any of them it is likely he paid pretty well for them, but these officers being found a great nuisance both to the king and country, were laid aside.

Robert Mather married a gentlewoman whose surname was Wollascott; she was descended of that ancient and worthy family of the Wollascotts of Wollascott, an ancient farm near Preston Gubballs; he purchased the reversion of a lease in Preston, off one Lewis, and after took a new lease of it. He had issue, one son, viz. Thomas Mather, and several daughters, which were married to several persons of good quality. One was married to one Twisse, of Hadnall, of an ancient and substantial family. Another to one George Huffa, a rich man. His father was Phillip Huffa, a blacksmith, who, by his own labour and industry, got a great estate; I dare not say he got it ill; for I never heard any person speak ill of him, but always commend him, but I can say that his estate had the fate of illgotten estates, for it did not continue three crops.

A third daughter was married to Mr. Turner, then minister of Hadnall, and after of Great Boylas. Thomas Mather, the son, married a daughter of one Bunbery, a gentleman in Cheshire; she was but a sickly woman, but she was a religious person, and a good housekeeper; he has one son, Robert Mather, who married Elizabeth, daughter of Roger Hodden, of Broughton; he died March 21st, 1705.

The tenants of Billmarsh farm have a share in this pew; this farm is the Earl of Bridgewater's land. It was formerly a common, as appears, in that every man that has land adjoining to it, does enclose from it, except a little piece of common called Billmarsh Green, and from this Billmarsh farm does make hayment, and therefore it may seem that this little green is part of Billmarsh farm, and that it was left out when the rest was enclosed. There was one George Watson, who was bailiff of the manor of Myddle, in the later end of the Derby's time; this Watson did enclose two pieces out of the north side of Billmarsh common, which are now called the Marle pieces, and these two pieces are not part of Billmarsh farm.

Before this common was wholly enclosed, there were two little houses or cottages upon it near the south-west corner of the common, and some small encroachments adjoined to them. One Towers, a tailor, dwelt in one of them, and one Edward Grestocke, alias Newton, lived and sold ale in the other, and his wife made cakes, which were accounted the best in this country, so that two or three of Grestocke's cakes was a very acceptable present to a friend. These two families are extinct in this parish.

Mr. Osmary Hill (about the beginning of the Earl of Bridgewater's time), took a lease of this common and enclosed it; he pulled down the cottages, and built a fair house upon it. He was bred up a scholar and kept a very flourishing school at his own house, where many gentlemen's sons of good quality were his scholars; he purchased a piece of freehold land that adjoined up to his house and was called the land piece. He bought a little meadow called the Partridge meadow, it lies at the west end of Sleape Gorse; he had also a lease of a tenement in Withyford, under Mr. Charleton of Apley. He had one son, whose name was Francis, he had several daughters, who were servants to gentlemen whose sons were his scholars. He had one daughter who was servant to a gentleman who lived near Wellington, and as this young woman was holding water for her master to wash his hands in the kitchen, he cast a little water from off his finger into her face, which her mistress (who was present), seeing, and conceiving it too familiar an action, she in a rage took up the cleaver, and gave her such a blow on the head that she died. This Mr. Osmary Hill died at Billmarsh, and lies buried in Myddle churchyard, under a plain gravestone which lies by the wayside that leads from the church to Mr. Gittins' house. I do not know whether any one has been since buried under that stone. His son Francis succeeded him, and married a daughter of Mr. Joshua Richardson's, of Broughton; he sold his lease of Billmarsh, and the lands which his father bought, unto George Reve, a Cheshire man, who came into this country to live at Sleape Hall, as I said before.

Francis Hill removed to Withyford, and there died — he left behind him a son, named Francis, and a daughter who is married to Mr. William Gittins of Myddle.

George Reve was a wealthy farmer, and held this farm during the life of Francis Hill, and afterwards took a lease of it for twenty-one years (for at that time the Earl of Bridgewater would set no leases for lives). This George Reve had but one son, whose name was Nathaniel; to him he gave his lease, and the purchased land, but he had several daughters who were married to good substantial persons in this country.

Nathaniel Reve married a daughter of one Jackson of Ash near Prees Heath — he had a hundred pound portion with her. He purchased some land near Billmarsh (adjoining to that piece which his father bought). The lands were called Little Billmarsh; he purchased them off Michael Baugh of Clive. When the lease of Billmarsh was expired Nathaniel Reve refused to take a new lease unless he could have it at his own rate — and therefore it was leased for twenty-one years to Thomas Hayward of Tylley — and Nathaniel Reve removed to Broughton and lived there a tenant to Richard Lister, Esq.; this Nathaniel built a new house at Billmarsh upon his purchased land, but there is no seat in church belonging to this house. He died at Broughton; he was such a notorious liar that he was scarce believed in any thing that he spoke . . .

Nathaniel Reve had four sons and several daughters (but I can give an account but of one that married one George Job of Tylley). He gave his lands unto Nathaniel, his eldest son, and thirty pounds a piece for portions to his other children. I will give a short account of George, his second son, and thereby of the ruin of the whole family, for it had been good for them if he had never been born.

> Well, better is rotten apple out of hoard,
> Than that it should rott all that's stored — *Chaucer.*

This George Reve was a cripple from his mother's womb, he was born with one of his legs shorter and lesser than the other (the old proverb says, Beware of him whom God hath marked). When he was about six or seven years old, by the help of steel plates fastened to his leg, he was able to walk and his leg received strength, but was always shorter than the other. He was set apprentice to a shoemaker and came to be an expert workman — but Mercury's boon was given him, that he should spend a groat before he had got two pence. He soon spent his portion, and afterward married one of the daughters and co-heirs of John Hilton, who had an estate in lands, of about thirty pounds per annum in Clive. This John Hilton being a bad husband, sold his estate for his life, and went a soldier beyond sea, but could not sell the inheritance from his two daughters, of which Reve married one. George Reve sued for this land, and having got proof that John Hilton is dead, recovered it, but the costs and charges in law, and his extravagant expenses, were so great, and the buying of the other daughter's part, that he had borrowed great sums of money, and his other brothers were deeply engaged for him, and soon after this George and his brother Nathaniel were brought to prison: the other two brothers fled out of the country, one of them left a wife and child behind him, which have relief out of Broughton parish. George sold his land in Clive, and having some money spare removed himself into the Fleet, where he now continues. Nathaniel sold his lands at Billmarsh and now holds it on the rack rent.

Thomas Hayward was the next tenant; he was son of Thomas Hayward of Tylley, who married a daughter of Mr. Thomas Kinaston of Ruyton — they were both dead, but the grandfather John Hayward was living and kept the house and most of the lands at Tylley from him, and therefore he took this farm. He married a daughter of Mr. Edward Onslow of Acton; her mother was one of the youngest daughters of Sir Andrew Corbett . . . When John Hayward died, this Thomas Hayward sold his lease to John Wareing of Shrewsbury, and removed to Tylley, where he wasted much of his estate and then died; his wife died some years after him. They left a son and a daughter, very hopeful children.

John Wareing was an attorney, bred up under Mr. John Edwards of Nesse: his master could not get him to write a good hand, nor to learn the practical part of the law thoroughly, yet he could make large bills, and was not inferior therein to the worst attorneys. He married one Hayward's daughter, a weaver in Shrewsbury, and had a considerable fortune in money with her.

He purchased Mr. Crosse's lands in Yorton, and sold his lease of this farm to Crosse, that he might have a place to live in. This John Wareing died before he had fully completed the purchase, and his brother-in-law John Chambre of Wolverley, went through with it, and now has the land.

William Crosse was the next tenant (for a while), he was descended of poor parentage; his father was Adam Crosse of Yorton, of an ancient and substantial family there; his mother was a daughter of Mr. Joshua Richardson of Broughton, and although his father died and left him but young, yet his careful mother caused him to have good education, under his uncle Mr. Joshua Richardson (some time Rector of Myddle). This William Crosse had a good estate in lands and a fair house in Yorton. He married Judith, the daughter of Mr. Francis Whitcombe of Berwicke. But that which sowered all, was that this William Crosse and his wife were both overmuch addicted to drunkenness, and it is no marvel that they consumed the marriage portion (which was considerable), in a short time, and afterwards the lands. When William Crosse had sold his lands in Yorton he came to Billmarsh, where he followed the same way of drinking as before, for he and his wife went daily to the ale-house, and soon after the cows went thither also; and when his stock was spent he sold his lease to Nathaniel Reve, and removed to Shrewsbury, where he took a little house on the rack rent, and there followed the same way of drinking.

He died soon after he went to Shrewsbury, and as his life was extravagant, so his end was strange, for as he sat in an ale-house cellar upon the stand that holds the barrels, and whilst another was drawing drink by him, he was taken with an apoplexy, and fell down dead. The other man thought he was playing the wag, and said, arise, why dost thou play the fool? — but when the other man went to him he found that he was dead, and called in neighbours, but he could not be recovered.

Nathaniel Reve had a desire to be tenant of this farm, because his grandfather and father had been tenants to it before, and therefore he bought the lease of Mr. Crosse for £20, and borrowed the money off Mr. Robert Finch, of Cockshutt, and gave his lease in mortgage for security of the £20. But Reve was soon after taken to jail for debt (as I said before), and Finch entered on the farm, and is now tenant of it. To buy land, and borrow all the money that pays for it is such a precipitate thing that hardly prospers.

I have been long in speaking of this fourth pew on the south side of the north aisle, and am now come to Mr. Hayward's tenement in Newton on the Hill. This tenement, and another tenement, and several lands in Newton, did belong to that worthy family of the Corbetts, of Stanwardine in the Wood; and it is likely that this estate did belong formerly to the Kinaston's of Walford, and that Robert Corbett, of Stanwardine, had it by the marriage of Jane, one of the daughters and co-heirs of Kinaston, and seeing that Kinaston came to the estate of Walford, and Stanwardine, and several other lands in this parish by the marriage of the sole daughter and heiress of John Hoard, Lord of Walford, it is possible that these lands in Newton did formerly belong to the family of Whoards, or Hords.

Robert Corbett, of Stanwardine, Esq. (with whom I was a servant several years, and under him had my best education), gave these lands in Newton unto Thomas Hayward, of Balderton, in exchange for a tenement and lands in Balderton; and Mr. Corbett was to have £20 in money for owelty of partition, which £20 was unpaid when I served Mr. Corbett, and I was sent to demand it. It was unpaid forty years at least. Mr. Corbett complained that Hayward had circumvented him in this bargain, when he was a young man, and did not well understand the worth of his lands.

Thomas Hayward gave these lands to Thomas, his eldest son, and he sold them to Thomas Hall, of Balderton. Hall borrowed all the money at interest which paid for the purchase, which caused Thomas Hayward (who was a discreet man), to say, that the buying of these lands in Newton would cause Mr. Hall to sell Balderton.

Thomas Hall sold one of these tenements in Newton unto me, and the greater part of the lands. At the time of my purchase, it was agreed, that the share in this pew should belong to that tenement which Thomas Hall did reserve, and that I should have that share in the sixth pew on the south side of the north aisle which belonged to these lands in Newton. Thomas Hall afterwards sold the other tenement in Newton, and the lands belonging to it, unto Robert Hayward, now (1701) owner of it; and to this tenement the seat I am now speaking of belongs.

But since I have undertaken to write of the antiquities and some old accidents that have happened in this parish, it will be needful to say somewhat of the tenants of these lands, and I do find that the family of the Newtons were formerly tenants of these lands, and that one John Newton, who was the last of that name here, had a daughter, named Jane, who was married to one Griffith ap Reece, of the parish of Baschurch, anno 1581. But there were two houses upon these lands, and one William Parkes lived in one of them. He was a weaver, and had many children, whereof Mr. Kinaston took one and maintained her, as I said before; and this is observable, that although this Parkes was a poor weaver, and had eleven children, yet neither he nor any of his children were chargeable to the parish.

Although this family was numerous, yet it is now wholly extinct in this parish. I knew but one of Parkes' children: her name was Anne. She was taken in her youth with that distemper which is called the ricketts; she could not go or walk until she was nineteen years of age. Afterwards her limbs received strength, and she was able to walk. She learned to knit stockings and gloves, in which employment she was very expert and laborious, and thereby maintained herself after the death of her parents. She was never married. She died at Daniel Tildley's house in Newton, and had twenty shillings in her coffer when she died, which she said she kept to pay for her funeral; and it may be she was never worth more all her life.

But now I return to Griffith ap Reece, the other tenant. He was a careful, laborious person and lived plentifully. He had three sons — John, Richard, and William, and one daughter, named Elizabeth. John was married, and lived in Harlescott. He had a son, named John, who lived in Yorton, who had a son named Thomas. He is now a freemason, and a good workman. He had a daughter, who was first married to one Thomas Owen, of Myddle, and is now married to one Samuel Davis, a sow-gelter in Myddle.

Richard, the second son, married a wife, whose name was Gwen. He lived some while in Newton, as tenant to Mr. Gittins, and after removed to Broughton, and held a farm under Sir Thomas Lister, of Rowton. This Sir Thomas presented King Charles I with a purse of gold when the king was at Shrewsbury, an. dom. 1642, and there the king knighted him.

This Richard Preece had a son named Richard (he married Margaret, the daughter of one Taylor, of Broughton), and had a daughter, called Jane, who was married to one Roger Clarke, a butcher in Ellesmere, and was very rich. But Richard Preece, the second, proved the saddest drunkard that ever I heard of. He would never (by his goodwill) drink less than a pint or a quart of strong ale at a draught.

He destroyed himself and his estate by drink and after his death, his sister Jane, of mere charity, maintained his widow. He left behind him a son, named Richard, who married Mary

Hancocke, of Wem, an ale-woman. She was thought to be a light housewife, and he proved to be a light-fingered person, and at last he was sent to Shrewsbury jail for fellony, where he hired a silly boy to procure him instruments to break prison. The boy brought him a bar of iron and a broken broom hook, and with these he pulled out several stones, and made a hole through the stone wall of the dungeon, and so escaped, but left the tools behind him. It was found that the silly boy had these things from a neighbour's house the day before; and so the poor boy was hanged, and Preece escaped and went out of this country.

William Preece (who was called Scoggan), I have mentioned before — how he was a soldier in the low countries, and at his return married one Katherine Chetwall, of Peplow. Of his three sons I have spoken. What I have to add is, that after his return from the low countries, he was made a sergeant in the trained bands for this county, in that company whereof Sir Richard Hussey, of Abright Hussey, was captain. But when King Charles came to Shrewsbury, he listed himself a soldier in the king's service, and because he was a stout and experienced soldier, he was there made a sergeant. He was lame, but not by any hurt in the wars; but endeavouring to rob Baylie Downton's orchard he fell down from a pear tree, and broke his leg, which was ever afterwards crooked. In the wartime he came to Peplow, to visit his wife's friends, and was there taken prisoner by the parliament soldiers, and brought to Wem; but he broke prison, and escaped the first night to Myddle, and there sheltered himself the day following in the tower or staircase of Myddle Castle, and the next night went to Shrewsbury. At that time the garrison soldiers of Wem made their outroads many times almost to the walls of Shrewsbury; and to prevent this insolence, the governor of Shrewsbury placed a garrison at Abright Hussey and Scoggan was governor of it. I remember the soldiers fetched bedding from Newton for the use of the soldiers there. They took only one coarse bed hilling from my father. A party of horse, of the parliament side, came on a Sunday, in the afternoon, and faced this garrison, and Scoggan, standing in a window, in an upper room, cried aloud, that the others heard him say, "Let such a number go to such a place, and so many to such a place; and let twenty come with me:" (but he had but eight in all in the house). And Scoggan, seeing one Phillip Bunny among the enemies, who was a tailor, born in Hadnall, he took a fowling gun, and called to Bunny, and said, "Bunny, have at thee!" and shot him through the leg, and killed his horse. The parliament soldiers took up Bunny, and departed. Soon after, this garrison was recalled at the request of Mr. Pelham Corbett, who feared that the parliament soldiers would come and fire his buildings. This Scoggan married a second wife, and boarded her with John Matthews (whom they called Great John Matthews), who then lived in a house of my father's called Whitrish House, and there she died. Scoggan continued a soldier in the king's service until the king's party was vanquished and dispersed, and the king, by wicked hands, had lost his life . . .

This Scoggan, after the wars, came to Whixall, and there married a third wife. He was not troubled by the parliament party, as many others were; for he that sits on the ground can fall no lower. So he died in peace.

But yet Elizabeth, the daughter of Griffith ap Reece, is not to be forgotten.

She was married unto one Thomas Hodden, of Myddle, and therefore I will speak more of her when I come to the seat that belongs to his tenement.

After the death of Griffith ap Reece, Thomas Hayward came to be owner of Mr. Corbett's lands in Newton, and he placed Thomas Tildsley in one tenement, and one Robert Smith dwelt in the other, who came there upon the death of William Parkes. This Robert Smith was born of good parentage in Acton Reynold. He married a Welsh woman, whose name was Jane, and by her had two daughters — Jane and Alice. This Alice was married to Richard Owen, the youngest son of John Owen of Myddle. This Richard took a lease off Mr. Adam Crosse, of Yorton, of a little house and piece of ground, called the Gothornes, or Goddins, formerly called Goldburn's piece, and there died, and his son William is now tenant there. Thomas Tildsley, that held the other tenement, and married Jane, the eldest daughter of Robert Smith. This was one of the Tildsleys, of Merington. He had a son, named Daniel, and soon after died. His widow held the tenement for some time; and afterward Thomas Hayward held it in his own hands until he sold it to Thomas Hall. This Mr. Hall pulled down the chief house, and set it up again at the end of the lane which leads from Newton to Haremeare Heath, and afterwards sold it to me, with his part in the sixth seat on the south side of the north aisle, and when I came to that seat I will speak more of this tenement. Mr. Hall pulled down the house and building wherein Robert Smith had lived, and set it up where the other had been and Daniel, the son of Thomas Tildsley, came to be tenant to it. He was a peaceable and religious person, he married a servant of Mr. Hall's, her name was Katherine Jones. She was born in Wales, near a place called the Mould. They are both dead, and one John Williams, who was born at a place called Coidyrath, near St. Martin's and married Mary, the daughter of Daniel Tildsley, is now tenant of it, under Mr. Robert Hayward, who purchased it off Mr. Hall.

The fifth pew on the south side of the north aisle belongs to Shotton

I have spoken already of that loving and lovely family.

CHAPTER 5

He . . . Got A Wench With Child, And Fled Away

The sixth pew on the south side of the north aisle

This belongs to Mr. Cotton's farm in Alderton; to Richard Gough's tenement, which he purchased off Mr. Hall, in Newton; to Richard Groome, in Marton; and Thomas Shaw, off the same. Of this pew I have spoken somewhat already, how upon a difference between John Downton, of Alderton, and William Formeston, of Marton, there was a parish meeting appointed and an order was made whereby John Downton was to have one-half of the seat, Thomas Hall a quarter, and Richard Groome and William Formeston, one kneeling apiece. That part of the seat which did belong to John Downton, does now belong to Mr. Phillip Cotton, who purchased John Downton's farm, and it seems to me, that it was intended by those that made the order, that John Downton should have the chief kneeling, because he is first named, and is named before Mr. Hall, as in other cases he is not. There is now (1701) some contest between William Groome, tenant to Mr. Cotton, and his brother, Richard Groome, about the superiority in this seat, and William Groome has made several large complaints to his landlord about it. But he loves himself and his money too well to spend labour and charges in such matters; but his tenant must trust to himself. Whether Mr. Cotton do well in it, I will not say . . .

Thomas Hall, by the order, had a quarter of the seat. He sold his part to me, by agreement, when I purchased one of his tenements in Newton. This house, or tenement, stood at the end of the lane which leads from Newton to Haremeare Heath, and one Robert Ored lived in it, and sold ale. He was born in Wirrall, in Cheshire, and coming into this country, married one Elinor Gorstilow; he had two sons by her at one birth, which he named Moses and Aaron. He removed hence with his wife and family a little before I bought the tenement, and went again to Wirrall.

When I purchased it, one Thomas Hancocks, who was born in Broughton, and had married Joan, the daughter of Thomas Whitfield, a tanner in Tylley, near Wem, dwelt in the house, and sold ale. But he disliking the place, I removed the house to another piece, called the Old Field, which I at the same time purchased off Mr. Hall. (The piece from whence the house was removed is to this day called Ored's Piece.) The house was set by the roadside that leads from Wem to Shrewsbury, and one Walter Greenwoller, who was born in Market Drayton, married Sarah, the daughter of Thomas Hancocks, is now tenant of it.

Of Richard Groome's family, I have spoken before, and of Shaw I hope to speak of when I come to his chief seat, because I think he has little to do with this seat, and if we believe John Downton, he has nothing at all in it.

The seventh pew on the south side of the north aisle belongs wholly to the whole town or farm of Hulston

Hulston is a hamlet in the township of Myddle; there is a constable, but neither pound nor stocks, nor ever was (as I believe). This was one entire farm, and belonged to the Lord Strang, and was granted to some chaplain or servant. There was a hall in this town, and therefore it was called Hullston, for hull, in old Saxon, is a hall. There is a piece of ground in this township, called the hall yard in which are ploughed and dug up some foundation stones and other things which show that there have been large buildings. It is conceived by most that know this town or farm, that it fell among five sisters, and that William Wicherley, Esq., hath two sisters' parts; Sir Francis Edwards Bart., hath one sister's part; Mr. Richard Lloyd, clerk, hath one sister's part, and Mr. Thomas Gittins, now Vicar of Loppington, one sister's part. These four tenements contain the whole town — I cannot say to which of them the chief seat or kneeling belongs, but I will speak of them in the order I have named them.

Mr. Wicherley's tenement was formerly the estate of one Mr. Aupert, a Cheshire gentleman. Mr. Gittins of Myddle (grandfather to the vicar) was about to buy it, and a meeting for that purpose was to be at Whitchurch. It happened that the night before the meeting Mr. Gittins' horses were broke out of the pasture and got into Mr. Hotchkis' ground, in Webscott, and Mr. Hotchkis' servants had put them in the common land, and they were strayed to Meriton Green, so that Mr. Gittins' servants were a great part of the day seeking them, and James Wicherley of Yorton came betimes to Whitchurch and purchased the tenement in Hullston of Mr. Aupert before Mr. Gittins came. I have not heard that James Wicherley was blamed for anticipating Mr. Gittins, but I can say that James Wicherley's estate had the fate of goods not well gotten, which our English proverb says, "will not last three crops" . . . But it is an erroneous way to judge of things by the event.

James Wicherley was a wealthy man, very provident and sparing, or as some would say covetous. He had two sons, James and Richard. This James fell in love with a sister of Adam Crosse, his next neighbour. She was a beautiful gentlewoman of good parts and education, but because her portion was inferior to old James' expectation he would in no case agree to the match, and did what he could to prevent his son coming near her. But love will cause boldness though attended with danger, for this young James was endeavouring to come to his mistress, and passing through some outbuildings that he might not be seen, he fell and broke his thigh and died. Richard, the second son, married Margaret, a daughter of that ancient and substantial family of the Fewtrells of Easthope. This Richard was heir to his father's patrimony and parsimony. I never heard that he was commended either for his charity to the poor, his hospitality to his neighbours, nor his plentiful housekeeping for his servants. He was troubled in the time of the wars (temp. Car. I) with the outrages and plunderings of soldiers on both parties (as all rich men were), and seeing his goods and horses taken away, and his money consumed in paying taxes, he took an extreme grief and died. He had no child, and therefore he adopted a kinsman named Richard Wicherley, to be his heir, who after his decease entered upon the one half of the estate throughout with the widow. He was a quiet man, and lived peaceably with the widow, for she ruled all things and did what she pleased. He was given to no vice, nor seemed to be proud; he never altered the fashion of his clothes, for he never had but one and the same suit during all the time that I knew him, which was about ten years. This Richard Wicherley the second was never married, and therefore he adopted Richard Wicherley (son of his brother Thomas Wicherley of Crockshutt), to be his heir, and put him to school to Mr. Suger of Broughton, at which time I was a scholar there. He was very dull at learning, which caused Mr. Suger to say very often he had no guts in his brains, but it seems he had gear in his breeches, for he got one of his uncle's servant maids with child, and thereupon his uncle sent him to London and bound him an apprentice there to a person that used some small trade about stuffs and serjeys. Before his time was fully expired, he married his maid; his uncle soon after died, and awhile after the widow died. There was a widow who had been wife to one Thomas Hulston of Kenwick's Park, and sister's daughter to old Richard Wicherley. This widow Hulston came to the funeral of the widow Wicherley, and brought with her some persons whom she could trust and were privy to her design, and when the corpse were taken out of the house and the company was gone, this widow Hulston and her confederates did shut the doors and kept possession. This news was sent to Richard Wicherley (the third of that name), to London, but he being unskilful in the law and destitute of money (for I think he had no portion with his wife), sold his lands to Daniel Wicherley, of Clive, Esq., who soon outed the widow Hulston. It is said the lands were sold at an easy value, and I partly believe it, for he that sold them knew not the worth of them.

Daniel Wicherley, Esq., was eldest son of Daniel Wicherley of Clive, gent., who married the daughter of one William Wolph of Acton Reynold. She was a proper comely and ingenious person, but her husband was a spare lean person, whose countenance showed that he was a passionate cholerick man, and his actions proved him so; for he was always at strife with his neighbours, and much in debt. He mortgaged all his estate in Clive to Mr. Gardner, os Sansaw, and gave it him in possession, and lived on his wife's estate in Acton. This Daniel Wicherley, the son, was well educated with all sorts of learning that the country would afford, and having the advantage of a good natural wit and a strong memory, he was like to make a person fit for any weighty employment. He was sent to London in his youth and there served some person that belonged to the law, and after having a prospect of obtaining a teller's place in the king's exchequer, his father wanting money, his aunt, in Acton, furnished him with one hundred pounds, which procured the place, and then he began to gather money and to get great acquaintance. After some years he obtained a steward's place under the Marquis of Winchester (this was that family of whom it is said, that "every other heir is a wise man"). In this nobleman's service Mr. Wicherley got his estate — he married the marquis's gentlewoman who if she wanted beauty had a large share of tongue.

And now all the marquis' estate was sequestered, and he and his son secured in the Tower, because they had adhered to the king, and Mr. Wicherley must raise a vast sum of money to pay off the marquis' composition, Mr. Wicherley, by selling and leasing of lands, and by borrowing money in the city (for which he gave a land security), procured the money in time and caused the marquis and his son to be released and discharged. But during this time, the Earl of Arundel had sent his steward to Wem, upon the account of raising money to pay the earl's composition. This earl, like a right nobleman, caused notice to be given to all his copyholders, that if they pleased they might enfranchise their estates and make them fee simple. Many embraced this motion and made their land free, but some inconsiderate self-conceited persons refused, and conceived that a copyhold estate was better than a freehold, but they found the contrary, to the great damage of their families, and the ruin of some. The steward's name I think was Hassall. This Mr. Hassall and Mr. Wicherley, were of great acquaintance, and Mr. Wicherley sold lands to Mr. Hassall which were of the marquis' estate, and when the copyholders had done purchasing, Mr. Hassall sold the lordships of Wem and Loppington to Mr. Wicherley, and so Mr. Wicherley became Lord of the Manor of Wem, and was by some persons called my Lord Wicherley. Soon after he was made a commissioner for the raising of the royal aid, and after was put in the commission of the peace for this county, and wrote himself Esq., and now I have brought this esquire to his zenith, or vertical point.

The justices of the peace of this county endeavoured to have him put out of the commission, and to that end preferred certain articles and a petition to the king and counsel. Mr. Wicherley was summoned to answer them. The then Lord Newport assisted the justices, and then was a privy counsellor; at the time of hearing, the king was present in counsel, and many things were proved against Mr. Wicherley, but the chief was that he had granted a replevin for a horse that was distrained and impounded by virtue of a warrant from the deputies lieutenants of this county, for not paying of a trained soldier's pay. This seemed a contempt of his majesty's deputies lieutenant's power; at last a short petition against Mr. Wicherley was read, which was signed by several hundreds of freeholders. During this hearing, the Earl of Bridgewater (then one of the king's counsel), took notes of all the chief things that were proved against Mr. Wicherley, intending as it was thought to make a speech, and sum up the whole matter, and deliver his judgment of it; but the king spared him that labour; for the king rising up said to the lord president, "I think we must put him out," to which all the rest agreed, and it was done. But this is not all . . .

The old Marquis of Winchester being dead, his son called Mr. Wicherley to give an account of his stewardship. This proved a long and chargeable suit; what the young marquis got I cannot say, but I have heard that Mr. Wicherley parted with all the leases which he had of the marquis' land and what houses he had in London; but this is not an end of trouble.

Mr. Wicherley had a long and chargeable suit with his copyholders of Wem lordship; they alleged that their custom for payment of fines at every decease and at surrenders, was to be one year's rent, according to the chief rent which was paid yearly to the lord of the manor. But Mr. Wicherley pretended that it was arbitrary, not exceeding three years' rent, according to the improved rent on the full value; after a tedious suit, it was decreed that the fine should be arbitrary, but should not exceed one year's rent on the improved rent. And the copyholders repented too late, that they had not made their land free. When Sir George Jeffries was made keeper of the great seal, he was only a bare knight, but when Mr. Wicherley had settled his customs in the manors of Wem and Loppington, he sold them to Sir George, and because Wem had been an ancient baronry, he was created Baron of Wem, and made lord chancellor; after that Mr. Wicherley was no more called my Lord Wicherley . . .

His son, William Wicherley, Esq., succeeds him — a person as highly educated as any in this county, and excellently skilled in dramatical poetry. The Earl of Rochester, in his poem of the poets of our time, gives a great encomium of him, and terms him the restorer of true comedy, and after hath these verses of him —

> Wicherley earns hard for what he gains;
> He wants no judgment, and he spares no pains;
> He often times excels, and at the best
> Commits less faults than any of the rest.

This Mr. Wicherley was once married to an Irish countess; she was heiress or widow (I know not whether) to Earl Roberts, sometime lord deputy of Ireland. He had no issue by her; she is dead, he is a widower, and being impaired in body by age and sickness, it is likely he will not marry again.

The next tenement belongs to Sir Francis Edwards; this is a family of baronet's degree, and I believe made so when the king was at Shrewsbury, anno '42. I have nothing memorable to say of this family; they are a sort of quiet mild persons, and make no great figure either in town or country, but I will speak somewhat of the tenant.

There were two families of the Pickstocks in this side of Myddle Parish. The one held this tenement. The other dwelt in Brandwood, but whichever of these was the elder family, I know not, but these families are now both extinct in this parish, for families have their fate, as well as other things.

The last of them that was tenant in Hulston, was George Pickstock; he was very infamous for reselling of stolen goods. His ground was overgrown with wood and thorns, and, lying in an obscure place, was a fit receptacle for stolen beasts and horses. His wife's name was Dorothy; whether she was fair or not I know not, but it seems she did not observe the counsel of an old woman to her daughter, "Si non castè tamen cautè." George Pickstock had two children, John and Elizabeth; John was somewhile servant to my father; he was an able and active person in husbandry; he afterward served Samuel Formestone of Brandwood, and got a wench with child and fled away, and by chance came to my father-in-law, William Wood of Peplow, and was hired with him, but the wench enquired him out, and came to apprehend him, but he fled from thence, but I know not whither. After the death of George Pickstock, William Bickley was tenant of this tenement, and after him, William Tyler, of Balderton, and after him Samuel Formestone, and now James Fewtrell, who married a daughter of Samuel Formestone's, is tenant of it. All the buildings are fallen, save only some part of the dwelling-house which is made use of to put hay and fodder in.

The next is Mr. Richard Lloyd's tenement; of his family I have spoken before, and as concerning his tenants here there is nothing worth mentioning.

Mr. Gittins' tenement, was formerly the lands of one Tong, but of what place I know not, for there was one Tong who was Rector of Myddle, and another of the same name lived in Myddle. There was also one Tong of Marton, and another Tong of Weston Lullingfield, who was a mean lord of the manor of Weston Lullingfield; he had several lands in other towns, but all is sold, and the family is gone or extinct. This Tong sold his manor of Weston to Sir Thomas Scriven of Froadsley, and he again sold it to my old master, Robert Corbett of Stanwardine, Esq., and now it is all the estate of Thomas Corbett, Esq., late of Stanwardine. This manor contains about eight or nine farms, and tenements, with some cottages and several chief rents — but I digress.

I hope to speak of Mr. Gittins' family, when I come to the seat belonging to the Castle Farm. In the meantime, a word or two of the tenants of this tenement in Hulston.

I find that one Reynold Aston was tenant to it, and I have heard that he married a daughter of the family of the Tylers of Balderton. He had a son named John, and two daughters, Mary and Anne. This Anne is long since dead: Mary was married to one William Groome; I know not of what family he was, but I find there was one William Groome, a weaver, in Hulston, and it may be he was son to this weaver. This William had two sons, John and Daniel, and a daughter named Mary, who now lives in Myddle. She is very old, but not much chargeable to the parish. Daniel is married and lives well. John is married and has no child by his wife. He built a pretty little house on this tenement, and lived in a good condition for many years. He was always a sober man, and a painful labourer; but his wife is now blind, and he is old and indeed an object of charity. He is now tenant to Mr. Gittins.

But I must not forget John Aston, because many in the parish have reason to remember him. He was a sort of a silly fellow, very idle and much given to stealing of poultry and small things. He was many times caught in the fact, and sometimes well cajoled by those that would trouble themselves no further with him. But at last he grew unsufferable, and made it his common practice to steal hens in the night and bring them to Shrewsbury, where he had confederates to receive them at any time of night. He was at last imprisoned and indicted for stealing twenty-four cocks and hens. The judge, seeing him a silly man, told the jury that the matter of fact was so fully proved that they must find the prisoner guilty, but they would do well to consider of the value, and thereupon the jury found him guilty of fellony to the value of eleven pence, at which the judge laughed heartily and said he was glad to hear that cocks and hens were so cheap in this country. This made John Aston more careful, but he left not his old trade wholly.

This John Aston was a person of a deformed countenance and a mis-shapen body; his pace or gate was directly such as if he had studied to imitate the peacock . . .

This town of Houlston, or Hulston (I suppose), took its name from a hall that was formerly in it (perhaps when it was one entire farm). There is a place in this town called the hall yard, in which are many times dug and ploughed up some foundation stones and other stones of ancient buildings, but I forget myself having written this before.

The eighth seat on the south side of the north aisle

This pew belongs to Mr. Gittins' freehold lands in Myddle, to John Horton's tenement in Myddle. Concerning the family of the Gittinses I intend to speak at large hereafter. This tenement is accounted an half tenement, and it seems to me, by an ancient recovery now in my keeping, that it was formerly the lands of the Banasters of Hadnall. The family of the Mathews was for a long time tenants of it. One William Mathews, who had a lease under Mr. Banaster, lived in this tenement (which is called the house at the higher well), when Mr. Gittins bought it. William Mathews had two brethren, John and Edward; this Edward was a blind man, but I conceive he was not born blind, for he could go all over this part of the parish a begging, and so maintained himself with meat. But the parish maintained him with clothes. He was the only person that was then chargeable to the parish; so that I have heard my father say that the first year that he was married (which was about the year 1633), he paid only four pence to the poor, and now I pay almost twenty shillings per annum. This Edward Mathews was a strong man, and did wind up the stones for the building of Myddle steeple. John Mathews was commonly called great John Mathews, for there was another family of the Mathewses in Myddle, and the master of it was called little John Mathews. This great John Mathews was so miserably covetous that he would not allow himself necessary meat and clothing, and yet he had still monies aforehand. He had one daughter, named Elizabeth, who was married to one Habbakuk Heylin, a bastard son of Mr. John Heylin, of Alderton, in Shawardine parish. This Mr. Heylin was descended of a good, but yet a decaying family. He was a very strong man; and I have heard it reported that he would take a three-penny horseshoe and with his two hands would draw it straight. He was a captain in the army of King Charles I. He had a daughter, named Golibra. She was servant to a lady in the west of England. The lady was blind; and, by her maid's persuasion, she came to live in Shrewsbury for the wholesomeness of the air. At that time, Mr. Heylin was an officer in the garrison in Shrewsbury Castle, (temp. Car. I). He came often to visit this lady, and would sit by her discoursing half a day. At last she gave him his table, and afterward was married to him, and then he took her to her own country again. Habbakuk Heylin's wife died without issue. William Mathews, that held the tenement of which I am speaking had likewise a lease of a piece of land called the Wood Leasow, which he held under the Earl of Bridgewater. He had one daughter, named Alice. When he died, the tenement fell to Mr. Gittins, but the lease of the Wood Leasow fell to his daughter Alice, who was then a servant to Mr. Gittins in Myddle. She renewed her lease, and besides her own life, she put in the lives of Daniel Gittins, second son of Mr. Gittins, and Mr. Morgan Win, eldest son of Mr. Richard Win, of Pentre Morgan. She married one Evan Jones, a tanner, servant to Mr. Atcherley, of Marton, and was commonly called Evan the tanner. He built a house on the Wood

Leasow, and divided it into four pieces, and so made it a pretty tenement. He and his wife were both laborious and provident persons, and lived in a wealthy condition. They had only one daughter. Alice died before Evan, and soon after the burial some malicious persons spread a rumour abroad that Evan had beaten and abused her, which caused her death. There was not many that believed the report; nevertheless the coroner was sent for (I believe, by Evan himself). When the coroner came, he summoned a jury, according to the custom in such cases, and caused the clerk to open the grave. When the corpse was uncovered, the coroner required the clerk to draw the winding sheet a little aside, that they might see the face; which being done, the coroner said, he had seen enough, but if the jury would see further they might; but they would not. Then those witnesses were sworn and examined, but nothing material was proved, and Evan was acquitted. He died some years after, and his daughter married one Richards, of Wykey, and removing thither, they sold their lease to me, at which time one Mr. Morgan Win's life was in it, who was much about my age; I held it four years; but being troubled with a bad tenant, whose name was Thomas Jones, son of Francis Jones, of Marton, and I having made a greater purchase, I sold this to Richard Rogers, a tailor, who then lived in Petton, and soon after Mr. Morgan Win died; but Rogers took a new lease, and now this spring sold it to William Willet, who now lives in it. Thus you see this ancient family of the Mathewses is wholly extinct in this parish.

John Horton is tenant to the Earl of Bridgewater of a tenement in Myddle, to which a share of this pew belongs. The house stands over against the church lich gates. This tenement was held by the family of the Heddens, which was an ancient family in Myddle; and there was another family in Myddle, of the same name, who lived in Hunt's tenement. The last of the Hoddens, save one (that were tenants of Horton's tenement), was Thomas Hodden, who married Elizabeth, the daughter of Griffith ap Reece, of Newton. He had issue by her, Thomas Hodden, and soon after died, leaving his wife a young wanton widow, who soon after married with one Onslow, a quiet, peaceable man; but she soon grew into dislike of him, and was willing to be shot of him. There were other women in Myddle, at that time, that were weary of their husbands, and it was reported that this woman and two more made an agreement to poison their husbands all in one night; which (as it is said) was attempted by them all; but Onslow only died; the other two escaped very hardly. This wicked act was soon blazed abroad and Elizabeth Onslow fled into

Wales, to her father's relations; but being pursued, she was found upon a holiday, dancing on the top of a hill amongst a company of young people. She was apprehended and brought to Shrewsbury, and there tried for her life. Her father spared neither purse nor pains to save her; and, as some say, by the assistance of Sir Richard Hussey of Adbright Hussey, to whom she had formerly been a servant, she escaped the gallows. But her next husband did not escape so, for he was the falsest thief that ever I heard of in this parish. His name was John Owen. His common practice was to sleep in the daytime, and to walk abroad in the night; sometimes near home, and sometimes farther off, and whatsoever was found loose was a prize for him. Among these many mischiefs which I have heard that he did, I will mention but one. It was thus:— there was one Jukes that kept an inn in Myddle, and it was usually the way of the Newport butchers to go to Oswestry fair, and there to buy fat cattle, and to come the same day back to Myddle and to lie at this inn all night. It happened one day, as these butchers came with their cattle to the inn, that this Owen was drinking there, and he went out to see the cattle put into the back side, and among the rest there was a delicate pied heifer, which was exceedingly fat. John Owen came in with the butchers, and sat drinking until they were gone to bed; and in the night this John Owen and one of Jukes' sons went and caught the heifer, and thrust a wire into her throat, so that she bled inwardly. In the morning, when the butchers arose, they found John Owen sitting in the corner at the inn where they left him. One of the butchers went out to see the cattle, and came in and told them that the pied heifer was dead; and they all concluded that, being so very fat, she had been overdriven, and so died. They went all to see her, and Owen went with them, and told them he thought that poor people would be glad of the meat and therefore he would buy her, hide and all, which accordingly he did for a little money; and when they were gone, he dressed her, and he and the innkeeper had a great deal of good beef. I will omit the rest of these evil things that I have heard of him, and hasten to that which hastened his end. I have mentioned before how George Pickstock, of Hulston, had rough ground, and thither this Owen brought his stolen cattle and horses. But the potsherd that goes often to the well, comes home broken at last. For there was a stolen horse found in Pickstock's ground, and Pickstock was apprehended, and said it was John Owen's horse; but Owen was missing. He had lately sold another to a person towards Atcham, and that horse was killed in the pasture that night that Pickstock was apprehended, and it was thought that Owen killed him. The next day Owen came home and was apprehended; he confessed that the horse was his, and made that idle excuse which every silly thief will do, that he bought him off a stranger upon the road. He was tried and condemned at Shrewsbury. At his trial, a list of articles of many of his villainies was presented to the judge, who, upon reading of them said, it was a great shame that such a man should live. Great numbers of people went to see his execution and to hear his confession, which they say was very large, and discovered all the villainies that he could remember that ever he had done, among which were several felonies that other persons had been blamed or suspected for; and in the conclusion, he said, that a lewd and wicked woman in this parish had brought him to that end, and said, that she tempted him to kill his wife, and that he once designed it, and to that end, he enticed her, on a Sunday afternoon, to come with him into the cornfields, to see if the corn was ripe; and as they were walking along between two lands, or butts of corn, he had a hammer in his pocket to knock her on the head, and then he turned back again to do it, but she smiling, and talking lovingly to him, he could not find in his heart to do it. Thus John Owen was hanged, and pity it was that the lewd woman had not been hanged with him . . .

By this time, Thomas Hodden, the younger, was grown up unto years of discretion. He was a careful, sober, laborious person. He married Frances, a servant of Mr. Robert Moores, of Myddle. She was a Yorkshire woman and came hither with Mrs. Moore. He had two daughters by her — Elizabeth and Alice. He took a new lease of this tenement, and to his own life he added the lives of Frances his wife, and Elizabeth, his eldest daughter, and soon after died. His widow afterwards was married to one John Williams, a Welshman, who could neither speak good Welsh nor good English. He was sometime servant to Mr. Gittins, of Myddle. This John Williams had issue by her a son, named John (who married a daughter of one Coalen, of Shawbury parish, and had two daughters by her, and then outran her, and was never heard of), and a daughter named Sarah, who was married to one Hayward, a weaver, who then lived in Myddle, and after removed to Weston under Redde Castle, and from thence to Bletchley, where by entertaining a guest (for they kept an inn) she was infected with the French measles; she got the distemper healed, but her husband died. They had one son, an untowardly person. He stole away, and married the daughter of Mr. Goldsbury, of a place called the Rye Bancke, in Wem parish; and after being suspected of felony (perhaps not without cause) he fled his country.

Elizabeth, eldest daughter of Thomas Hodden, Jnr., when she was grown up was married to one Richard Maddocks (son of Henry Maddocks, of Haston). He gave his father-in-law, John Williams, and Frances, his wife, several pieces of land that did belong to this tenement to hold for the life of Frances, his wife. The cunning Welshman would not build a house upon any of the pieces of land, fearing that his wife might die before him, but he built a house on the top of Myddle Hill, near to some of the lands; and now his wife, being long since dead, he lives in it. Richard Maddocks was a carpenter by trade, and an ingenious workman, but he was very slow, or as some said idle, so that few men employed him, and therefore he left his trade and turned carrier; but the death of an old horse broke him. He pulled down the barn which was at his house over against the lich gates, and set it up for a dwelling-house (on a piece of ground that belonged to his tenement) at the foot of Myddle Hill, near Penbrooke's gate, and there he sold ale, and at a time when a sad fever was in Myddle, he and his wife both died within a week together, and left two sons, Richard and Thomas, and three daughters behind them. Upon the death of Elizabeth, the wife of Richard Maddocks, the lease of this tenement expired, and Richard Maddocks, Jnr., who was a shoemaker by trade, took a new lease on the rack rent, and after sold it to John Horton, or Haughton, of Shrewsbury, who is now tenant to the Lord of the Manor, and his subtenants are John Plungen, at the house over against the lich gates, and John Bennion, at the house at the foot of Myddle Hill. Thus that ancient family of the Hoddens is wholly extinct in this parish.

A share of this pew belongs to the widow Mansells' tenement which is the lands of the Earl of Bridgewater. I find that the family of the Mansells have been tenants of it 101 years; and before them, the family of the Dods were tenants of it for many generations — of which family I find nothing memorable, but that one William Dod, was constable of Myddle Castle in the later end of the reign of King Henry VIII, as appears by an ancient deed, now in my keeping. And I find by the parish register, that in the year 1587, one Richard Dod was parish clerk of Myddle. He had a daughter, named Elizabeth, who in the year 1600 was married to one Walter Mansell, of the parish of Lillshull, and so the family of the Mansells came to be tenants of this tenement. This Walter Mansell had a son, named Bartholomew, who was cook many years to Mr. Chambre, of Petton; and after the decease of Walter his father, he married Dorothy, the daughter of one Houle, of Shawbury. This Bartholomew was very serviceable to his neighbours in dressing meat at feasts, and in slaughtering beef and swine, all which he did at a very reasonable rate. He had issue, a son, named Bartholomew, and two daughters, viz. Priscilla and Elleanor.

Elleanor Mansell was many years a servant and housekeeper to Mr. Chambre, of Petton, and was married to John Dod (born at Estwicke or Easton, in Ellesmere parish), who was chief servant or bailiff to Mr. Chambre. She was very useful and indeed famous for her skill in surgery (which I believe she learned of her young mistresses, the daughters of Mr. Chambre), and in that way she did much good in the country. Her husband and she lived very lovingly together, but they had no child. She died not many years ago, and lies buried in Myddle churchyard, and her loving husband has caused a fair gravestone to be laid upon her. We may almost call it a little monument. It is raised upon stone about two feet above ground. John Dod intends to be buried near his wife, and therefore he has left £10, the interest to be dealt in bread among the poor on this part of the parish. Priscilla married with one John George, a person blameable for nothing that I know, but that he was idle. His father-in-law Bartholomew Mansell gave him liberty to erect a house at the lower end of Myddle, upon a piece of ground which belongs to this tenement, and there he and his wife died, and left a son behind them, named John George, who married Ann the daughter of Thomas Pye, sometime cook to Sir Richard Newport, and after to my Lord Newport, now Earl of Bradford. She is yet living, but he is dead, and left two sons — Thomas, who was brought up by John Dod, whom I named before; and James, who is now apprentice to a carpenter. Bartholomew Mansell the second, married first with a daughter of one Nightingale of Leaton, and had two daughters by her, both which were brought up by their kind uncle, John Dod, and by him preferred in marriage, the one to a kinsman of his, named William Dod, the other to William, the son of William Edgerley of Burleton. They are both handsome, orderly, and modest women, and with them their uncle gave considerable portions. This Bartholomew married a second wife, whose name is Jane. She was daughter-in-law to one Richard Waters of Burleton, but what her father's name was I know not. This Bartholomew was for some years bailiff of the manor of Myddle, in which office he behaved himself justly. He died of a dropsical distemper, and left a son, named Bartholomew, which he had by his second wife, and she is yet living.

CHAPTER 6

Tormented With A Crew Of Fanatical Persons . . . Termed Anabaptists And Dippers

The ninth pew on the south side of the north aisle

This pew belongs to my ancient tenement in Newton on the Hill; to Wolf's tenement in Myddle; and to Hunt's tenement in Myddle.

Richard Gough, the first, was descended of that ancient family of the Goughs of Tylley, who were copyholders of about £60 per annum; he was a lease tenant in Newton of the tenement wherein I now dwell, and held it under that worthy family of the Banasters, of Hadnall. His wife's name was Anne, but of what family I cannot certainly say; and yet, by what I heard, I may rationally guess, that she was the daughter of one Hayward, of Aston, near Wem, who was owner of a copyhold estate there, which, by marriage of a daughter of one of the Haywards, came to the Menloves, and is now in the possession of Margaret Menlove, widow. This Richard Gough had issue, two sons — Richard and Roger. This Roger had a wife, whose name was Gwen, he had a lease under Mr. Banaster, of that tenement in Newton, which is now the vicar Gittins'. This Roger died without issue.

Richard Gough, the second, purchased the tenement wherein I dwell, of Richard Banaster, of Hadnall, Esq., and Peter, his son. This Richard had a wife, whose name was likewise Gwen. He had by her two sons — Richard and Thomas — and a daughter, named Margaret; she was married to Richard Paine, of Eardeston, one of the eleven towns. He was a good freeholder, and his heirs continue there to this day; but because I shall sometimes mention the eleven towns, I will here give some account of what they are; and first, their names are Old Ruyton, Cotton, Shelvocke, Shottatton, Wykey, Eardeston, Tedsmeare, Rednall, Haughton, Sutton and Felton. These eleven towns make up the manor or lordship of Ruyton, and they are an allotment in the hundred of Oswestry.

But to return. Thomas Gough married a wife in Weston Lullingfield, and held a considerable farm there; but his family is wholly extinct.

Richard Gough the third married with Elizabeth, the daughter and only child of William Crump, of Acton Reynold, who was tenant there to the worthy family of the Corbetts, of Morton Corbett. This William Crump was a strong and a stout man, one instance I will briefly relate. In the time when Shrewsbury was a bailiff town (for it was not made a mayor town until the reign of King Charles I), there was a tax imposed upon Acton Reynold (which is in their liberties), which William Crump conceiving to be a wrong one, refused to pay, and therefore the bailiff sent two officers to distrain, who took two oxen of William Crump's, who, having notice of it, rode after them with a good cudgel, and as soon as he overtook them, he knocked down one of them, and the other ran away. And William Crump called to him and said, "Commend me to thy masters, and tell them if thou wast my man, the first thing I did, I would hang thee, because thou sawest thy partner knocked down and didst run away." The next day the bailiff sent twelve officers who brought Crump to jail, but Sir Andrew Corbett hearing of it, went straight to Ludlow (which court was in full power at that time, and Sir Andrew was one of the prince's counsel there), and brought an order to release Crump. Not long after the bailiffs of Shrewsbury sent two cunning tradesmen to Crump's house, and desired to speak with him on the backside, and there they offered him four nobles, for his false imprisonment, and desired him to take it privately, that it might not be a bad example to others. But he told them he was not brought to jail in private, nor would he receive the money in private, but if they would pay him in the open street, he would take it. As they were paying him in the street, he called with a loud voice to his neighbours, and said, "Come hither quickly!" and the people came in all haste, and he showed them the money, and said, "See here, the bailiffs of Shrewsbury have sent me four nobles for false imprisonment — I pray bear witness that I have received it." This Richard Gough, the third, had only one son by William Crump's daughter, named Richard Gough. He was the fourth of that name. His mother died in child-bed of him, and William Crump brought him up until he came to man's estate.

Richard Gough, the third, married a second wife, whose name was Anne. She was the widow of one Thomas Baker, of Weston Lullingfield. She had a son named Thomas Baker by her first husband, and Richard Gough the third, had three sons by her, viz. John, Roger, and William, and one daughter, called Elizabeth.

This Richard Gough lived to a great age, and was dark twenty years before he died, and yet was very healthful. Before I speak more of the children of Richard Gough, the third, it will not be amiss to say somewhat of Thomas Baker, the son-in-law of this Richard; for although he was born at Weston Lullingfield, yet he was brought up and maintained at Newton on the Hill, until he came to man's estate; and from whence he had that help and assistance, which put him in a way to get an estate. This Thomas Baker was a wild and careless young man, wholly addicted to dice, and such gaming, insomuch that when he came to full age and had received the portion which his father, Baker, left him, he soon spent and consumed it in gaming, and afterward went to be a servant unto Mr. Andrew Chambre, of Sweeney, near Oswestry, where he was employed to gather tithes. This Andrew Chambre was a sleepy drone of a man; he was never married, and his servants consumed all the profits of his estate, and put him also into debt. Thomas Baker began now to bethink himself that it was time to provide somewhat for the future, and therefore he bargained with Mr. Chambre for the tithes of one town (I think it was Maesbury), but Richard Gough, the third, lent the purchase money to Thomas Baker, and had the tithes for security. But Baker had an easy purchase of it (for as I have heard) he paid the purchase money out of the profits of the tithes in two years. Thomas Baker afterwards married with Mr. Chambre's housekeeper, and then he became rich and covetous.

Soon after this, Thomas Baker took a lease of Sweeney Hall and the demesnes belonging to it, of Mr. Andrew Chambre, for the life of Mr. Chambre, for this estate was to descend to the Chambres, of Petton, after the decease of Andrew Chambre, who was now grown poor, and would say, "formerly it was Mr. Chambre and Tom Baker, but now it is Mr. Baker and Andrew Chambre."

Mr. Andrew Chambre went to Petton, and was there maintained upon charity. Not long after, my uncle, William Gough, the youngest son of my great grandfather, went to live with his half brother, Thomas Baker, at Sweeney, and these two joined their monies together, and took a lease for three lives of Sweeney Hall and the demesnes of Mr. Chambre, of Petton, and afterward Thomas Baker purchased the reversion. He still grew richer, and purchased a good farm near Oswestry called Coyd Dugon, a place very pleasantly shadowed with stately woods. He purchased several lands in Weston Riu, and many houses in Oswestry. He had (when he died), £1,000 upon a mortgage of Mr. Pope's farm, called the Luin, near Oswestry. He had £1,000 upon a mortgage of another farm in Sweeney, called Old Sweeney; and besides these he had several other debts owing to him.

This Thomas Baker gave by his last will a certain annual sum of money to the parish of Baschurch (in which he was born) for the buying of bread to be dealt amongst the poor of the parish upon every Lord's day in the year. He had two sons, and one daughter. His eldest son (whose name I have forgotten), was a very hopeful young man, a comely person, and endued with extraordinary good natural parts. His father was not wanting in giving him the best education that could be had, but he died before he came to maturity.

The daughter's name I have likewise forgotten, but I think it was Anne. She was a lovely, handsome woman, and was married (more to please her father than herself), to a neighbouring gentleman of a good (but of a decaying) estate. She had one son by him, and then left him, and went away with a captain, who promised to take her over into Ireland, but he left her at Chester.

She made some shift to come to Newton from Chester, and my great grandfather being then old and dark sighted, sent my grandfather to Sweeney, to make up the breach, which was done by giving a second portion. She returned again to her husband, but died not long after, in the lifetime of her father, so that Thomas Baker, when he died, had one son living, whose name was Thomas.

Thomas Baker, Jnr., was no comely person of body, nor of great parts, and little education, but he was very rich in lands, woods, money and goods. Howbeit, he married with a lovely gentlewoman of a masculine spirit and no mean beauty; I saw no inducement that she had to marry him, save his riches.

Her name was Elizabeth, and her maiden name was Fenwicke; she was descended of a good family, and well educated. Judge Mackworth married her sister. She had a brother that was a colonel in the parliament army, a comely proper gentleman. He was somewhile governor of a small garrison in the castle at Moreton Corbett, which he fortified with a mud wall, and there manfully withstood a sharp assault of his enemies. What countryman he was I know not, but I have heard that the name of Fenwicke is very usual in the north of England.

This Mr. Thomas Baker (for so I must now call him) erected a new fair house in Sweeney, a handsome pile of building, the contriver's name was Baker, he was a disbanded captain. I have heard Mr. Baker say it was wholly built in sixteen weeks.

Mr. Baker was made a justice of peace in the parliament time (and so continued until the restoration of King Charles II), and wrote himself esquire. But it was little trouble to him, and his clerk had a fair life, and, indeed, was not fit for much business. I cannot tell whether he knew where the bench was where the sessions were kept, for I never saw him there.

He was made high sheriff of the county, and kept a very noble sheriff's house. He behaved himself among the gentlemen of the county with much commendation, even to admiration. He was a great patron and benefactor to all independent preachers, such as Vavaser Powell, who commonly preached every day in the week. I have heard him pray and preach four hours together in the dining room at Sweeney, where many persons came to hear him; and when the people departed they had everyone a quarter of a twopenny bun or cake, and everyone a glass of beer, of about half a pint.

And to say the truth of Mr. Baker he kept good hospitality, and was very charitable to the poor. He seldom changed his servants but when they married away, and then he sent them not away without a reward; but all this was thought to be done by the discretion of Mrs. Baker. And now I come to the apex of Mr. Baker's dignity. He was chosen by the protector to be a parliament man. The other knight for this shire chosen also by the protector, was John Browne, of Little Nesse, a self-conceited, confident person, but one that Mr. Baker had a great respect for, because he favoured the Independent party. This parliament was picked by the protector through the whole kingdom, and not chosen by the freeholders, as usual. It was thought that the protector, chose this parliament on purpose that they might make him king; but this parliament was too wise to do that, although the protector, when he turned them out, called them a parliament of fools. They made one act only, which was, that all persons should be married by justices of the peace; of which act Mr. Culpepper said merrily —

> An act for marriages, from heaven sure sent,
> The only business of one parliament.

I have now brought Mr. Baker to his meridian; as he increased in dignity, so he decreased in riches, which wasted faster than his father got them. He had spent all the money that his father left him, and, having no child, he began to consider of an heir to his estate, and first he designed his sister's son, and to that end sent him to Oxford to learn university reading; but he proved extravagant, and got much in debt, and profited nothing in learning, and therefore the uncle paid his debts and cast him off.

When he came home, he married a wife of no fortune, and hardly a good name, and this alienated Mr. Baker's affection wholly from him.

Afterwards Mr. Baker designed a son of Judge Mackworth's for his heir, but the young man died before he came to maturity; and then Thomas Browne, the eldest son of John Browne, of Little Nesse (Mr. Baker's oracle), married with my cousin, Mary Gough, eldest daughter of my uncle, John Gough, of Besford, half brother to old Thomas Baker, and had a son by her, named Thomas Browne, and this young man Mr. Baker made choice of to be his heir.

I have not heard that Mr. Baker sold any lands, but he had contracted much debt, and therefore he ordered some lands to be sold after his death for the payment of debts, which was accordingly done by Mrs. Baker (for she survived him). The rest descended to my cousin, Thomas Browne the younger, which was Sweeney Hall, and the demesnes, lands in Weston Rin, and houses in Oswestry. It is almost incredible how great the fortune was that Thomas Browne the elder had with my cousin, Mary Gough. It is reported that she had little less than £3,000, and yet he has sold all the lands that he had with her in Besford, and all the lands which his father gave him in Little Nesse and Millford, and yet he and his son are not free from debts, and those, I doubt, considerable . . .

And now I come to speak of the children, which my great grandfather Richard Gough the third had by his second wife, which, as I said before, were John, Roger, and William, and a daughter named Elizabeth. This Elizabeth was married to Michael Baugh of Clive alias Cliffe. He was a person of an ancient family there, and of a good estate. He was an understanding man, of a smooth and ingenious discourse, and never blamed, as I know of, for any vicious living and yet although he had a good portion with his wife and several helps from my great grandfather, from my grandfather, from my uncle Roger Gough, from my uncle William Gough of Sweeney, and from my father, yet his estate was always in a decaying condition.

Michael Baugh had issue, Thomas Baugh and several daughters. Some of which daughters married happily and some unfortunately. Thomas Baugh's first wife, was a daughter of Thomas Spendlove of Clive, who was a crafty contriving old fellow, a great surveyor and measurer of lands. (My old schoolmaster, Mr. William Sugar did usually call him, Longo limite mensor.) Thomas Baugh had a second wife, but I cannot say who she was; she lived with him but awhile: he afterwards married the widow of one Bagley, of Bagley, and had a daughter by her named Mary, who is now wife to Samuel Braine of Myddle. This Thomas Baugh had a son named Michael Baugh who is yet living. Now when all the benefactors of Michael Baugh and his son Thomas were dead, they mortgaged their lands so deeply to Daniel Wicherley of Clive, Esq., that they were at last constrained to take a lease for lives of part of it, and release the rest and the reversion after the lease to Mr. Wicherley. Michael the son of Thomas holds that part which is leased for his life and then all is gone.

John Gough, the eldest son of my great grandfather, Richard Gough, the third by his second wife, was a diligent laborious person, and sparing almost to a fault. He married with Katherine, the daughter of one Hopkins of Besford in Shawbury Parish. This Hopkins was a wealthy farmer under the right honourable family of the Corbetts of Moreton Corbett. This John Gough had a lease of two pieces of land in Brandwood in this parish, called the High Hursts. The lease was for ninety-nine years determinable upon the lives of Richard his son, Mary his daughter and my life. He sold this lease to Richard Nightingale of Myddle, and Nightingale sold the lease to Samuel Formestone late of Brandwood, who exchanged the lives, and James Fewtrell now holds them, and the lease which Samuel Formestone took is still in being. It is now above sixty years since my uncle John Gough took the lease, and two of the lives are yet living. But I have heard of a lease that was taken for ninety-nine years determinable upon three lives, and that one of the lives survived the ninety-nine years, and so the lease expired before the lives were dead. Two of the lives that were in my uncle John Gough's lease are yet (1706) living; it is forty years since Formestone renewed the lease.

In the close of the wars (temp. Car. I), when the king's field army was dispersed and most of his garrisons taken, his majesty went privately down to Scotland (his native country), in hopes of having assistance from his own countrymen, but his hopes were disappointed, and they sent him in nature of a prisoner to the parliament of England who sent him to Uxbridge, and there began a treaty with him, by their commissioners, which was concluded at the Isle of Wight, and the commissioners made a report of their proceedings to the House of Commons, for there was then no House of Lords; the Commons had voted them useless, and the army would not suffer them to sit, and made an act, that no person that had taken arms for the king should come within twenty miles of London.

An act, and London may go shake her ears,
She twenty miles must live from Cavaliers — *Culpepper*.

When the commissioners had made their report to the parliament, it was straightaway put to the vote whether the king's condescensions were satisfactory. And was carried in the affirmative by no great number of over voices; but the army being displeased at these proceedings, there was a band of soldiers placed at the parliament door who kept out all that had voted for the king, the rest were suffered to go in, and these were called the rump of a parliament. This rump presently brought his majesty to a trial, and after to an untimely end, and then made a vote that all persons who had adhered to the king's party should be proceeded against as traitors to the commonwealth of England. But here came a little sprinkle of mercy from them, which was, that every such person should be acquitted upon paying of a certain sum of money for his composition money. Which sums were set down by this parliament and were unalterable.

And now Sir Vincent Corbett, of Moreton Corbett who had been a loyal subject to his majesty and had several times adventured his life in his majesty's service, was put to pay a great sum of money for his ransom; for the raising whereof, he sold several lands in Preston Brockhurst, and among the rest, one very good farm, which had been held for several generations by the family of the Dawsons (gentlemen of good account). These lands were sold to Mr. Wingfield of Shrewsbury, who pulled down the hall wherein old Mr. Dawson lived, and built there, a fair hall of freestone, and therein his son Thomas Wingfield, Esq., now dwells.

At this time, and on this occasion, Sir Vincent Corbett sold to my uncle, John Gough of Besford, the tenement in Besford wherein my uncle then lived and another tenement in the town wherein one Harrison dwelt, so that he had in Besford, about £50 per annum, freehold land. But these lands were bought in the name of my uncle William Gough of Sweeney, for my uncle John Gough had been in actual arms for the king, under Sir Vincent Corbett, and he was afraid that this parliament would, after the great ones, call the little ones to account; and beside my uncle William living at Sweeney, could shelter himself under Mr. Baker, who then began to be of some account among that party, and under Judge Mackworth, who as is reported was one of Oliver Cromwell's creatures.

Not long after this purchase, my uncle John Gough died; but my aunt Katherine, survived him. She was so extremely fat, that she could not go straight forward through some of the inward doors in the house, but turned her body sideways; and yet she would go upstairs and down again, and to and fro in the house and yard as nimbly, and tread as light as a girl of twenty or thirty years of age. This, perhaps, to some, may seem idle to speak of; but, indeed, I thought it a very strange thing.

My uncle, John Gough, had three children — Richard, Mary, and Elizabeth. Mary was married to Thomas, the son of John Brown, of Little Nesse, I have spoken of them before. They are both now living at Sweeney. Elizabeth was married to Mr. Richard Glover, of Measbury, near Oswestry. My uncle Gough gave with her certain lands in Measbury, called Measa Cland, which are worth between £20 and £30 per annum. She died after a few years, and left two children behind her — John and Katherine. This Katherine proved a wanton, light woman, to her own ruin, and the great disgrace of her friends. My brother-in-law, Richard Glover (for so I must now call him, because he took my sister to be his second wife), was very indulgent of his son John, and therefore spared no pains nor costs in his education. He placed him in the best schools in this country, that he might be well educated in good literature, but he profited little.

When his father took him from school, he had a great desire to go with his uncle, one Mr. Godolphin, to be a trooper in the king's guards; and to that end his father furnished him with a good horse, and all things necessary. He was entertained in the king's guards, and for some time well approved of; but afterwards he took to much drinking, he sold his horse, and spent the money, and then came to his father's house in the night and my sister kept him close and sent for a tailor, and furnished him with a new suit and other necessaries before he could adventure to come in his father's sight. And when his father saw him, he was much enraged; though the young man pretended his horse was dead, and that the king did usually go so fast in his flying coach from London to Newmarket, that many troopers had killed their horses in keeping pace with him. But within few days his name came down in the gazette for outrunning his colours. Then his father cast him off; but my sister sent him into Wales, to some of his father's relations, and gave him money to bear his charges thither, and sent a man with him; but he went no further than a mile beyond Oswestry, and there got into an ale-house and spent his money, and the man returned and said, he could get him to go no further. Mr. Glover had at that time a good horse, of about £10 price. His son takes this horse in the night, and returns to London, and continues in the king's guards until he was forced to sell his horse to pay for ale-house scores, and then he came down to my cousin Browne, of Sweeney. It was long before his father would be reconciled to him; but at last he took him, put him in a very gentile habit, gave him a good horse, and sent him to court a gentlewoman who was likely to be a good wife for him. But this match failed: and soon after an unlucky match was made between him and a sister of Mr. Lloyd's, a Montgomeryshire gentleman. My brother, Glover, gave him £100 per annum at marriage, and £100 per annum at his decease; but some years after, great difference happened between the father and son, and also between the son and his wife and mother-in-law. But in some kind humour his wife's friends persuaded him to take a yearly sum to maintain him, and to part with his wife; and the annuity being too little to supply his extravagancies, he lives meanly.

Richard, the son of my uncle, John Gough was never married; he was an honest, just man, and well-beloved. When he was somewhat past his middle age, he got a distemper called the scurvey; he took several medicines in hopes to cure it, but they heightened the distemper, so that in one years' time all his teeth dropped out of his mouth, and then he grew to have a precipitate consumption, and died. His lands descended to his sisters, Mary and Elizabeth, and their husbands, who first sold the timber and wood, and then sold the lands, to Mr. Roger Griffiths, a wealthy alderman of Shrewsbury.

Roger, the second son of my great grandfather, Richard Gough the third, by his second wife, died without issue, and I have nothing memorable to say of him. William Gough, the youngest son of my great grandfather, by his second wife. was the wealthiest man of our family. I have said before that he took a lease of half the demesnes belonging to Sweeney Hall; he purchased a farm in Trevlech; he purchased a farm in Sweeney, called the Nant, which is rich land, and has coal and limestone in it; he purchased several houses and lands in and about Oswestry and Measbury. I have heard that he had £500 per annum in lands and leases before he died. He never married until the sixty-eighth year of his age, and then he took a wife, Mrs. Dorothy Griffiths, a jolly widow in Oswestry, she had two daughters by a former husband — Dorothy and Elizabeth. Dorothy married Roger Eavans, Esq., who had been a captain in the parliament army, and was a justice of peace in the protector's time. He was a discreet and prudent man, and therefore was made justice in the time of King Charles II. The second daughter of my Aunt Goughs was married to one Captain Griffiths, an apothecary in Chester. He was first a captain in the parliament army, and after he was captain of the county troop in Cheshire. He was one of the commissioners that tried and condemned the Right Hon. Earl of Derby for meeting his majesty at Worcester fight. Judge Mackworth, of Betton, was judge of that court. The good earl was beheaded at Chester, and one Captain Sawyer, one of the tallest men in England, and a very valiant man was condemned by this court, and hanged. This Captain Griffiths was afterwards chosen a burgess in parliament for the city of Chester, and now he was come to his height. When King Charles II was restored, Mr. Griffiths was put under the black rod. He escaped with life, but his estate was utterly ruined; so that my uncle maintained him, his wife, and children, but Mr. Griffiths died soon after.

My uncle, William Gough, by his last will (which he called his wife's will), gave all his lands to his wife's friends (except such as he had given to my brother, Glover). He left some small crumbs of legacies in money to his relations; nevertheless he left £5 per annum for ever to the parish of Myddle, for setting out of apprentices, and the like yearly sum for the like use, to the parish of Oswestry; and a noble yearly to a minister, to preach a sermon in the English tongue, in Oswestry on St. Stephen's Day, because he was told that he was born on that day; but I believe it was a mistake, for I find by the register that he was baptized on the 23rd of February, and I believe they did not keep him above two months after he was born before they baptised him . . .

Richard Gough, the fourth, my grandfather, was born and brought up at Acton Reynold. He was bailiff almost twenty years to Sir Andrew Corbett, that right worshipful knight who was the chief deputy lieutenant of the county, and most commonly one of the knights of this shire in parliament, and one of his highness the Prince of Wales' counsel in the marches of Wales.

Richard Gough, the fourth, married with Katherine, the daughter of Trustan Turner, who dwelt in a farm called the Wall, near Adeney, in this county. He was a proper tall man, and she a very little woman. He had two sons by her — Richard Gough, the fifth, and William Gough, and three daughters, Elizabeth, Joan and Judith. This Judith was a comely woman, and accounted a great beauty. She was taken with a palsy as she was making of hay in Haremeare. She was lame many years, and then died. Joan married unhappily, and soon after died. Elizabeth married a rich old widower in Acton Reynold, whose name was William Wakeley. He was a person of good account in his time. He had one daughter by my aunt, named Margery. She married with Arthur Noneley, son of John Noneley, of Nonely, and had issue one daughter, who married Henry, the son of Arthur Hatchett, of Burleton, and had issue one daughter named Margaret, who is yet unmarried. William Gough married with Elizabeth, the daughter of one Reynold Dicher, of Edgbolton, and had several sons by her, and a daughter, named Katherine, who was married to one William Blakemoare, of High Hatton. William, the eldest son, married a daughter of my uncle, Richard Groome, of Marton. He had two sons by her who are both living and one daughter, all of them unmarried. Richard, his second son, is a tanner by trade; he married Martha, the daughter of ——— of Childs Arcoll, and has several children by her. He lives in Acton Reynold, he was many years bailiff to my Lady Corbett, of Acton, and to Captain Corbett, of Moreton Corbett, but has now given this up and follows his trade. My grandfather, Richard Gough the fourth, was thick of hearing for many years before he died, and in his old age was taken with a palsy, and was lame some years, and then died at Acton Reynold, and was buried at Shawbury.

Richard Gough the fifth, my father, was a man of a middle stature, very active of body, and of a nimble strength. He purchased a piece of land of Sir Richard Lea, called the Whitrishes, and added it to his estate. He married with Dorothy, the daughter of one Richard Jenks of Cockshutt and Crowsemeare. Her mother, Elizabeth, was daughter of John Groome, a lease tenant of Sleape Hall, he had also a good estate of freehold lands in Sleape town. He was Abavus, i.e. the greatgrandfather's father of Thomas Groome, now of Sleape. This Richard Gough had issue one son, who wrote these memoirs, and one daughter named Dorothy; she was married to Andrew Bradoke, of Cayhowell, gentleman. This farm I have spoken of before at large. Andrew Bradoke died, and left a son and daughter, which both died without issue. The farm is sold to Captain Simon Hanmer, who pays rent to my sister for part of it, which is her jointure. After the death of Mr. Bradoke, my sister (against consent of friends), married Mr. Richard Glover, of Measbury. She had issue by him a son named Richard (who some while served as an attorney, and is unmarried), and a daughter named Dorothy. She is married to Mr. John Vaughan, of Lluin y Groise. This couple when they were married were so young, that they could not make passing thirty years between them, and yet neither of them were constrained by parents to marry, but they going to school together fell in love with one another, and so married. They live lovingly together, and have many children. My father died at Cayhowell, and lies buried in the church at Kinnerley that belongs to Cayhowell.

And now I come to speak somewhat of myself, who am the sixth Richard of our family. I married Joanne, the daughter of William Wood, of Peplow; he was descended of that ancient family of the Woods of Muckleton. Her mother was Joyce, the daughter of Mr. John Baddeley, of Ellerton Grange, in Staffordshire. She died at my house in Newton, and lies buried in Myddle Chancel. I had issue, Richard, my eldest son, who was the seventh Richard of our family; but he died before his middle age, and lies buried in Myddle Chancel. Baddeley Gough, my second son, was apprentice to Mr. Johnson, a dyer in Shropshire, and died of the smallpox, and lies interred in St. Aulkmond's Church there. William, my youngest son, is a grocer in Shropshire. He married Elizabeth, the daughter of Mr. Richard Hatchett, of Lee, who has a son by her named Richard. I have omitted to say anything of two children that I had which died in their childhood. I have three daughters — Joyce, Anne, and Dorothy. Anne is married to John Palin, of Baschurch. My dear wife died at Shrewsbury, where she went to take physic. She was brought to Myddle, and lies buried in the Chancel under the same stone with her mother.

Another share of this ninth pew on the south side of the north aisle belongs to Wolph's tenement in Myddle, now in the holding of Mr. Dale, Rector of Myddle. This is the Earl of Bridgewater's land, and is one of those which they call half tenements in Myddle. It was formerly held by the family of the Wolph's, which was an ancient family in this parish. I could name many of them; but since I can say nothing memorable of them until I come to Richard Wolph, I will begin with him. He married Anne, the daughter of one Humphrey Parbin, of Myddle, Anno Domini, 1587. He had issue by her three sons — Richard, Thomas, and Zacharias. This Zacharias was a blacksmith, and built a smiths shop on the side of Myddle Hill, near the town's end (where now Martin Cheshire dwells), and there he died, and was never married. Thomas Wolph was a shoemaker in Ellesmere. He was a good religious man, of a sober and discreet discourse, but he was somewhat tormented with a crew of fanatical persons in that town, which were termed anabaptists, and dippers. The ringleader of them was John Capper, a glover, but I believe they are now extinct in that place.

Richard, the eldest son, was tenant of this small tenement, and had a lease under William, Earl of Derby. He had two sons — Richard and Arthur, and two daughters. Elizabeth was the youngest and I have forgotten the name of the other. Richard was under cook to Richard Hunt, servant to Sir Richard Lea, of Langley. He went to London, and was there received into very good services. I met with him in London about forty years ago, and he took me to his master's house, who was a Scottish lord, and lived in Lincoln's Inn Square. He sent for his brother Arthur, and preferred him in service, but whether both or either of them be living, I know not. Elizabeth was married to one Edward Owen, a servant in Myddle. Arthur Owen, a tailor, who lives at Myddle town's end next the hill, is a son by that match. After the death of Edward Owen, she was married to one Richard Clarke, of whom there is many remarkable things to be spoken.

This Richard Clarke was the son of Richard Clarke, of Myddle Wood. He was naturally ingenious. He had a smooth way of flattering discourse, and was a perfect master in the art of dissembling. He was listed for a soldier on the parliament side in Wem, whilst he was yet but a mere boy. There was nothing of manhood or valor in him, and yet he was serviceable to the officers of that garrison by carrying of letters to their friends and correspondents that were in garrisons of the adverse party. He had an old ragged coat on purpose which he would put on, and go as a beggar boy. He carried a short stick, such as boys call, a dog staff. There was a hole bored in the end of it, and there the letters were put, and a peg after them, and that end he put in the dirt. If he met with soldiers, he would throw his stick at birds, so that it might go over the hedge, and then go over to fetch it. When he came to the garrison, he would beg from door to door, and consort himself with beggars until he came to the place where he was to deliver his letter. When a maid came to the door, he would desire to speak with the master, from a friend. When the master came, he would give him his stick, and go to clean the stable until the master brought his stick, and then return begging as before. After the wars, he married a wife that lived beyond Ellesmere, her maiden name was Phillips. She was very thick of hearing, but yet she was a comely woman, and had a portion in money, which Clarke quickly spent, for he was a very drunken fellow if he could get money to spend. After he had spent his wife's portion, he came to Newton on the Hill, in a little house there under Mr. Gittins and there he set up a trade of making spinning wheels. He was not put apprentice to any trade, and yet he was very ingenious in working at any handicraft trade. He had a little smith's forge, in which he made his own tools, and likewise knives and other small things of iron. He had several children by his first wife. The eldest he named Jonathan, who now lives in Wem, and is as ingenious at working as his father, and as thick of hearing as his mother. This Richard Clarke, after the death of his first wife, married Anne Onslow, of Clive. She was descended of good parentage, and was a comely and good humoured woman. About this time that fanatical, self-conceited sort of people called quakers began to start up here and there in this country. This Clarke, merely out of design, had a mind to join with these persons. He went to one Gefferies, of Stanton (who was a topping quaker), who received this new proselyte very gladly, and entertained him all night very kindly. He came home the next day a perfect quaker in appearance, and had got their canting way of discourse as readily as if he had been seven years apprentice.

This Clarke was for a while of some repute among the quakers, till at last he had borrowed several sums of money among them, which, when they required, he at first gave fair promises, but at last utterly refused, telling them he was not able, and they were worse than devils if they sued him. Upon this, at a general meeting of the quakers, he was excommunicated. This Clarke, whilst he was in favour with the quakers, had sadly abused our ministers with his scurrilous language, calling them hirelings, dumb dogs, and Baal's priests. He was once bound to the behaviour for saying the protector was the Beast, and the Whore did ride him. When Clarke was cast off by the quakers, he thought the protestants would not receive him, and therefore he turned papist, but was not regarded by that party. This Clarke had several children by his first wife, all which died while he was a quaker (except his son Jonathan), and were buried by him in his orchard. When his second wife Anne was in travail of a child, the midwife told him that the child was dead in the womb, and unless it were drawn from the woman, she would die also; and thereupon Clarke made iron hooks in his little smith's forge, according to the midwife's direction, and therewith she eased the woman of her birth, and the woman recovered. But when she was with child again, and the woman was in the same condition, he would not suffer the midwife to do the like, so the woman died; and very quickly after he married this Elizabeth, daughter of Richard Wolph. Richard Wolph was now grown old, and his wife was dead: this Clarke, by fair and flattering speeches, persuaded the old man to deliver all his estate to him, on condition of being maintained while he lived. Clarke having now got an estate, followed his old way of drinking; and when he came home drunk, he would so abuse the old man, that he made him a weary of his life; and, therefore, in a melancholic fit of grief, he went on foot to Wem, and bought poison, which he eat up as he came homeward; and when he came home he was extremely sick, and vomited exceedingly: he told what he had done, and would fain have lived; but no antidote could immediately be had, so he died. The coroner's inquest found him a *felo de se;* and he was buried on Myddle Hill, at that crossway where the roadway from Ellesmere to Shrewsbury, called the Lower-way, goes over cross the way that goes from Myddle toward the Red Bull, but was removed next night: and some say he was interred in a rye field of his own, which is over against John Benion's, in that corner of the piece next the place where Penbrook's gate stood. Thus ended Wolph's lease, which was one of the last of William, Earl of Derby's leases in this lordship. Thus Wolph ended his life, and Clarke lost his estate.

After the death of Richard Wolph, Mr. William Hollway, then Rector of Myddle, took a lease of this tenement, and Clarke removed to Ellesmere, where some papists lived nigh: but they regarded him not. However, when King James II began his reign, Clarke looked as big as any of the papists — "We apples swim quoth the horse-turd."

At that time a limner was employed to beautify the parish church at Ellesmere. This Clarke went to see his work, and said, "You do well to leave the church in good repair for us; for you had it from us in good order." The limner (knowing him to be a papist) said, "What, do you think the papists must have the church?" "Yes, I do," says Clarke. Then says the limner, "What do you think shall become of us protestants?" Then Clarke answered, "I hope to see all the protestants fry in their own grease before Michaelmas next." The limner proved these words before Mr. Kinaston, of Oatley, a justice of peace: Clarke was committed to prison, and indicted at next assizes, for these seditious words: and judgement was given against him, that he should stand on the pillory at three market towns, on three several market days — viz., at Shrewsbury, at Ellesmere, and at Oswestry. He was set on the pillory at Shrewsbury: but the under-sheriff (knowing how enraged the people were against him), suffered him to stand without fastening of his head through the penance-board.

The people, by pelting him with eggs, turnips, carrots, stones and dirt, used him so hardly, that the under-sheriff took him down, for fear he should be killed outright. The people followed him to the jail door, and pelted him all the way. He lay some while sick and sore at Shrewsbury, and after he was brought to Ellesmere and there put to stand on the pillory, where he found the like favour from the under-sheriff, and the like hard usage, or worse, from the people; and hereupon the high sheriff wrote a letter to the judge, and acquainted him what he had done, and with all told him, that he could promise to put Clarke upon the pillory at Oswestry, but could not promise to bring him alive from amongst the enraged Welshmen; and thereupon the rest of the punishment was remitted. Clarke lay in jail afterwards for some time, and then came to Ellesmere, where he lived a few years, and then died. His wife sold all his tools and household goods, and went into Ireland; but she returned very poor, and so died. I have mentioned before, how Mr. Hollway took a lease of Wolph's tenement, and, when he died, he bequeathed it to his son, Barnabas Hollway, who sold his title to Mr. Hugh Dale, who is present tenant of it.

Another share of this seat belongs to that tenement in Myddle which we call Hunt's tenement. It is the Earl of Bridgewater's land, and one of those that are accounted half-tenements in Myddle. The tenants of it formerly were the family of the Hoddens: and I find that one Roger Hunt, of Uffington, married Jane, the daughter of Thomas Hodden, A.D. 1581, and so became tenant here. This Roger Hunt had two sons — William, who was born 1590, and Richard, born A.D. 1586. William Hunt was parish clerk of Myddle: of him I have spoken at large before: he died without issue. Richard Hunt was cook to Sir Humphry Lea, first at Lea Hall, and then at Langley. This Richard Hunt was very famous for his skill in the art of cookery, and therefore was much employed by the sheriffs of this county, for dressing of their dinners at the assizes. He had a lease of a tenement in Ruckley, perhaps given by his master: he likewise had a lease of this tenement in Myddle, and now it is held by lease by some of his family. As for the under-tenants of it, there is nothing memorable but that one Ralph Astley, and Elizabeth, his wife, lived many years in it. This Elizabeth was a midwife of very great account in her time. The reason that Ralph Astley and his wife held it was this. This Elizabeth, in her youth, was servant to Sir Richard Lea, of Lea Hall, and had a daughter by him: and Sir Richard Lea, at his decease, gave this daughter a lease for life of a tenement in Ruckley of about 10 pound per annum: and this tenement lying near to a tenement which Hunt had a lease of, he gave this tenement in Myddle (which he then had a lease of), in exchange for that in Ruckley for life of this daughter of Elizabeth Astley; and so Ralph Astley and Elizabeth, his wife, came to be tenants of it during the life of that daughter; and now it is in lease to some of the family of the Hunts of Ruckley.

Mr. Richard Lloyd, of Myddle, claims some privilege in this

seat, for his tenant, who lives in a house not long since erected on a piece of land called the Hill Leasow, but he has no right here; and it is not a strange thing for Mr. Lloyd to impose upon his neighbours, as appears by his stopping of a footway over his back side, for which he was sued and cast, and by his claiming a way over Mr. Gittins' ground, near Penbrooke, and cutting open the gate, for which he was forced to make satisfaction. But I will not contend in a small matter . . .

CHAPTER 7

She Went Daily To The Ale-house

The tenth pew on the south side of the north aisle

This belongs to Mr. Hatchett's tenement in Newton, of which I will speak when I come to speak of the chief seat belonging to that seat which is the chief seat belonging to that tenement. This seat belongs likewise to Tyler's tenement in Balderton, which family of Tylers is very ancient in this parish; but I will lay the era of my discourse (concerning this family) with William Tyler, who was great grandfather of this Richard Tyler now living, of whom I may say, many had done wickedly, but he excelled them all. He was a person of a mean stature, lank hair, and a manly countenance . . . I have mentioned before, how this William Tyler debauched Hussey's wife, and caused them to part; she went to Little Drayton, and there this Tyler visited her sometimes, and at last had a child by her, which was commonly called Nell Hussey: when she was grown up, and able to do service, Tyler took her to be his housekeeper, and had a bastard by her. I need mention no more of his villainies.

This William Tyler built a new house in Balderton, and converted his old house into a bakehouse. He married his only son, Richard, to Mary, the daughter of Thomas Bradocke, purchaser of Cayhowell; and by some way or other this William Tyler became indebted to Thomas Bradocke, brother of Mary, but neglected or refused to pay it; and thereupon Mr. Bradocke sent for a writ for Tyler. In those times there was not such a pack of beagles as we have now, who make it their trade to serve writs; but it was usual to put some stout strong person in the sheriff's warrant, and such were called special bailiffs. Thomas Bradocke employed Reece Wenlocke to serve William Tyler with a writ; and Reece met with him at Loppington Court, and quietly in the street, he served him with the sheriff's warrant. Tyler, by fair words, persuaded Reece to come to Thomas Pickering's house; and Tyler stepping into the house, shut the door, but Reece had got his leg in, and Tyler with his knife, struck Reece in the leg; but Reece being a strong man, burst open the door, broke the knife (but cut his own fingers by so doing), he got Tyler down on the floor, and fell to beating of him. Pickering's wife, who was Tyler's sister, made an outcry, and the people came out of the court, and when they came in, Tyler fained himself dead; and the people seeing his face and hair all bloody, with the blood of Reece's hands, apprehended Reece and put him under the constable's hands and so Tyler escaped. Afterwards Mr. Bradocke sent his tenant, William Byron (a little man, but stout of his hands), to serve Tyler with another warrant. Byron came (upon Sunday) to Myddle Church to morning prayer (for in those days all writs and processes might be served on the Lord's day). William Tyler came to church with a good backsword by his side, which then was not usual. After service, Byron stood at the church stile; and as soon as Tyler was gone over the stile, Byron leapt on his back, and cast him down. Many of Tyler's companions, and some women of his relations, came to rescue Tyler; but the high constable, Mr. Hatchett, a bold and discreet man, was present, some say on purpose, and he quieted the people. Roger Sandford, of Newton (who married Mary Bradocke, aunt to Mr. Bradocke), was there, with his servants and friends, to assist Byron; and one William Hussey, servant to Roger Sandford, came to assist Byron; and Tyler got Hussey's thumb in his mouth, and worried all the flesh to the bare bone: but Hugh Suker, a weaver, standing by with a pikestaff in his hand, put the pikes into Tyler's mouth and wrenched open his teeth, and released Hussey. At last Tyler was set on horseback, and Byron leapt up behind him to hold him there, and William Hussey led the horse, and thus Tyler went toward the jail. But the consternation and lamentation of Tyler's friends, especially the women, was such as I cannot easily demonstrate . . .

All the company followed William Tyler out of town; and at the town's end there, upon a bank near the pinfold, stood John Gossage and several others of Tyler's drunken companions, with a pailful of ale. Gossage cried, "Ah, Will! art going to the jail?" Tyler said, "It is too true." Then says Gossage, "Come, boys; fall on!" but Tyler cried, "Hold, hold. It is to no purpose;" so they took him away. When they came a little below the Lea Hall, the miller of the windmill met them, carrying a sword on his shoulder, with the hilt behind him; Tyler put his hand in the hilt of the sword and drew it out, and struck at Hussey; but Byron soon pitched him beside the horse, and took the sword from him. Byron would not give the sword to the miller; and Hussey carried the naked sword in his hand, and led the horse; and so Tyler was brought to jail.

This William Tyler gave his tenement in Balderton to his son Richard, and went to Houlston, where he lived some time as a tenant to Sir Francis Edwards, and afterwards removed to Weston Lullingfield, and lived in a tenement under John Nonely, of Nonely; but when Nonely came for his rent, Tyler, knowing him to be a quiet peaceable man, began to curse and swear and call him rogue, and swore he would be the death of him, if he came upon his ground; and told him, he had taken the tenement for three years, if he lived so long, and swore he would pay no rent till he saw whether he should live so long. Nonely knew not what to do, it being in the heat of the wars; but Nonely employed friends to compound with Tyler to be gone; and Nonely forgave him what rent was behind, and gave him 10 pound for the corn of the ground, and for planting and grafting some fruit trees, in which work Tyler was very skilful and took much delight. Tyler removed to a place called Sherd Oake, and lived in a tenement under Mr. Francis Finch. Tyler lived there many years, during which time his son Richard died.

William Tyler lived to a very great age; and when he had wasted most of his estate, he came back to Balderton, and lived in the old house, which was then made use of for a bakehouse. He had a little flock of sheep, which he kept on the commons: his employment was to walk among his sheep, with a shepherd's crook in his hand, and if he saw a fat wether of his neighbour's, he would catch him with his crook, and carry him home and slaughter him for himself. He had been accustomed to stealing all his lifetime, and could not forbear in his old age.

At this time Tyler was detected stealing a fat wether of my father's, and one of Richard Eaton's of Myddle, for which they indicted him at the country sessions, but his grandchild Thomas Tyler being the chief witness, the jury conceived it malicious, and blamed him for offering to hang his grandfather; and so old Tyler was acquitted. Not long after, William Tyler died at Balderton, and had hardly estate left sufficient to defray the charges of a mean funeral.

William Tyler had a son named Richard, and two daughters — Elizabeth and Anne. This Anne was married to Richard Cleaton, of whom I have spoken before. She died at Allen Challoner's, in Myddle; and was buried without any service or ceremony (according to those times). All the speech which was made at her grave, was several sad curses which her father gave against those that had brought her to her end.

Elizabeth was married to William Bickley of Brandwood, of him I hope to speak hereafter. She was accounted a lewd woman, and had several daughters who had no better a repute. She died at Myddle, and her daughter Susan with her, at what time there was a rageing fever in that town. Richard the son of William Tyler married with Mary Bradocke, as I said before. He was a handsome little man and very different from his father in his morals; he was peaceable and well reputed among his neighbours, he died about his middle age, and many years before his father. His widow was soon after married to one Robert Morrall, of Hopton; a strong robusteous person of a rude bawling carriage. Old William Tyler was his utter enemy, and often threatened to be his death, but Morrall was too hard for him. They met accidently at a stile in Houlston, and discoursing friendly, they sat down on each side of the stile; but Tyler having a halter in his hand, cast it about Morrall's neck and drew him over the stile, and was likely to have hanged him: but Morrall by his strength and agility freed himself, and did not forbear to beat Tyler severely. Robert Morrall removed from Balderton to Hopton, near Hodnett.

Richard Tyler left behind him two sons, Thomas and Richard; and a daughter named Mary — I cannot say for certain, but I think Mary was married unto one Anchors of Hodnett, who kept a little mercer's shop. Richard was goggle-eyed and short sighted, I knew him when I was at school, but have not seen him since. Thomas, the eldest son, married with Joan, the daughter of Roger Gough, of Forton, near Montford Bridge. This Thomas did imitate his grandfather's morals, and not his father's: and I believe had he lived, he would have been worse than ever his grandfather was: but he lived not half his days, for about the twenty-seventh year of his age he was killed with a cart, at a place called Double Gates, which is between Balderton and Newton. His widow afterward married with Arthur, the eldest son of Rowland Plungin. This Arthur and his wife, are both living at the end of Balderton, in a little house which was built of part of Tyler's old house.

Thomas Tyler had issue, one son named Richard, and two daughters, Elinor and Sarah, all of them very young at his decease.

Sarah, as she said (and some believed), was married to Robert Outram, a stranger who was a journeyman joiner in Shrewsbury, where she then lived in service. When she was found to be with child, her master turned her away, and she and Outram came to Balderton and dwelt with her father-in-law until she was brought a bed; and afterwards, he pretended that he would go again to Shrewsbury to work journey work, and would take a chamber and send for his wife. He bought a hundred, or half a hundred of cheese off Richard Tyler, brother to Sarah, and borrowed his horse to carry them to Shrewsbury; and because the way was foul, he borrowed Tyler's boots, and borrowed a pair of spurs and a bridle of Mr. Robert Hayward. He went to Shrewsbury and sold the cheese there and went away with the horse, and neither they nor I ever heard of him after. Not long after, Sarah went to service again in Shrewsbury, and married a soldier who stayed not long with her. But when she was found to be with child, the parish officer came to her to know who was father to her child; and she declared that she was married to a soldier that was gone, and that Mr. Clarke, parson of Fitz, did marry them at a place called the Bull in the Barn, which is at the end of Frankwell, one of the suburbs of Shrewsbury. Clarke was cited to Lichfield, and the thing being made apparent, Clarke was suspended for three years, which had almost ruined him: but I hope he will take better care for the future.

Elleanor, the eldest daughter of Thomas Tyler, was married to one Foster, an ale seller; and they both are living at a place called the Red Bull, near Broughton. Richard, the son of Thomas Tyler, married with Martha, the daughter of one Francis Smith, of Balderton, and has many children by her. They are both living, and are tenants to Richard Hatchett, of a tenement in Newton; which he holds by lease under the Earl of Bridgewater.

The eleventh pew on the south side of the north aisle

Belongs to Mr. Muckleston's tenement in Alderton, and to Guest's tenement in Myddle . . .

Guest's tenement is the Earl of Bridgewater's land; the house was built by George Watson, bailiff of this manor. He enclosed several pieces out of the common moors, and out of the common, called Divlin Wood; and so made a small tenement about the house: but I think he had made no outhouses before his untimely death, for he was drowned at Haremeare.

After the death of Watson, one Thomas Guest took a lease of this tenement. I have nothing to mention of him, but that he procured leave to erect this seat, because this being a new house, no seat did belong to it; and, that by his wife Margaret he had two sons, Ralph and Richard. This Richard was a tailor, and lived in Market Drayton; he had a son who was a barber, and did live, and perhaps does still live in Drayton. He had also a daughter named Mary, who was a servant to Sir Henry Vernon, of Hodnett. His only son, Mr. Thomas Vernon, was over familiar with her, and had a child or more by her. Sir Henry Vernon had only a son and a daughter; his daughter was married to Mr. Cholmley of Tale Royal, and his son soon after married with Mr. Cholmley's sister, a beautiful and well accomplished lady. There was great feasting and joy at the solemnization of this marriage; but all was quashed on a sudden, for Moll Guest openly declared that she was married to Mr. Thomas Vernon, and several children she had born him, and soon after, a suit was commenced in the consistory court at Lichfield, in *causa matrimonii,* which came to commission to examine witnesses. The commission was executed in the parish church of Ellesmere, where old Canon Comins of Preece, was commissioner for Moll Guest, and Dr. Powell, the Rector of Hodnett was commissioner for Mr. Vernon; some say that the evidence for the marriage was too apparent, and that Sir Henry Vernon returned from Ellesmere in great grief and discontent; but this I know, that he soon after died. Soon after the death of Sir Henry, his son Sir Thomas made an agreement with Madam Guest (for so people called her) and gave her a yearly salary or annuity and so she went to London, and (for ought I know) is yet living (1701).

Ralph, the eldest son of Thomas Guest, was a sober peaceable man; his employment was buying corn in one market town, and selling it in another which is called badgeing. His wife's name was Anne, she was a decent housekeeper. They lived lovingly, and in good repute. He had a son named Richard, who succeeded him as tenant of this small tenement, who married with Hannah, the daughter of one Thomas . . . of Burleton. He died some years past, and his widow is married to Francis Watson, of Myddle Wood; what children Ralph Guest had beside Richard, and what children Richard left behind him, I can give no perfect account of.

The twelfth pew on the south side of the north aisle

Was a supernumerary pew at the uniforming of the seats, and no man could claim any right to it. But Margaret, the daughter of Allen Challoner, of Myddle, a blacksmith, did usually sit in it; and now, Thomas Highway, her husband, claims a right to it. But he has another kneeling beside this, and it is not likely, that he being a cottager and paying but a 6d. leawan, should have one whole pew and a kneeling in another pew. Thomas Highway did usually give liberty to other cottagers to sit in this seat, on condition they should pay him money yearly for such liberty. This was a thing never done in this parish before, and therefore Highway was blamed for doing wrong to the parish.

There was one Francis Davis, son of Thomas Davis, of Marton, to whom his father gave a lease which he had, of a piece of land, near Myddle Wood, which piece was called Clare's Lesow. Francis Davis erected a house upon it, and divided it into several pieces, and made a small tenement of it. He complained to the churchwardens that he paid a 4d. leawan, and had no seat in church; and thereupon Richard Eaton, then warden, placed him in this seat. Highway complained of it, but had no relief by the parish; at last, Highway and Davis agreed that Davis should have one kneeling in this seat, and that neither of them should give liberty to any other to sit in that pew without consent of the parish. But Highway does not keep his word in this.

This Francis Davis was a rich man, and served many offices in the parish; and although he had two or three wives, yet he died without issue. He left his little tenement to his nephew, Thomas Davis, of Newton, who now lives in it. He left his personal estate among his poor relations, who quickly spent it.

The thirteenth pew on the south side of the north aisle belongs wholly to Freeman's tenement in Marton

About forty years past, Thomas Freeman, a younger brother of the family of the Freemans of Hambridge came into this parish and married Elizabeth, the eldest daughter of my uncle Richard Groome of Marton, who gave him half his farm or tenement in Marton during his lease. This Thomas Freeman was a person slow of speech, provident, and laborious, yet delighted much in bargaining and more in building. He purchased half that land that belonged to Wright's tenement in Marton and for the raising of money to pay for it, he sold his part of my uncle Richard Groome's farm to Richard, son of John Groome of Sleape, who had married the youngest daughter of my uncle Richard Groome of Marton. Thomas Freeman built a house upon the land which he purchased of Wright and gave it at marriage to his son Richard Freeman. Whilst Thomas Wright lived this Richard Freeman did usually sit in that pew which belongs to Wright's tenement without interruption. But when Thomas Wright was dead, his widow and his eldest son Joseph being cross, litigious persons, would not permit Richard Freeman to sit in that seat, and he being a peaceable man desired of the parish that he might have liberty to erect a seat for himself in some vacant place in the church and it was condescended to by the minister, church and parish officers, and several of the parishioners, that he should at his own charges, remove the font to the place where it now stands near the north door, and should erect a seat for him and his family in the place where the font then stood. All this was done accordingly, and this is the thirteenth seat on the south side of the north aisle and stands opposite to the north door. This Richard Freeman died of the smallpox about the fortieth year of his age. He was a peaceable, honest man and left a good name behind him.

Seats adjoining to the south aisle

The first pew on the north side of the south aisle belongs to Broomhurst farm. This is the Earl of Bridgewater's land. It was formerly in lease to William Nicholas and after to Mr. Chambre of Petton. And about twenty years past Mr. George Chambre of Loppington, took a lease of it and built a house upon it. And when he died gave it to his eldest daughter, Mrs. Mary Chambre, but charged it with payment of debts. This Mary Chambre was married to one William Heath (or William of Heath as he was called in his own county for he was a Staffordshire man). This William Heath much improved this farm and enlarged the buildings, but took no care to pay the debts that were charged upon it; but sought rather to avoid and delay the payment thereof by subtle tricks and slights in law which proved so chargeable to him that he was forced to sell his lease of this farm and leave his country. When he was gone all his personal estate was seized upon by creditors . . .

The third pew on the north side of the south aisle belongs wholly to the Castle Farm in Myddle

I have mentioned before that Sir Roger Kinaston was castle keeper of Myddle Castle, and had a lease of this farm in the time of the Earls of Derby. And that his youngest son Humphrey dwelt in the castle after him, and as it is reported was the last inhabitant of Myddle Castle, because he suffered it to go to ruin. I find that after Humphrey Kinaston, one Richard Moore was tenant of this farm and bailiff of the manor of Myddle, and it may be reasonably supposed that he built the farmhouse.

After Mr. Richard Moore, one Mr. Morgan ap Robert was tenant of this farm, and bailiff of the manor of Myddle, and was commonly called Baylie Morgan. He had no child and therefore he adopted a young kinswoman of his (whose name was Alice) to be his heiress. In Baylie Morgan's time Richard Gittins, a wealthy tradesman's son of Shrewsbury, came to dwell in Myddle, and took a lease under the Earl of Derby of that tenement in Myddle, wherein Thomas Moore now dwells, and is commonly called the Eagle Farm. This Richard Gittins was rich in money and purchased off Mr. Banister of Hadnall, a tenement in Newton on the Hill. He also purchased Mathews' tenement in Myddle, called the House at the Higher Well, and also lands in Houlston, which formerly did belong to one Tong — but where this Tong lived I have not heard. There was one Thomas Tong who about this time was Rector of Myddle. There was another person at that time in Myddle named Tong, and another in Marton; and there was then one Tong who was lord of Weston Lullingfield, who had lands in Cockshutt and Crowsmeare and in several other places. But he sold them all and it is likely that Mr. Gittins bought this in Houlston off this Tong of Weston.

Richard Gittins had three sons — Richard Gittins the second of that name in Myddle — Ralph and William — of this William I cannot give much account. I find there was one William Gittins, a tanner in Shrewsbury, and perhaps this was the same person. Ralph was brought up a scholar, and indeed his natural genius inclined him thereunto, and by his diligent study and reserved life he was very eminent in his time. He was somewhile high school master of the free schools in Shrewsbury. But how he lost his place I cannot tell unless it were for adhering to the king's party (tempore Cari. primi). He had a natural facility to poetry. His verses were commonly rhyming verses such as the monks used to write. And these usually came from him extempore . . .

Richard Gittins the second, married with Alice, the kinswoman and adopted child of Mr. Morgan ap Robert, tenant of the Castle farm of Myddle. And so the family of the Gittinses came to be tenants of this farm. This Richard the second was a mild and peaceable man, very charitable and so willing to forgive injuries that he passed by many without seeming to take notice of them. He had two sons — Richard who was the third of that name — and Daniel and a daughter whose name I think was Mary. She was married to Mr. Richard Win of Pentre Morgan, a gentleman of an ancient and good family and great repute in the country. Daniel was a merchant tailor in London. I never heard that he was married or that he made any great figure in the world.

Richard Gittins the third, married with Margery the daughter of Francis Peplow, a wealthy farmer in Fenemeare — tenant to Sir Richard Newport, father of the now Earl of Bradford. This Richard the third was of good account in his time but he was too sociable and kind-hearted: and by striking hands in suretiship, he much damnified himself and family. He did not at all derogate from the charitable, meek and commendable morals of his father.

He was somewhat fair of complexion and his wife was very black (our English proverb says that a black woman is a pearl in a fair man's eye). He had seven children, five of them were of his complexion and those are all dead.

Richard the eldest and the fourth of that name and was a good country scholar, and had a strong and almost miraculous memory. He was a very religious person but he was too talkative. He died unmarried and his death was somewhat sudden and surprising. He served on the grand jury for this county of Shropshire: and amongst others I was one of his partners. And when the grand jury was discharged I came home that night and left him in good health. He intended to stay with some friends until next day, but as he was walking with some friends under the market hall in Shrewsbury, that evening, he was suddenly taken with an apoplectic fit or some other distemper (what pleased God) which took not away his speech for he cried out suddenly (not sudden death good Lord). He was had into a house hard by and lay on a bed. Mr. Arthur Hatchett of Burleton being then in town went to visit him, who told me that he never heard more devout prayers, nor more heavenly expressions come from any man. He died that night and was buried at Myddle amongst his ancestors. Daniel the second son of Richard the third succeeded his brother as heir to the freehold lands of the Gittenses. He died unmarried when he had survived his brother about one year. And so the lands descended to Thomas the third son, who then was and now (1701) is Vicar of Loppington. He married Sarah, the daughter of John Downeton of Nonely, and has issue by her, Thomas and Mary, who is yet unmarried. Thomas, the son of Vicar Gittins, married Mary, the daughter of John Nonely, of Nonely. They are both living and do dwell in Myddle, in that house which is called the House at the Higher Well. The barn and house that stood here some years past was burnt, and it was no less than a miracle that in so violent a fury of fire the house of John Eaton, which was on the other side of the street and not above twenty yards distant was preserved, and that Mr. William Gittins' house, which was above two hundred yards distant, took fire and was burnt down and all the buildings belonging to it except the backhouse.

And that the parish church of Myddle which stood partly between the two houses was preserved.

The fourth and fifth sons of Richard Gittins the third were twins (viz.) Ralph and Nathaniel — Ralph died before he came to maturity. Nathaniel was brought up at Oxford, and was afterwards Vicar of Ellesmere where he was much loved by his parishioners. He married a daughter of Mr. Roger Gough's of the Marsh. He died at Ellesmere and left behind him a son named Nathaniel, who is now a captain under our gracious King William III. William the first and youngest son of Richard the third is now tenant of the Castle Farm. He married with Sarah, the daughter of Francis Hill of Withyford, formerly tenant of Billmarsh Farm as I said before. The eldest son of this William is Richard the fifth of that name in Myddle. He is my godson. I pray God give him his blessing, and grant that by him the name and family of the Gittinses may be propagated in the parish. Richard Gittins the third had one daughter named Mary. She was a person of a comely countenance but somewhat crooked of body. She was a modest and religious woman and died unmarried.

The fourth pew on the north side of the south aisle

This belongs wholly to Webscot Farm (the first pillar stands in this seat). This farm is in Balderton township, but there is a small chief rent due to the Earl of Bridgwater for this farm. It was formerly the estate of that ancient and worthy family of the Thornses of Shelvoke. Thomas Thorns, Esq., the last of that family (for the family is extinct) sold it to Mr. Thomas Price who married his sister and is now owner of it. As for the tenant of this farm I find that one Godfrey Thomas was tenant of it, who it is likely was a younger brother of the family of Shelvoke. And after him Mr. Thomas Hoskins (who had a good estate in lands and houses in Ruyton) was tenant here. But I must not forget that there were formerly two dwelling-houses upon this farm — the one called the Higher Webscott where this Mr. Hoskins dwelt, and the other the Lower Webscott where one Twisse dwelt. This Twisse was a rich man and had no child. His first wife died when he was an old man, and yet he married again with his servant maid, a wanton gadding dame, who had neither goods nor good name. She was commonly called Besse Benion. This Twisse removed from Webscott to Eaton in Baschurch parish, where one Peter Braine (an excellent beast leech) became very familiar with this Besse Benion (for so she was always called). At last she had a son who was named Francis. He was very like Braine, but Twisse was very fond of him. Afterwards Braine's wife died and he married again with a rich widow in that town, which so enraged Besse Benion that she swore the death of her and said that Braine had promised to marry her when old Twisse was dead. Braine's wife being afraid of her life procured a warrant for her and brought her before Sir Edward Kinaston and his fellow justice at a monthly meeting. Old Twisse came with his wife but was so weak and old that he could not stand before the gentlemen, and therefore they caused a chair brought for him to sit down. When the complaint was proved against his wife he begged several times that what punishment his wife deserved might be laid upon him which caused much laughter amongst the gentlemen and the company, and Besse was acquitted.

After Twisse had left the Lower Webscott, one Robert Orred came thither and sold ale. That time there was a fall of timber in Myddle Park, and that merry parson, Mr. Bing, was then curate to Mr. Moore, at Myddle, and he gave it the name of Robins Rowst, which name it carried until William Higginson pulled it down and brought it to the Higher Webscott.

Mr. Thomas Hodgkins had a son named Thomas and a daughter who was named Elizabeth. I have heard that she was second wife to Baylie Downton, and that Thomas her brother married a sister of Baylie Downton's. Thomas the son was well educated — he was a good father and a good farmer, a good clerk, and a good companion, and that marred all. He spent his estate faster than his ancestors got it, and took no care to leave somewhat to maintain him in his old age, but was kept on charity by his son-in-law, Mr. Edward Tong. This Mr. Hodgkins when his first wife was dead married with a rich widow in Newton. She was widow to Roger Langford. She had a farm there of thirty pound for her life. She was rich in cattle, corn, and goods. Mr. Hodgkins as soon as he had married this widow sold his lease of Webscott to Mr. Thorns, and in few years he spent all the estate that Mr. Sandford had; he sold the title of the lease and all the household goods even to the wainscot. He went to his son-in-law, Tong, and she poor woman went to live in the lodge, on Haremeare Heath, and had nothing to maintain herself but what neighbours sent: and thus she that was descended of good parentage being sister to Mr. Thomas Bradocke, purchaser of Cayhowell, she that had lived in a plentiful condition in her first husband's time, she who maintained the best hospitality and good housekeeping of anyone in Myddle parish; she I say died in a poor cottage in great poverty and want, if not for want.

This Mr. Hodgkins made it his practice to go to the ale-house daily, and when he came home drunk he could go as well as when he was sober; but he could not speak as others might understand him and at last he had got a habit of mashing at all times, so that when he was sober a man could hardly understand him. He had two children, a son named Thomas, a pretty gentle, handsome man. He married a widow beyond Shrewsbury who maintained him handsomely. And a daughter who was married to Edward Tong, an attorney in Shrewsbury, who maintained him when he had spent his estate. After Mr. Hodgkins, John Downton son of John Downton by his second wife was tenant of this farm for some years, and after him Richard Nightingale until he had married Alice Fletcher kinswoman of John Lloyd of Myddle (as I said before). After him William Higginson, a painful laborious man and a good husband, took a lease of it at an easy rack rent for three lives, but after his death his son John proved not so good a husband as his father; and having contracted some debt he sold his lease to the landlord Mr. Price, who repaired it and set it for three years to William Jenks of Stockett, and now one Ralph Vaughan is tenant.

The fifth pew on the north side of the south aisle

This belongs to that tenement in Balderton which is the ancient inheritance of the Haywards. And to that messuage in Alderton which Rowland Muckleston lately purchased of Thomas Downton, and to Braine's tenement in Myddle, of which family I have spoken formerly. Hayward's tenement did formerly belong to the Abbey of Lilshull, and was sold by the abbot long before the dissolution of the abbeys in England — reserving about £12 or £14 per annum chief rent and optimum animal for an heriot at every principal tenant's decease. I find that the family of the Haywards is very ancient in this parish, and that John Hayward and Roger his son were both buried on the same day (viz.) April 7th, 1578. Thomas succeeded them (I believe he was the son of Roger). He married with Susanna the daughter of one Somerfield of High Hatton, alias Hatton Hineheath, a wealthy tenant of the Corbetts of Morton Corbett. He had issue by her, Thomas the second of that name, Henry and Richard and two daughters, Margaret and Mary. The youngest was married to one John Moody a fair conditioned honest man; but he was kept under the hatches by debts that lay heavy upon him. Margaret was married to David Higley. He was a good husband by fits. What he got with hard labour he spent idly in the ale-house. A rude person and fit company for Bearewards and such like persons. He lived at Parkegate near Cockshutt.

Richard Hayward when he was a boy desired to be a cook. His indulgent father put him to serve Richard Hunt, an able cook servant to Sir Humphrey Lea, of Langley, who kept a noble house. In this family Richard Hayward served seven years as a scholarian boy, and seven years as master cook, and then went to London where by the assistance of Mr. Walter Bromley (the cook to his majesty King Charles I), he was preferred to the service of Dr. Juxton, then Bishop of London, and Lord Treasurer of England. But when the parliament had got the upper hand of the king all bishops were displaced, and the Bishop of London betook himself to his pad nag and went to Lambeth, his paternal estate, and discharged most of his servants, and Cook Hayward amongst the rest, who at his departure begged his master's advice whether he might do well to go and serve Mr. William Peirpoint, a parliament man, to whom the bishop answered, I will commend you to him as the best of parliament men. Cook Hayward immediately goes to Mr. Peirpoint and told that he heard that he wanted a cook, and that he was commended to his service by his lord and master Bishop Juxon, whom he had served many years. Mr. Peirpoint answered he would willingly accept of a servant that had served so noble a person who was the best of bishops. Mr. Peirpoint told the cook he must be both cook and caterer. He must provide eight dishes every day for dinner, and keep him at eight leawan per week for flesh meat and salt. And if the protector or any great person came to dine with him he must not increase his number of dishes but make them the fuller and richer, and put in the margin of his bill what was augmented on that day.

Cook Hayward covenanted that if his lord and master were restored he might be at liberty at any time to return to his service which Mr. Peirpoint easily granted.

Cook Hayward served Mr. Peirpoint twelve years, and then King Charles II was restored, and Doctor Juxon then living was made Archbishop of Canterbury (Dr. Wren, Bishop of Lincoln, was likewise living and restored to his place: all the rest of the bishops were dead). Cook Hayward (according to agreement) went to his old lord and master, then archbishop, and served him several years, during which time his eldest brother Thomas (having consumed most part of his estate and being still in debt) sold his lease of this tenement in Balderton, to this Cook Hayward.

He growing old and almost unfit for service desired of his lord and master that he might go and spend the remaining part of his days in his own country. And so he came to Balderton and purchased the reversion of this tenement of my old master Robert Corbett, Esq. This Cook Hayward lived several years at Balderton in good repute amongst his neighbours. He gave in his lifetime ten leawan to the poor of this side of the parish of Myddle, the interest to be dealt in bread upon every first Lord's day in the month, yearly, for ever. He gave this tenement to Robert Hayward, his eldest brother's eldest son. And when he was blamed by some gentleman of his acquaintance for so doing because he the cook was a true son of the Church of England and Robert Hayward, his nephew was a dissenter from the church, he answered that it was God that had given him an estate and according to the laws of this land which he believed were founded upon the laws of God, this young man was his heir; and he did not find by the law that he ought to disinherit him because he was different from him in some opinions.

Henry Hayward, second son of Thomas Hayward the first, was a woodmonger in London. He took a house and a fuel yard, and his brother the cook engaged for the rent and lent him money to buy a stack. He made a great figure for a while, but at last he broke, left the key under the door and went into Ireland. The cook lost his money and was forced to pay the arrears of rent.

Thomas Hayward the second was a handsome gentleman, a good country scholar and a pretty clerk. He was a person well reputed in his country and of a general acquaintance. He was just and faithful in affirming or denying any matter in controversy, so that less credit was given to some men's oath than to his bare word. He was well skilled in the art of good husbandry. His father left him a farm of thirty pounds (fee simple) in Newton on the Hill and the lease of this farm in Balderton. He had eight pounds (land in fee simple) left him by an uncle in Whixhall. He married with Alice, the daughter of Mr. Wihen, high school master, in Shrewsbury. He had a good fortune with her in money, besides houses in town of considerable yearly value. She was a comely woman, but highly bred and unfit for a country life, besides she was shrewd with tongue, so that they lived unquietly and uncomfortably, and their estate consumed insensibly.

He had little quietness at home which caused him to frequent public houses merely for his natural sustenance, and there meeting with company and being generally well beloved he stayed often too long. His intimate friend was Mr. Hotchkins of Webscott, and indeed there seemed to be a natural sympathy between them for they were both of them very just honest persons and well beloved — but their deportment when they were in drink was very different for Mr. Hodgkins could go but not speak, and Mr. Hayward could speak as well and seemed to be more acute and witty in his drink then at other times but could not go.

This Thomas Hayward sold and consumed all his estate and was afterwards maintained on charity by his eldest son. He had two sons Robert and Thomas and a daughter named Elizabeth. She was a comely good humoured young woman, but her father having no portion to give her she was constrained to betake herself to service.

She married with one Roberts a pretty ingenious young man who was clerk to a gentleman whom she served. He was son to one Roberts, an innkeeper in Oreton Maddocke in Flintshire. This new married pair having little to begin with kept a little ale-house in Oreton, but the husband soon after died, and she having no child went to London and there married a second husband and (as I have heard) lived very well. Thomas the youngest son was put apprentice to a silver-wire drawer in London. He has two sons, Thomas and Robert. Robert the eldest son of Thomas Hayward the second was put apprentice to a refiner of silver in London. His master was a person of fanatical opinions and one that was of the sort of the millinarians or fifth monarch-men. His apprentice had soon imbibed the rudiments of his master.

Not long after the restoration of our late gracious sovereign King Charles II, the enthusiastical leaders or teachers of this sect persuaded their hearers that now the critical time of the millennium was come and their prayers were not only necessary, but their arms for bringing on of this work and encouraged them by telling that one of them should chase a 1,000, etc.

These deluded people made an insurrection in London and having got themselves well armed broke out into open rebellion, and marched along the streets making some sort of a proclamation. But they were soon surrounded by the city militia (some say that they fought desperately for awhile) but they were all taken and the city prisons were filled with them (amongst this rout was this Mister and apprentice). But such was the clemency of that merciful king that they were all pardoned except their ringleader who I think was hanged.

This master refiner had by this means consumed his estate, and when he was set at liberty he went into Wales, and was there entertained as a factor to the Dutch merchants in their employment about lead ore. After his death his apprentice Robert Hayward was employed in the same post. And sometimes in his vacation came to visit his friends and made courtship to Mrs. Margery Muckleston, eldest daughter of Mr. Edward Muckleston of Meriton, and after married her. She was short-sighted and of no commendable beauty but she was a virtuous and religious woman. They lived somewhile in Shrewsbury. They had no child and lived very comfortably. When his uncle the cook was dead and had given him this tenement in Balderton, then they came to live there, and there Robert Hayward laid out his wife's portion (which was considerable) in purchasing some of that farm in Newton, which his father had formerly sold to Mr. Hall, and afterwards he purchased Balderton Hall and all the lands that Mr. Hall had in Balderton. He has taken Robert the youngest son of his brother Thomas to be his heir. He set him apprentice to a white draper in Shrewsbury (the wealthiest trade in town) and now he follows that trade, and also the same employment that his uncle had about the lead ore in Wales. Mrs. Hayward is dead and Robert is yet living in Shrewsbury, and still retains his former opinions.

The next share in this pew belong to that tenement in Alderton which Mr. Rowland Muckleston of Meriton lately purchased of Thomas Downton. William Downton was formerly owner of it. He was a person well to pass in the world. He had a son named Samuel who was crook-backed, had a grim swarthy complexion and long . . . black hair. But he was not so deformed in body as debauched in behaviour. His prudent father observing the idle and lewd courses of his son sought out a wife for him in time. He married with one Botfield's daughter of Nonely, and had a good portion with her in money and lands. During her lifetime this Samuel lived in good fashion. He had one son by her named Thomas and four daughters. She died before her children were brought up to maturity. He hired a servant maid to look after his children. She was but a young girl of obscure parentage, but somewhat fair. He married this servant which his children were much troubled at. And therefore his son left him and went to serve Captain Richardson. The daughters all left him as soon as they were able for service. He quickly contracted more debts than he was able to pay. He sold the lands he had by his first wife but this tenement he could not sell (being settled at his first marriage). But he was about to sell it for his life which his son hearing of procured money by the assistance of Mr. Richardson and bought it off his father, who immediately left Alderton and went to Cockshutt where he kept an ale-house and had great custom —

perhaps for his wife's sake whom the people there called white legs because she commonly went without stockings.

After some years this Samuel Downton and his wife (having sold some of their household goods) got away from Cockshutt in the night-time and left all their children behind them — four of which were after maintained by the parish of Ellesmere. They went into Staffordshire and there he went a begging like an old decrepit person and she carried a box with pins and laces. But after a while she got a new spark that travelled the country and went away with him, and then this Samuel came again to Alderton to his son Thomas who maintained him during his life.

Thomas Downton, by his parsimonious living, had spared so much out of his rent of this tenement, as had paid all the money he borrowed to pay his father and had got a good stock of cattle, and was in a condition to live well; but unexpectedly he married a wife with nothing. Her name is Judith — she was brought up all her lifetime as a servant in some ale-house or other, and she proved such a drunken woman as hath scarce been heard of; she spent her husband's estate so fast that it seemed incredible.

This Thomas Downton was a sickly aged man when he married, and had no child, and it was no matter, for his wife was sufficient to spend his estate — she went daily to the ale-house. Her husband paid ten leawan at a time for ale-house scores; but to be short (for she made but a short work of it), in few years her husband was so far in debt, that he sold this tenement and land to Mr. Muckleston, reserving a lease for his own life; and he left sixty leawan in Mr. Muckleston's hands to be paid at his decease to his wife if she survived him, and if she died before him then to such persons as he by his last will should bequeath it. He took up ten leawan of this sixty leawan before he died, to pay ale-house scores, and then he died. The inventory of his goods, together with the fifty leawan that was in Mr. Muckleston's hands, did amount to about one hundred and twenty leawan and now she sets out in earnest to spend this, and with hard shift, spent most of it in about two years, and now lives poorly in a little house in Myddle.

Rowland Muckleston, is son of Edward Muckleston, a gentleman of an ancient family. He had a fair house, and an estate of about one hundred and twenty leawan per annum where he was born at a place called Pen-y-Llan, near Oswestry. He married the daughter of one Mr. Corbett of Meriton, she was an heiress of a good estate in lands, in Meriton. She was a provident housekeeper, if not too parsimonious, but he proved not a careful husband, for he sold part of his wife's lands in Meriton, to Sir Humphrey Lea, and they say his wife never consented to it, however (though some suits have been brought concerning it), yet it was never recovered.

This Edward Muckleston had three sons — John, Richard, and Rowland; and four daughters — Margery, Mary, Anne, and Martha. This Martha was married to John Harewood, a grocer in Shrewsbury, he was an excellent tradesman, and died very rich in lands and goods, she is yet living. Anne was married to Robert Higginson, of Ellesmere, a mercer. they lived plentiful but are both dead. Mary was married to Francis Lloyd of Cockshutt, a gentleman of an ancient family but very low in the world at the time of his marriage; for his father's debts and the mortgages of his lands were so great, that his son did not know whether it was best to enter on his father's estate, or take his wife's portion and let the creditors take the lands and estate. However, he by his labour and industry, and by his parsimonious living retrieved all and afterward became very rich in lands; there was no servant in the town that went more mean in habit, that fared hardier in diet, or that worked harder at any slavish labour than he did.

Margery the eldest daughter of Mr. Edward Muckleston, was married to Robert Hayward, as I said before. John Muckleston was no comely person, nor had a plausible way of speaking, but he was wise in his own conceit, and yet there was as much hope of a fool as of him. He died without issue, and by his last will devised the lands at Pen-y-Llan to his brother Richard, and the lands in Meriton, to his youngest brother Rowland. He loved Rowland, but cared not much for Richard.

Richard Muckleston was a tanner in Shrewsbury, he was a provident man, a careful tradesman, and purchased a great estate in lands. He had three sons, Richard, Edward, and Joseph. He gave to Richard above two hundred leawan per annum in lands, and married him with a daughter of John Taylor, of Rodington, Esq. with whom he had 1,200 guineas, and as much silver as made her portion 1,400 leawan, all paid on the wedding day. Edward is a tanner, and he gave him several lands and houses in Shrewsbury. Joseph is a grocer in Shrewsbury, and to him he gave the lands in Meriton which he purchased of Mr. Colfex's daughters. He had also one daughter to whom he gave a great portion in money. She is married to Mr. John Edwards, Jnr., of Gt. Nesse.

This Richard Muckleston was a person of a bold and daring spirit; he could not break an injury offered him. He commenced a suit against the town of Shrewsbury for exacting an imposition upon him which they call tensorship, and did endeavour to make void their charter, but they gave him his burgesship to be quiet; he was accounted a just man in all his dealings.

Rowland Muckleston (who purchased this tenement in Alderton) had for his first wife, the daughter of one Andrew Bouldler, of Meriton; who gave with his daughter a lease of a tenement in Meriton which he held under Sir Richard Lea, and what money he gave I cannot tell, but it was so much, that afterwards he was able to do little for the rest of his children. She was a quiet low-spirited woman, and suffered her husband to concern himself with all things both within doors and without, so that their housekeeping was not commendable. She died, and left behind her one son named Edward, and two daughters. Afterwards he married (a second wife), the daughter of Mr. Cuthbert Hesketh of Kenwicke, commonly called Darter Hesketh; it was a hasty match and a small portion, but she was a very handsome gentlewoman and of a masculine spirit, and would not suffer him to intermeddle with her concerns within doors, and she endeavoured to keep a good house, but this caused them to keep an unquiet house, and many contests happened between them which ended not without blows. I think she never boasted of the victory for she had lost an eye in the battle. After that she had lived some few years with him she died and left no child behind her. His third wife was widow to one Maddox of Astley. (Her son likewise married the eldest daughter of Rowland Muckleston.) This wife is still living and I think she will not contest with her husband, for if she loses an eye she loseth all. They are both living but live not together, for he lives with his son at Meriton, and she with her son at Astley. Edward, the son of Rowland, married Anne, the daughter of John Joyce, of Cockshutt (her mother was a daughter of the family of the Pembertons, of Wrockwardine); she is a good discreet woman and a good housekeeper. They have many handsome lovely children, and do live very plentifully.

The youngest daughter of Rowland Muckleston was married to John Hayward, of a place called Wood-houses, in the township of Tylley, near Wem. He was a dissolute person, and died about his middle age; his widow afterwards married with Mr. John Collier, the second schoolmaster of the free schools in Wem. Of Braine's family I have spoken before.

CHAPTER 8

What Time A Violent Fever Raged In Myddle

The sixth pew on the north side of the south aisle

This belongs to Richard Hatchett's tenement in Newton, and to John Eaton's in Myddle. This tenement of Richard Hatchett's is the Earl of Bridgewater's land, and is all the lands that the earl has in Newton, and formerly the family of the Deakins was tenant to it; the last whereof was Thomas Deakin, who died A.D. 1611. He had no child, and therefore left his estate to Roger Sandford, his sister's son, who married with Mary, the sister of Mr. Thomas Bradocke, purchaser of Cayhowell. This Roger Sandford was a wealthy man. He had a lease of this tenement for his own life and his wife's. He kept the best hospitality of any man in this parish in his time. He had no child, and when he died, he left his widow very rich; but she, unadvisedly, married with Mr. Hodgkins, of Webscott, who sold the lease of this tenement to Thomas Newans, and after spent all her riches; so that she died poor, in Haremeare Lodge, as I said before.

Thomas Newans was a younger brother of that ancient family of the Newans, of Greensell. He was brought up a servant under Sir Andrew Corbett, and there he married his fellow-servant, Elizabeth, the daughter of Baylie Downton, by his second wife. When he had purchased Mr. Hodgkins' title in this tenement, he renewed the lease, and put in the lives of himself, his wife, and of Thomas his eldest son. This Thomas Newans was unskilled in husbandry, though he would talk much of it. He made a figure here and then stepped away into Ireland, when he had first made over his lease to his brother, John Newans, and his brother-in-law, John Downton, for some years, for the raising of money to pay his debts. At the end of the years he and his wife returned, and dwelt in Shrewsbury, and set this tenement to Francis Smith, of Balderton, who placed his son Daniel in it, when he had married Anne, the daughter of George Higginson, of Stoke Grange. During the time that Daniel Smith was tenant here, Thomas Newans, the younger died, and the elder died, and after them Elizabeth died, and not long after Daniel Smith died, when he was not much past the prime of his age.

After the expiration of this lease, my cousin, Richard Hatchett, took a lease for lives of this tenement and because my son married his sister, I will give some account of this family.

Richard Hatchett, great grandfather of this Richard Hatchett, was a wealthy farmer in Peplow, under Sir Robert Vernon, of Hodnett; at what time Sir Robert Vernon (who was owner of all Peplow and Ellerdine), had mortgaged the whole town of Ellerdine unto Sir Richard Newport, of High Erchall, for a great sum of money, which mortgage was expired, and the money called for. Now there were four tenants in Peplow which were very wealthy persons — viz., this Richard Hatchett, and also Mrs. Arnway, mother of Dr. Arnway and Robert Arnway, and great grandmother of Mr. John Gardner, late of Sandsaw; she was likewise mother to Mrs. Baddeley, of Ellerton Grange, and great grandmother to my wife. Another of these rich tenants was William Wood, my father-in-law; but what the fourth was called, I know not. To these four, Sir Robert sent to borrow the sum of money to pay off the mortgage; but they consulted together, and made excuses: and thereupon Sir Robert swore, that no child of any of the four persons should live upon his land, after their leases were expired: but Richard Hatchett removed before his lease was expired; for he was so plagued and plundered by the soldiers in the wartime, that he was forced to remove to Shrewsbury.

He bought several houses in town, and was made a burgess of that corporation. He had two sons — Stephen and John, and a daughter who was married to Mr. Jones, of Chilton. His son John married with Margaret, a bastard daughter of Mr. Ditcher's, of Muckleston; for this Ditcher had no legitimate child, but was very rich. This John Hatchett had a great fortune with his wife, beside that estate that was given him by his father: but he lived above it all, and therefore it was no marvel that he died poor. His widow after his decease, was placed in one of the alms-houses at Little Berwick, and there she died.

Stephen Hatchett dwelt at Lee, near Ellesmere, upon a farm there, which either his father or he purchased off one Mr. Charleton. I conceive this Charleton was some time steward to the Earl of Bridgewater, and kept his courts in his manors of Ellesmere, Myddle, Knockin, etc. I have heard that he was a corrupt man, a vicious liver, and always needy of money. But to return: Stephen Hatchett was a person of good repute in this country. He had a son, named Richard, who married a daughter of one

Lyth, of Lee. They are both yet living, and have two sons — Richard, who took this lease, and John, who is a grocer in Gloucester, and is unmarried; they have also two daughters, the eldest married one Higginson, and lives in Haughton Farm, near Ellesmere. The youngest married to my son. Richard Hatchett, Jnr., is married with the daughter-in-law of one Francis Morrice, of Techell. He had a great fortune with her; but that which is worth all, she is a loving wife, a discreet woman, and an excellent housewife. They have one son, named Edward, and two daughters, Mary and Elizabeth. He is now receiver of the rents of the Earl of Bridgewater, for the lordships of Ellesmere and Myddle, and is generally well spoken of by the tenants, for his gentle dealing and forbearance . . .

The seventh pew on the north side of the south aisle

Belong to Ames' tenement in Alderton, and Bickley's tenement in Brandwood.

The first of the family of Ames, in this place was Walter Ames, born in Herefordshire. He married the daughter of a wealthy farmer that held this tenement. This Walter had a lease of it for ninety-nine years absolute, and after purchased it. He had lands in Isombridge which he sold, and purchased lands in Loppington parish. He had issue, Thomas Ames, who married a daughter of that ancient and substantial family of the Woods of Muckleton; and had issue by her, Robert Ames, who married a daughter of one Lyth, of Lee; and had issue by her, William Ames, who married with Julian, the sister of Sir Gerard Eaton, of Eaton, in Flintshire. This William Ames was very serviceable to this parish, in serving the office of churchwarden very often, which office he discharged with much carefulness and fidelity; yet I have heard him blamed for that he spent more in treating of workmen about parish work than the parish was willing to pay, or his own occasions would permit him to do. As for Mrs. Julian Ames, she was very helpful to her neighbours in chirurgery in which she was very skilful and successful. They had issue — Robert, Richard, and Thomas. I begin with the youngest, Thomas. He was a shoemaker by trade, but went for a soldier under Oliver Cromwell. He was a soldier at the fight at Dunbar, in Scotland, which was on the third day of September, 1650. And here I think it is not amiss to mention, that some persons that give over much credit to the occult philosophy, have accounted the third day of September to be a critical day for England, and have numbered up a great catalogue of very remarkable things that concerned England in general, which have happened on that day. I will only name such as have happened during the time of memory:—

Upon the 3rd of September, 1650, King Charles II was routed at Dunbar.

On the 3rd of September, 1651, he was routed at Worcester.

On the 3rd of September, 1658, Oliver, the protector, died.

On the 3rd of September, 1666, was the greatest of the conflagration of the terrible fire in London.

And on the 3rd of September, 1701, our late King James died: for our newsletters said that he died September the 14th, stilo novo, which is according to the Gregorian foreign new account: but we in England, who follow the Julian or old account, do begin one month eleven days after theirs. But I doubt I am mistaken one day in this.

But to return. After the protector had peace at home, he lent several troops to the King of France, to assist him against the King of Spain in Flanders: and this Thomas Ames went into Flanders in one of these troops, or companies. He was at the taking of Mardike and Dunkirk. When King Charles II was restored, this Thomas Ames was disbanded, and came to Wem, where he built a house and married a wife: and there he died, and was buried at Myddle. At which time there were three corpses buried in Myddle Churchyard at one time, by two ministers. One minister stood between two of the graves which were near together, and read the office for both together.

Richard Ames was a shoemaker in Shrewsbury. He was crier or martial of the town court and town sessions, which place he obtained by favour, but served in it but ill-favouredly, for he could never speak plain. He was many years crier at Batlefield Fair whilst I was steward there: and at proclaiming of the fair, he made the gentleman much sport by his blunders. He died in Shrewsbury.

1701. Robert Ames the eldest son of William, is yet living, and is of so great age that he is almost childish. He married the daughter of one Raulston, of Dunnington, near Lillshull. He had issue by her three sons — William, Kenricke, and Robert, and two daughters, Julian and Elizabeth. This Elizabeth married one Hamson, a Cheshire man, but no good husband. They are both living in Cheshire, near Durtwich. Julian married with William, the son of John Turner, of a place called Wood Houses, near Shiffnal. This William Turner came to live at Alderton, and died there when he was churchwarden of Myddle. He left no child behind him. She is yet living and is a widow. Robert, the youngest son, has lived in several nobleman's services. He is still unmarried, and has got an estate in service. Kenricke was a baker, and served his apprenticeship in Shropshire, and then removed to London, where he married and lived in good fashion. He is dead, and left some small children behind him. Old Robert Ames died March 13th, 1702, aged, by his own reckoning 100 years abating seven.

William Ames, the eldest son of Robert, married Elizabeth, the daughter of Mr. Adam Crosse, of Yorton. Her mother was Mary, the sister of Captain Richardson, of Broughton, a discreet gentlewoman and a good housekeeper. William had issue two daughters — Mary and Martha, and then his wife died. Mary, the eldest daughter married Samuel the son of Thomas Wright, of Marton, without her father's consent, which so displeased him that he gave his lands to Martha, the younger daughter, and married her to Edward Jenks, eldest son of William Jenks, of Stockett, who now lives in this tenement. William Ames is still living, but his wife is long since dead.

Another share in this seat belongs to Bickley's tenement in Brandwood. The family of the Bickleys is very ancient in this parish. The tenement is the land of the Earl of Bridgewater, and has been held for many ages by the Bickleys. There was more lands belonging to it, of which I will speak hereafter. Roger Bickley had issue Thomas, who had issue Andrew, born A.D. 1573. Andrew had two sons Richard, born 1602, and William. This Richard died young, and William was tenant of this farm. William was a fair dealing person, and well to pass, but he was unfortunate in his marriage with Elizabeth, daughter of William Tyler, of Balderton. She was more commendable for her beauty than her chastity, and was the ruin of the family.

William Bickley had two sons — Thomas and William, and three daughters — Mary, Elizabeth, and Susan. Thomas practised his father's virtues, William imitated his grandfather's villanies, and the three daughters followed the mother's vices. I will begin with Thomas, who deserves not to be named amongst the rest. He married a daughter of one Baylie Wilkinson, of Wolverley, and lives now in Horton in good repute. Susan, the youngest daughter, had a bastard by John Billingsley, Vicar of Kinnerley. This Billingsley was born in Meriton, and was son to a sister of one Edward Paine of that town. He went into Ireland in his youth, and it is said he was a mountebank there. He returned into England about twenty years past, and came to be parson of Preston Gobballs for a while, and then went to be curate to Dr. Fulke, at Kinnerley, and at last came to be vicar there. He produced his ordination by a Scottish bishop: but it was thought to be a piece of forgery. He married a kinswoman of the Bickleys, and when she lay in childbed, this Susan went to tend her, and then this Billingsley got her with child. Soon after this the parishioners preferred many articles against him which were proved, and he was silenced, and went out of this country. Susan came to Myddle, and lived there with her mother, and there was brought a bed, and not long after she and her mother died together, what time a violent fever raged in Myddle; and this parish maintained the bastard.

Elizabeth, the second daughter, had a bastard by Thomas Hall of Balderton, born in his house: he caused him to be brought up till he was able for service; and then he fell lame, and had his leg cut off, and was cured at the parish charge, which cost almost twenty leawan. He wears a wooden leg; and going to London, he met with a woman there, whom he brought down with him, and says she is his wife. He has three children by her, and lives in the cave in Haremeare Hill, and has maintenance out of the parish. This Elizabeth afterwards married with Arthur, a son of Robert Morralls, of Hopton near Hodnett: he fell out of a tree, and broke his neck. She lives in Hodnett, very poor.

Mary, the eldest daughter, married George Reve, one of the Reves of Fennimere. They are both living at a place called the Wone-house, near Preston Brockhurst. She was the comeliest of all the daughters, but had no better a name than the rest. Her daughters are so infamous for their lewdness, that I even loathe to say more of them.

He that would publish their lewd fame (I think),
Must write with something nastier than ink.

William, the younger son of William Bickley, to whom the father gave the lease of this tenement, married with Sarah, the daughter of Francis Smith, of Balderton. He died in May last. His way of living and his demeanour are fresh in memory. I need say no more of him. He left two daughters behind him, Anne the eldest, does not at all degenerate from the ways of her female kindred. The youngest is a sickly crooked girl, and more modest than the other.

The eighth pew on the north side of the south aisle

Has the middle arch or pillar standing in it, and also a post, which supports a large beam that goes over across the south side of the church; so that there is only room for two persons to sit there, but none can claim any right to it.

The ninth pew on the north side of the south aisle

Belongs to James Fewtrell's tenement in Brandwood, and to Noneley's tenement and Hill's tenement of the same. But this being not the chief seat I will speak of them hereafter.

The tenth pew on the north side of the south aisle

This pew belongs to Edward Garland's tenement in Newton, and to Hordley's tenement which is in the lane that goes from Myddle to Burleton. This tenement is the Earl of Bridgewater's land, and has been long in the tenure of the family of the Hordley's. The first that I can give any account of was John Hordley, a tailor. He married with Katherine, the daughter of Richard Ash, of Marton. He had issue, Andrew, who married a daughter of the family of the Formeston's, of Marton. She was a very orderly and neat housekeeper. She nursed Mrs. Lettice, eldest daughter of my old master, Robert Corbett, of Stanwardine, Esq., and Mrs. Elizabeth, his second daughter, who is now Mrs. Clive, of Walford. Andrew Hordley had three sons: Thomas, Andrew, and John, and one daughter, who was married to one Gittins, of Ruyton. This Andrew Hordley died long since, and his widow survived him many years. The two eldest sons continued bachelors, and managed their mother's concerns. They were rich and always had money beforehand. These three persons died almost together. Thomas died first, and his brother Andrew took such grief at his death, that he was almost senseless; and about a week after, he was found dead in a small deep hole of water on the back side of the house, where they used to fetch water for the use of the house. The coroner's inquest found it an accident; and, that (as they believed) he was going to wash his hands and face, and so slipped in and was drowned. Joane Hordley, the widow, died soon after; and so the lease and estate fell to John.

John Hordley had for his first wife, Alice, the daughter of Francis Cleaton, of Hollins; she would sometimes refresh herself with a cup of ale. His second wife is a daughter of George Hinks, of Burleton; her mother was sister to Mr. George Chambre, of Loppington, grandfather of George Chambre, now living. This second wife was a widow when he married her and had been married to one May, a tradesman in London. She has a daughter named Honora, which she had by her first husband.

The eleventh pew on the north side of the south aisle

Belongs wholly to Edward Cooper for his two messuages in Myddle, which are the lands of the Earl of Bridgewater. One of these messuages is in Myddle town, and John Hewitt the younger dwells in it. The other is at the north corner of Myddle Wood Common; and there Edward Cooper dwells. That messuage in the town, was built by Mr. Wilton, some time Rector of Myddle; and was called Mr. Wilton's new house. There is a piece of ground (belonging to this house) which was taken out of Myddle Wood Common, and lies on the north side of Mr. Lloyd's back side, and I suppose it was enclosed by Mr. Wilton. After the death of Mr. Wilton, one William Goslin or Geslin took a lease of this messuage and piece, and also of that messuage in the wood; but who was tenant of this before Goslin, I know not. This Goslin was a covetous, rich old fellow. He had two daughters, Mary and Elizabeth. The eldest was married to Roger Jukes, a shoemaker, in Shrewsbury, he was as excellent a workman as any in town; he had a house and shop on his own land, and a good fortune with his wife, and had no child; and yet being given to drink, he was never rich. Elizabeth was married to Peter Lloyd, who was husbandman to Mr. Gittins, of Myddle. This Peter was descended of a good gentleman's family, in Oswestry; his eldest brother was a captain, in the service of King Charles I, in those wars. Peter was many years bailiff of this manor, and discharged his place with much faithfulness, and was not only just to his master, but also favourable to the tenants; which caused him to be generally well beloved and of good account. Peter Lloyd had two sons, Peter and William, and a daughter named Alice. The eldest son died unmarried. The second son, William, was apprentice with his uncle Jukes, who gave him his house, shop, and lands, in Shrewsbury. This William married a daughter of one Stanley, a dyer in Shrewsbury, who was some time a person of good account, and married a daughter of Mr. Hanmer of Marton; but afterward, became a drunken sot, so that I believe he gave but little with his daughter. Alice, the daughter of Peter Lloyd, was sometimes a servant to Mr. Harcourt Leighton, of Plash; and there she married with Thomas Lovett, who was keeper of Plash Park for Mr. Leighton. After their marriage they both came to Myddle, and lived with Peter Lloyd. And after his decease Thomas Lovett was bailiff of this manor; and discharged his place with like care and commendation as his father-in-law had done. This Thomas Lovett was a person of an upright straight stature, of a comely and handsome complexion, skilful and ingenious in any work that he undertook, and of a mild, courteous, and honest disposition.

He died when he was somewhat past his middle age, and left behind him two sons, Thomas and William, and two daughters, Elizabeth and Alice. This Alice did marry with one Shingler, a Staffordshireman; and Elizabeth married with John Huett, Jnr., of Myddle, blacksmith; who now dwells in the house in Myddle which was called Mr. Wilton's new house. William Lovett was a soldier some while under King William III, in Flanders: and at his return was entertained in service in London: where (for ought that I know) he now dwells. Thomas Lovett, Jnr., was entertained (when he was very young) in the service of Mr. Gower, of Chilleton, in Staffordshire, a papist. And this young man became a proselyte of theirs, and leaving the religion wherein he was born and baptised, he betook himself to his beads.

Alice, the widow of Thomas Lovett, married Edward Cooper, who was some time husbandman to Mr. Mackworth, of Betton; he is a careful laborious man. They are both yet (1701) living at the house in Myddle Wood.

The twelfth pew

Is an old pew which was not broken at the uniforming of the seats. And Evan Jones, and Francis Davis, who had built new houses upon lands taken out of Myddle Wood, sat in this pew, because they had no seats in church; and now Richard Rogers who has Evan Jones' house, and Thomas Davis, who has Francis Davis' house, claim a right in it by long usage.

Seats adjoining to the south wall of Myddle Church

The uppermost pew belongs wholly to Mr. Phillip Cotton's farm in Alderton, formerly called Alderton Hall. This little town of Alderton lies within the liberties of Shrewsbury, and . . . contains only three farms or tenements — viz., Mr. Cotton's, late John Downton's; Amies' tenement; and Mr. Muckleston's, late Thomas Downton's. These are of unequal value, for if the town be divided into seven parts, Mr. Cotton has four; Amies has two; and Muckleston has one; and according to this division all leawans were formerly paid. This town as I said formerly belonged to Wombridge Priory; at which time Downton, Amies, and Downton were tenants here. At the dissolution of abbeys and priories, this town was sold to one Selman. Some say his name was Wike. Some say he was called Selman Wike. However he kept it not long, but sold it to the tenants. And now I come to speak of the owner of this farm, who late were the Downtons, for I have spoken of the Amies' family and the other Downtons before.

The family of the Downtons is so ancient in this town, that I have not heard of any that were tenants of this farm before them; and such a numerous offspring has branched out of this family, that there were three families of the Downtons at one time in this town — viz., John Downton who lived in Alderton Hall; George Downton who lived in a house below Billmarsh which stood upon those lands belonging to this farm which lie between Billmarsh and Tylley Park, in which house (after George Downton), one Goldbarne dwelt. I do remember an old decayed house there, but now it is converted to a barn and beast houses. The third family was William Downton, who was owner of that tenement which is now Mr. Muckleston's. There was at the same time a family of the Downton's in Myddle, and another at Webscott; but now all these families are extinct, so that there is not one of that name now in this parish, except one widow; so that it appears that families have their fate and periods as well as particular persons — and no marvel, since families are made up of particulars.

John Downton (who I believe was purchaser of this farm), had a wife whose name was Ellen, and by her he had one son named Thomas, and two daughters, Jane and Mary. These two daughters were married both on one day, viz. June 4th, 1574. Jane was married to Arthur Butler, of the parish of Condover, and Mary was married to one Thomas Maddocks, of Astley, in the parish of St. Mary's. Thomas succeeded his father in this farm. He was bailiff of the manor of Myddle, and therefore called Baylie Downton. He built fair barns and beast houses upon this farm, which are still standing. He had a fair round tower of a dove house, which is now decayed. His wife's name was Elizabeth. She was daughter of one Marsh, of Clive. This Marsh had some pieces of land in this parish — viz., Marsh's Croft, sold to Mr. Chambre, of Petton; one piece of land adjoining to the Hall Marsh; and a little meadow, called the Partridge Meadow, both sold to Mr. Hill, and by his son sold to Reve. Nathaniel Reve built a house on the piece of land, and lately his son has sold it to one Godfrey Cooper. This Baylie Downton had issue, John Downton, whose first wife was daughter of one Greensell, of Astley, and by her he had Thomas and Dorothy, and after he married the daughter of Reynold Hotchkiss, of Webscott, and had issue by her John and Elizabeth. This John Downton fell sick in Myddle church, and was carried thence into Mr. Gittins' house in Myddle, and there died.

His widow was afterwards married to Dr. Evans, of Ruyton. He was a doctor of physic, and in his youth was of very great account, and had much practice among the best men in these parts. He gave all his physic in powders, and made up his composition with his own hands, not trusting to apothecaries. In his later age (for he lived very long), his practice failed and his estate decayed. He died at Ruyton.

Elizabeth, the daughter of John Downton by his second wife, was married to Thomas Leawns, as I said before. John, his son, was married with the daughter of one Arthur Podmoore, of Hawkston. This John purchased land in Nonely, and after sold it again to my cousin, Thomas Payne of Eastaston. Dorothy, the daughter of John Downton by his first wife, was married to Richard Cotton, of Haston. She lived until she was almost 100 years of age and died not long ago.

Thomas succeeded his father in this farm, he married first, with the sister of the said Richard Cotton, and had issue by her, John and Elizabeth, besides several other sons which I can give no account of. Elizabeth was first housekeeper to Mr. Richard Higginson, of Wem, and afterwards became his second wife, but died before him.

Thomas Downton married a second wife who was widow to one Alsope, who lived toward Bridgenorth. She had a son named Thomas, by her first husband. He was my school-fellow, and was a youth of good towardliness. John the son of this Thomas Downton, married Elizabeth the daughter of one George Causer, a joiner by trade, who lived in the parish of Priors Lee. He had this only child, and she was accounted a great fortune. Howbeit, all the money that John Downton had with his wife was given to Thomas, his father, and to his second wife, who gave up all their estate to this son; but when Thomas had consumed what he had, he returned to his son John, who maintained him until he died, which happened soon after his return. John Downton had issue Thomas Downton and Elizabeth, and several other children, which I can give no account of. He was at great charges in the education of his children. He gave £50 with his son Thomas to Mr. Graver, an attorney, to teach him that practice, but he proved not excellent in it. John Downton had great losses by paying money for suretiship. At last he got far in debt, and his son Thomas, married the daughter of one Mr. Clively, and had only £100 portion with her, which displeased the father, and he gave him no part of his land at present, so that he took his £100 and lived upon that and his practice at Wem. His wife proved a very discreet and provident woman, but their estate being wasted, she maintained them by selling ale. At last the father and son agreed together, and sold this farm to Mr. Phillip Cotton.

They left £400 of the purchase money in Mr. Cotton's hands, to be paid to the son Thomas at his father's decease, and the father to have the interest of it at five per cent to maintain him during his life. The son died before the father; and John Downton the father, married the widow of one Barnabas Bolton, an ale-woman in Wem, with whom he lived an unquiet life for some years, and after parted from her and soon after died. Elizabeth his daughter had only £20 of the purchase money for her portion, and some goods; she is a comely woman, and is married to one Thomas Vaughan, an innkeeper in Shawbury.

Mr. Cotton's first tenant was George Beacall, Snr., of Wollerton; his wife was a good, discreet woman — they were both peaceable and well beloved. His present tenant is William Groome, late of Sleape; but whether he will be so well beloved I know not.

The second pew adjoining to the south wall belongs wholly to Balderton Hall

This farm has been sold five times in little more than the space of one hundred years last past. The first owner of this farm that I can give any account of, was Roger Nicholas, and of him I can only say that his wife's name was Alice, and that he died A.D. 1572, and left behind him a son, named William, who was born A.D. 1550. William Nicholas built most part of Balderton Hall — viz. all except that cross building, called the kitchen end. There is likewise a fair dove house made of rough stone and plastered over with lime, which is supposed to be built by him. There is likewise a very deep draw well which he caused to be made, but now the spring is diverted and the well has become useless and the shed that was over it is pulled down; and the well is only covered with a flagstone. Some say that the drying up or diverting of the spring was caused by the making of a marl pit in a piece of land belonging to this farm, called the Within Hills — because this happened in the year that the pit was made; and this is like the reason that a man gave concerning Godwins Sands. It happened that in the reign of King Edward the Confessor, a great west wind in a dry season blowed great abundance of sand from the sea shore, which covered a great part of the lands of the wicked Earl Godwin, which to this day are called Godwin's Sands; and this happened in the year that Salisbury steeple was built; and therefore a man that was asked what was the reason of Godwin's Sands, answered, the building of Salisbury steeple.

But to return. This William Nicholas was never married that I know of, and by his great charges in building, he contracted much debt. Yet being addicted to projects, he became a timber man, and purchased all the timber in Kenwick's Park, thinking to enrich himself by it but it proved his ruin. It is reported that he bought all the oaks at 12d. a tree, and had the ash and underwood into the bargain, but he wanted sale for it. It is said that he would sell wood for fuel at 4d. per wain load, and because he wanted vent for cordwood, he erected a glass house to consume some of his charcoal, which house is called the glass house to this day. But in the end his creditors came so sharp upon him, that he sold Balderton Hall, and the demesnes and his lease of Broomhurst farm, to Mr. Chambre of Petton, and went out of the country and was never heard of. But some say there came an old man in beggar's habit (some years after his departure) to Balderton, late in the evening, and sat under the barn wall, and was found dead in the morning, and was thought to be this William Nicholas.

I have spoken of Mr. Chambre's family before, and how Mr. Arthur Chambre gave this farm and a lease of Broomhurst farm to his youngest son Michael, who sold Balderton Hall to John Nocke.

Mr. Arthur Chambre who purchased this estate in Balderton, had two sons, Arthur and Michael, and two daughters; the one of them was married to Mr. Albany, lord of the manor of Whittington, and had one daughter by him, and after his death she married with Mr. Hunt of Fernehill, and the daughter of Mr. Albany was married to Mr. Lloyd of Aston, and by that means the manor of Whittington came to the family of the Lloyds of Aston. The other daughter of Mr. Chambre was married to Mr. Kinnaston, a wool merchant in Shrewsbury. Mr. Arthur Chambre, the purchaser, gave this estate in Balderton unto his younger son Michael, and also a lease which he had taken of Broomhurst farm, and charged the lands with the payment of legacies to the two daughters, hoping (as reasonably he might) that Michael would take a wife with such a fortune as would discharge the legacies. But Michael intended nothing less; there was nothing commendable in him but that he was well descended, and that he was so blasted by his vicious life that he was a person of no account.

This Michael Chambre was wholly addicted to idleness, and therefore no marvel that he was lascivious. But the worst of this Michael was, that his lewd consorts were such ugly nasty bawds, that they might almost resemble ugliness itself, and such as were the very scorn of the greatest and vilest debauchees of those times, of which (the more the pity), there were too many in this parish. So prone is human nature to all vice. But to conclude, this Michael took no care to pay the legacies to his sisters, and being sued by his brothers-in-law and put in prison, he and they joining together sold Balderton Hall and the lands belonging to it to John Nocke. Michael reserved the lease of Broomhurst farm to maintain him and his pugs, but he lived not many years after.

John Nocke was a wealthy draper in Shrewsbury, but running the fate of many of such tradesmen, his factors or correspondents in London breaking, he was forced to pay great sums of money, for the raising whereof he mortgaged his estate in Balderton to Mr. Webbe, another rich draper in Shrewsbury, at which time my uncle Richard Gough, of Burlton, was tenant at Balderton Hall, and he leaving it, Mr. Webbe held it some while in his own hands. But he running the same fate that John Nocke had done before they both joined together, and sold it to Mr. Zanky, then Rector of Hodnet. Mr. Zanky was a person much commended for his virtue and piety.

Mr. Zanky died soon after he had made this purchase, and his widow came and lived some years in Balderton Hall. He left two sons Robert and Jerome. Robert, his eldest son, was clerk to Mr. John Birch, of Canke (who in his time was accounted the ablest attorney at law in England). He married Mr. Birch's daughter, a proud, passionate dame as ever lived. He went for a soldier in the parliament army, in the beginning of the wars in the reign of King Charles I, and was made a colonel, and his brother Jerome was a captain under him, but he died in the beginning of the wars, and his brother Jerome was made a colonel in his stead. This Jerome was a person of a mean stature, mild disposition, and accounted a very religious man. He continued his command in the army until the restoration of King Charles II. He was well respected by Oliver the protector, and served him in all his wars in Ireland and Scotland, and was by the protector made a knight and one of the four commissioners for the governing of the kingdom of Ireland, instead of a lord deputy. The other three commissioners were Miles Corbett, Edmund Ludlow (sometimes a major general), and Colonel John Jones. Sir Jerome Zanky (for so he was then called), had a brigade of soldiers under his command while he was in Ireland; and when Sir George Booth and Sir T. Middleton made an insurrection in Cheshire, this Colonel Zanky was sent for with his brigade out of Ireland, but a great part of his brigade was lost and cast away at sea, and the rest came not until the business was over. When King Charles II was restored, this Colonel Zanky was disbanded and all his brigade. He took the benefit of the king's declaration, which was sent from Bradaugh and sued out his pardon on course, and what became of him afterwards, I know not.

Robert Zanky, a little before his death, sold Balderton Hall to Mathew Lath.

Mathew Lath was born to no estate. He was a servant in husbandry, and married Mary, the daughter of Trustan Turner, who was brother to my grandmother Gough, so that Mary Lath and my father were first cousins, which we call cousin germans. This Mathew Lath lived as a tenant at a farm called the Wall near Adeney, in this county (where his father-in-law Turner had formerly dwelt and his ancestors), but when he had purchased Balderton Hall he removed thither. He had only one daughter whose name was Jane, and she being a great fortune had many suiters. But among the rest she was married to Thomas Hall of Isombridge, who had an estate there in lands from his father, and an estate in lands in Roddington, which was given him by his grandfather on the mother's side. He had one sister named Mary who was married to Edward Jenks of Cockshutt, my uncle who had a good tenement there for his life. But Thomas Hall gave him no portion with his sister, although it was said that she was to have a considerable portion, and for want of that, and she proving an idle housewife, that family, which was formerly one of the chiefest in that town, came to ruin.

Thomas Hall lived at Balderton with his father-in-law, and during his life he was a reasonably good husband, but after his decease he let loose the reins to many disorderly courses, as cocking, raising, drinking, and lewdness. He had one bastard born to him in his own house, by a daughter of William Bickley. This bastard when he was grown of age went to service, and there falling lame, he was at the charge of the parish put to a surgeon who cut off one of his legs and cured him; this cost the parish above £20; after he was healed he went to London, and from thence brought a wife, as he calls her. He now lives in the cave of Haremeare Hill, and has maintenance from the parish: he is called Richard Bickley, alias Hall. By these ill courses Thomas Hall consumed his estate; he sold his land in Isombridge and Roddington, and although he bought a considerable tenement in Newton, yet he sold it again, and after he sold Balderton Hall and the lands belonging to it unto Robert Heyward, and left £400 of the price in the purchaser's hands, to the intent that the interest of it might maintain him and his wife during their lives, out of which interest she whose portion was accounted worth £1500 had only £8, but she is dead, and willingly left this troublesome world.

This Thomas had six sons Thomas, Edward, William, Mathew, Andrew, and Humphrey, and two daughters Joanne and Anne, besides other children which died in their infancy. Anne lives now with her brother Edward, in that part of Balderton Hall which their father reserved for his habitation during his life; Joanne, a comely and good humoured young woman, was some while a servant to Daniell Wycherly of Clive, Esq., and there she was married unto William Paine, another servant of Mr. Wycherley's. This Paine was born in Wikey, and descended of good parentage. But I doubt his father-in-law Hall gave him but little with his daughter; they lived some while in Ellesmere and kept an inn, and after they went to Masbrooke, and there kept a little alehouse where William Paine died and left many small children, which she was not able to maintain, and there has assistance from the parish. Humphrey was a silversmith in London, and is there married; he is a strong man, and a skilful workman, but he loves drink too well to be rich.

Andrew, the fifth son, was set apprentice to a glover and skinner in Drayton. His master was an honest man, and a good substantial tradesman. And this Andrew came to be an excellent workman at his trade, insomuch that when his apprenticeship was ended, he was courted by the best tradesmen in Shrewsbury, to work as a journeyman with them, but he was so addicted to drinking that he quickly got in debt in Shrewsbury, so that he was forced to leave the town and went to London, and there died.

Mathew, the fourth son, was set apprentice unto Charles Booth, a shoemaker in Wem, and after his apprenticeship he worked journeywork in Shrewsbury; and his master dying, he married his mistress, and purchased his freedom in Shrewsbury, and lived in good estate during the life of his first wife; but when she was dead he married a second wife, and soon after grew sickly. He was a very religious person, moderate in drinking, but I cannot say so of his second wife, and therefore he lives in a mean condition.

William, the third son, married a gentlewoman who was servant to Mrs. Cleaton of Lea Hall. She is a papist. He had a considerable fortune with her, but soon made even with it; he now sells ale in Cockshutt, and is deputy bailiff of Pimhill hundred.

Edward, the second son, was warrener of Haremeare Warren; he had a lease of it for 21 years, but enriched himself nothing by it. He lives now in that part of Balderton Hall which his father reserved during life. He writes a good hand and gets somewhat by teaching to write.

Thomas, the eldest son, was a scholar to old Mr. Rd. Roderick of Wem, and being a youth of great diligence, his master took such a love to him, that having got about £20 off old Hall, to put him in an equipage for Oxford, he procured for him to be servitor to those two famous D. Drs., viz. Dr. Fell and Dr. Alestree, in whose service he gained such love and respect, that they preferred him to be chaplain to the Lady Button, where by his modest behaviour and diligent service he gained such a good repute, that the lady gave him a benefice of about £30 per annum, at a place called Abbington, in Oxfordshire, and besides that he married a gentlewoman with a good fortune, who was housekeeper to the Lady Button. He has no child, and his father now lives with him and is maintained by him.

Robert Hayward is now owner of this estate; he has no child, but has made Robert his brother's son, his heir, who is a draper in Shrewsbury. Thus you see how this estate has been sold five times in less than a century of years . . . Robert Hayward, senior, died December 3rd, 1705.

The third pew belongs to Wright's tenement in Marton and to Formeston's tenement in Marton.

Wright's tenement was formerly the lands of my old master, Robert Corbett, of Stanwardine, Esq., whose grandfather had it by the marriage of one of the daughters of Kynaston of Wallford, and seeing that Kynaston had the manor of Walford by the marriage of the daughter and heiress of John Hord, Lord of Walford, I may well conclude that this tenement did formerly belong to the family of the Hords.

The family of the Bakers were formerly tenants of this place, which was an ancient and flourishing family in Marton, insomuch that Mr. William Hanmer of Marton took a wife out of this family, but now this family is wholly extinct in this parish. After the decease of the last of the Bakers, one Thomas Wright took a lease of this tenement off Mr. Corbett, and afterwards purchased the fee simple, and then sold the one half of the lands to Thomas Freeman, who married Elizabeth, the eldest daughter of my uncle Richard Groome of Marton, but he had no part of the building nor any share in this seat. Thomas Wright had two sons, Allen and Thomas, and two daughters, Mary and Anne or Margery, I know not whether; she was married to a carpenter in Shrewsbury, but I have forgotten his name.

Mary married with James Dod, an ancient widower in Weston Lullingfield; he was a lease tenant to my old master. This Mary had one daughter before James Dod died and afterwards she married Arthur Wykey, a younger brother of that ancient family of the Wykeys of Weston.

Allen, the eldest son of Thomas Wright, was a pretty gentle young man; but he died unmarried.

Thomas Wright, the younger was a tanner by his trade, and served an apprenticeship with Thomas Acherley of Marton. He married Martha, the daughter of Robert Wilkinson, of Wolverley, who was bailiff to the Earl of Arundell in his manors of Wem and Loppington. He took more care to get money among the tenants, than to gain their love or preserve his own credit.

This Thomas Wright had three sons, Joseph, Samuel, and Robert, and two daughters, one of which is married to Richard Smyth, junior, of a place called New-house, in the township of Sansaw, near Yorton bridge. The other daughter is unmarried.

Robert, the youngest son, is a tanner, unmarried, and an untowardly man.

Samuel, the most hopeful of all the sons, married with Mary, the eldest daughter of William Amies, of Alderton, which so displeased her father that he disinherited her, and settled his lands upon his younger daughter. This match with Samuel Wright was carried on by the persuasion and encouragement of William Crosse, who was uncle to the young woman, but he deceived them sadly.

Joseph, the eldest son, is a drunken, rude, untowardly man; he married a widow in Shrewsbury, not unlike him in disposition, and yet these two live a very unquiet and ungodly life. This Joseph and his mother joining together, sold their estate in Marton about two years ago, to Richard Groome and Richard Freeman, both of Marton, who divided it between them, and the family of the Wrights is wholly extinct in this parish.

Another share of this seat belongs to Formeston's tenement in Marton; it is the lands of the Earl of Bridgewater. The family of the Formestons have been tenants of it about three or four generations, and is now almost extinct. The first that I can give any account of, was John Formeston. I find that he had two wives; the first was Anne, the second Dorothy. I find that afterwards there was one Thomas Formeston in Marton, who for ought I know, was son to John Formeston. This Thomas Formeston married with Margaret, the daughter of Allen Challoner of Myddle, blacksmith. He had issue four sons, Thomas, Stephen, William, and Samuel; he had a daughter named Susan, who was married to Bartholemew Pierce of Myddle. Besides, I know not whether he had another daughter, who was married to one Nicholas Chaloner, a blacksmith in Wem.

Thomas, the eldest son, was an ironmonger in London, he married there, and had a son named Thomas, who was grown up to man's estate before the plague happened in London, in the time of King Charles I. And when the plague broke out in London, he was sent down to Marton, and afterwards went for a soldier in the wars, temp Car. primi, and died in the wars.

Thomas Formeston, the ironmonger, died of the plague in London. His brother Samuel was with him at the time of his decease, and had the disposing of his estate, for he left no widow.

The next tenant was Stephen, the second son of Thomas. He had a son named Stephen, and a daughter who was married to one Nathaniel Simcocks, who is present tenant of this tenement. This Stephen the younger was never married, but was accounted to live a debauched life among lewd women; and now (viz. about Christmas 1701) a daughter of William Challoner has fathered a bastard on him, and he has fled out of the country. If he return not, this family as to males will be extinct in this parish. I shall have occasion to speak of William Formeston and Samuel hereafter.

CHAPTER 9

And There He And His Loving Wife Spent Their Old Age

The fourth pew adjoining to the south wall belongs to Tyler's tenement in Balderton, Nightingale's in Myddle, and Shaw's in Marton.

I have spoken already of Tyler's family and Nightingale's.

Shaw's tenement is the Earl of Bridgewater's lands. It was formerly held by the family of the Ashes. Richard Ash, the first that I can give any account of, had several daughters, and one son named Thomas. This Thomas Ash was a proper, comely person; his father gave him good country education, which, with the benefit of a good natural wit, a strong memory, a courteous and mild behaviour, a smooth and affable way of discourse, an honest and religious disposition, made him a complete and hopeful young man, insomuch as Mr. Edward Hanmer, of Marton, was easily induced to give him his daughter Elizabeth to wife. This was a very suitable match, for she was a lovely, proper gentlewoman, and so like to her husband in disposition, that it should seem there was a sympathy in nature between them, and therefore they lived a loving and comfortable life together. This Thomas Ash was not so much blamed for being too nice in observing the canons, as he called them, of the first counsel of the apostles at Jerusalem, in abstaining from blood and things strangled, as he was commended for avoiding that abominable sin of profane swearing. For this Thomas Ash was much in debt; but how it was contracted I cannot say, unless he was charged with the payment of portions to his sisters, and I doubt he had but little portion with his wife; however he bore an honest mind, and was willing to pay every man, and to that end he set his tenement to Edward Payne of Meriton, for raising of money to pay debts; and to shelter himself from the fatigue of duns, he listed himself soldier in the king's service in the wars, tempore Car. I, and continued a soldier until the king's forces were utterly dispersed, but never attained to any higher post than a corporal of foot. At his return, he brought nothing home but a crazy body and many scars, the symptoms of the dangerous service which he had performed, and besides, he found little of his debts paid, for the payment of taxes and charges of repairs had taken up most part of the rent; but he being minded that none should lose by him, sold his lease to William Formeston. He had some money to spare when he had satisfied his debts, and with that he took a lease off Mr. Crosse of Yorton, of several pieces of ground near Yorton Heath, and there he built a little warm house, made a neat little garden, planted a pretty orchard, built several out-houses, and made everything very handsome and convenient, and there he and his loving wife spent their old age, though not in a plentiful, yet in a peaceable and contented condition. There was but little space between the time of their deceases.

William Formeston, the third son of Thomas Formeston, as I said before, married with Alice, the daughter of Roger Jukes, who was tenant, under the Earl of Bridgewater, of a cottage near Houlston, but in the township of Myddle, where the family of the Jukes's had been tenants for many descents, and now this cottage came to William Formeston, by marriage; he was a weaver by trade, but when he had bought Ashe's lease he sold this to Bartholomew Peirce, of Myddle, who gave it by will to his youngest son, Nicholas Peirce, who now dwells in it.

William Formeston had three sons, Thomas, William, and John, and a daughter, named Margaret, who was married to William Challoner of Myddle, cooper. She was suspected to be but a light housewife, but never openly defamed; but she left three daughters, two of which are as impudent whores as any in this country; one of them has two bastards, and she being run out of the country, they are both maintained by the parish. The other is now (Jan. 20, 1701) great with a bastard, and at Christmas last was sent by order into Wem parish, where her last service and settlement was. She has fathered it on Stephen Formeston, her uncle's son, and he has fled.

John Formeston is an husbandman, and some sort of a gardener. He lives near Wikey, in the Eleven Towns.

William, the second son, was a hatter, but such an insatiable drunkard, that although he is a good workman, and was set up several times by his father, yet he still spent all, and sold his tools, and hardly keeps clothes on his back.

Thomas, the eldest son of William Formeston, succeeded his father as a tenant of this place; he married the widow of old Shaw of Stanwardine in the fields; she was a harmless and almost helpless woman, but he had a great fortune with her. She had a son by old Shaw named Thomas Shaw, to whom his father left a considerable fortune or portion, but Thomas Formeston got it all into his own hands, and while it lasted he lived very high. He put Thomas Shaw an apprentice to William Watson, a tailor in Myddle Wood, and this Shaw married William Watson's sister. But when Thomas Shaw came to age, money was wanting to pay his portion, and Thomas Formeston sold his lease to Shaw, and with a pretty good stock of cattle went to a farm near Oswestry called Corduga, which was formerly the lands of Mr. Baker, of Sweeney, but was sold to Edward Lloyd of Leaton. But when Formeston had stayed there about one year, all his effects were seized upon for rent, and he removed to Oswestry and sold ale there. But when he was so much in debt there that he could be trusted no longer, he fled to London and left his wife behind him. Thomas Shaw took her to Marton and maintained her during her life; and now Thomas Shaw is tenant of this tenement, and lives upon it in good fashion.

The fifth pew adjoining to the south wall

in Myddle Church belongs to James Fewtrell's tenement in Brandwood, to Noneley's tenement there, and to Taylor's tenement by the side of Divelin Lane.

James Fewtrell's tenement is the land of the Earl of Bridgewater; it was formerly held by the family of the Pickstockes, which was an ancient family in this parish, and of such repute that Mr. Chambre of Burleton (father of Mr. Arthur Chambre now living) took a daughter of this family to wife. The last of the Pickstockes was Richard Pickstocke, who married with the daughter of one Luskin, or Lovekin, a tanner in Tylley. This Lovekin had a copyhold estate in Tylley; his house stood near Wem Mill, for the township of Tylley goes to Wem mill wheel. He had only two daughters who were co-heirs to this copyhold, and Pickstocke married the eldest, and soon after died, and left her a young widow, and left no child behind him; and thus that ancient family was extinct in this part of Myddle parish; howbeit there is one Richard Pickstocke, who lives in Haston, whose father Seth Pickstocke was a younger brother of this family. About this time, Samuel Formeston, the youngest son of Thomas Formeston, of Marton, who was a glover by trade, was newly come from London, because of the plague. He was a swaggering brave young man and a crafty subtle person. He gained the love of this widow, and married her, which so displeased the younger sister, that she would not come near them; but the elder sister died not long after and left no child behind her, and then Margaret, the younger sister, who was so discontented with her sister for loving and marrying Samuel Formeston, was content to marry with him herself, which soon after was done. This Samuel Formeston enfranchised the copyhold lands of his wife in Tylley. He enlarged his tenement in Brandwood by the addition of two pieces of land called the High Hursts, which are the lands of the Earl of Bridgewater. These two pieces were formerly in lease to my greatgrandfather, who gave the lease of them to his second son, my uncle John Gough, and he took a new lease of them, and put in the lives of his son Richard, his daughter Mary, and my life (I suppose his daughter Elizabeth was not then born), but when my uncle John Gough had purchased his farm in Besford, he sold this lease to Richard Nightingale of Myddle, and not long after Richard Nightingale sold this lease to Samuel Formeston, who to make all sure renewed the lease and put in three lives of his own naming, viz. his own, his wife's, and his daughter Margaret; but he might have spared that money, for I and my cousin Mary are yet living, and his money was laid out abouty fifty years ago; and although two of the lives of his naming are yet living, yet one of them is about twenty years older than either of us. Besides, this Samuel Formeston about twenty years (for a sum of money) exchanged his own life for his sons, but his son died before him and so that money was lost. This Samuel Formeston had only one son, named Samuel (he lived to a man's estate and was an ingenious hopeful young man, but he died unmarried) and five daughters; Elizabeth who married with Francis Bayley, of Ellesmere, a tanner; Mary who married with Thomas Moore, of Myddle; Margaret who married James Fewtrell; Ellenor who was married to one Davies, of West Franckton, and he dying, she is now married to Samuel, the son of Captain Heneage, and sells ale in Ellesmere; Martha is married to John Jones, an attorney in B. R., he is now town clerk, or deputy town clerk of the corporation of Oswestry.

James Fewtrell, a younger brother of the ancient and substantial family of the Fewtrells of Easthope, by the marriage of Margaret, came to be tenant of this place, and so continues, but he has no child. *Note*, that the name of the Formestons is extinct in this parish, unless Stephen Formeston, whom I named before, does return.

Noneley's tenements (for now it is parted in two) did formerly belong to Bickley's tenement in Brandwood. It is the Earl of Bridgewater's land. There was one Bickley, whose name was Morgan, if I mistake not, who was charged with the payment of portions to two of his sisters; and being unable to raise money, he gave them some part of the lands of his tenement during his lease. The sisters divided it, and one of them married with one Illage; she had an ancient house upon her part. The other was married to one Serjeant, and he built a little house on his part, and after sold his part to Illage, who took a new lease of both parts, and made it one tenement. Illage after many years sold his lease to Thomas Noneley a younger brother of the family of the Noneleys, of Noneley; he married a daughter of one Tyler of Sleape, a freeholder of about £60 per annum, out of which lands in Sleape Mr. Gittins, the vicar, has a small yearly chief rent, but by what title or what cause I could never find. This Thomas Noneley was a cross, quarrelsome, and troublesome man among his neighbours, and therefore not well beloved. He lived pretty well in his wife's time, though he was then much given to drinking. But after his wife's decease he went all to nought, and was so far in debt that he was laid in jail and set his tenement, and his poor children were forced to trust to themselves, and work for their living. He was so poor in jail that he wanted clothes and meat, and therefore, to get a little money, he was hired to be hangman at the execution of Thomas Parbott of Franckton, who was hanged, though some say wrongfully, for the barbarous murder of a day labourer, at Marchamley. This was a disgrace to Noneley and his family ever after. Whether he died in prison, or was let out for pity, I cannot tell, but sure I am that he died very poor.

Thomas Noneley had two sons, Arthur and Francis; besides I know not whether he had a son called Richard, but I know not what came of him. He had three daughters, Joanne and Rachel, who married a baker in Shrewsbury, and another who was married to a man at Crosse Greene. Joanne was married to John Hill, a chandler in Wellington; she had no child, and they lived in pretty good condition. After the death of Thomas, this Hill being in possession at Brandwood, sought to take a lease of this tenement, but Arthur having married a wife whose maiden name was Rider, descended of a good but a decayed family in Montgomeryshire; and having many children, the parish took a lease for him of that house and land which did formerly belong to Serjeant; the parish paid the fine. John Hill took a lease of the other part and so it became two small tenements again. John, the son of Arthur, now lives in the one; and John Hill, his wife being dead, lives in the other house. But James Fewtrell holds the ground and maintains the old man, which I reckon is almost done of charity. Francis, the youngest son of Thomas Noneley, was servant in husbandry many years, but towards his later days he lived hereabouts and worked here about at day labour, and at harvest last he had been mowing for Mathew Win of Petton, and as he came homewards in the evening, and his cousin Thomas Noneley with him, when he was almost come to Burleton, he was taken with such an illness, that he could go no further, but desired his cousin to fetch a horse and bring him home. Some neighbours came to him, and he told them he was a dead man; he was taken by the way, and so at Burleton towns end, not far from the Smyth's shop, he died before his cousin could come with a horse.

Taylor's tenement is the Earl of Bridgewater's land. The information that I had from Abraham Taylor, the late tenant of this place, is this. When Divlin Wood was first enclosed, there was a considerable part of it left common on each side of the common way that leads between Myddle and Burleton, and that one Abraham Taylor took a lease of this waste or common ground, by the name of Divlin Lane, and built a house upon it and enclosed several pieces, leaving a sufficient lane or passage for a road. I do remember one long piece enclosed by the side of the road. This Abraham Taylor that took the lease had two sons, Henry and Richard. This son Richard was a tailor, and so famous in that trade, that he was of good repute in his time, and that he had much custom, and lived in a handsome condition; he lived in Loppington, and had one son very unlike in morals to his father, for the son was an idle drunken fellow, and for debt and some petty misdemeanours was compelled to leave his country.

Henry, the eldest son, was a weaver, and married Rose, the daughter of William Wagge, of Myddle Wood, carpenter, and during his wife's life he lived in some tolerable condition, but after her decease, he let loose the reins to such extravagant courses, that he soon spent his estate, and then hired himself as a servant in husbandry with Mr. Gittins of Myddle. This was before the wars, in the reign of King Charles I, at which time it was accounted a creditable employment to be a soldier in the county militia, and therefore many persons that were maintainers, did themselves serve as soldiers; and among the rest, Mr. Richard Gittins, father of Mr. Thomas Gittins, Vicar of Loppington, did trail a pike under Captain Corbett of Albright Hussey: but when the wars broke out, the maintainers hired others to serve in their stead, and Mr. Gittins hired this Henry Tayler at what time Sir William Brereton had made a garrison for the parliament at Nantwich, and when the militia for this county, and several new raised dragoons, were called together to attack Nantwich, this Henry Taylor marched with them. The army quartered all night at Whitchurch, and Sir William Brereton having notice of it, sent a party of horses to beat up their quarters, who came upon them in their beds and easily scattered them, and this Henry Tayler going out at a back door found a harrow under the wall, and taking it on his back, passed by the soldiers unsuspected and when he had carried the harrow about a mile, and saw that he was out of danger, he laid down the harrow and came home.

Henry Taylor had two sons, Thomas, who died in the wars, and Abraham, who was a tailor by trade. This Abraham was tenant of this tenement after his father, and had by his first wife Thomas, who married the daughter of James Chidley, and lives now in Chidley's tenement (of which hereafter) and a daughter named Mary, who went to London.

Abraham Taylor, by a second wife, had a son named John, and a daughter named Elizabeth; she married with Rowland Stanway, a widower, soon after the death of his first wife. This Stanway and his wife became poor in a short time, and Abraham Taylor gave them a piece of ground of this tenement during his lease, on which this Stanway built a little dwelling-house, and there lived and died; and here is to be noted that a daughter of this Rowland Stanway, which he had by his first wife, lived as a servant in Wem, at what time a very violent fever raged there, and coming homesick, although she recovered, yet her father, Rowland Stanway, caught the fever and died, and Abraham Taylor and his wife coming often to visit him, got the fever and both died; and John Taylor, their son, coming to see them in their sickness, fell sick and died. These four died all in about one month's space, about two or three years ago, and now Elizabeth, the widow of this Roland Stanway, is tenant of this tenement. She married with a Samuel Hordley, A.D. 1706, but had one bastard, if not more, before she married.

The sixth seat adjoining to the south wall

in Myddle church belongs to my ancient tenement in Newton, of which I have spoken before: and to Mansel's tenement in Myddle, of which I have likewise spoken before; and there was a house or cottage in Myddle wherein one John Lloyd lived. The tenants of this cottage did usually sit in this seat, but whether of right or by leave I know not: but I have heard that it was by leave. This cottage stood upon the lands of the Lloyds of Myddle, and was built for John Lloyd, a younger brother of that family, who was a weaver, and after him William Vaughan, a weaver, and Adam Dale, a mason, dwelt both together in this cottage. This William Vaughan was a Welshman, and was a soldier several years under King Charles I. He had a sister, named Margaret, who came into this country to be a servant to Mr. Kinaston, Rector of Myddle, and was married to Francis Cleaton, eldest son of William Cleaton, of the Hollins, and this brought William Vaughan into this parish. He was never married. He had a brother, named Reece or Eavan, I know not whether; and was a soldier, and killed in the wars.

Adam Dale was born at Cheswardine, in Staffordshire; he was apprentice with Michael Wright, a freemason, and an excellent workman. Adam was an honest, laborious man, but not so good a workman as his master. He was married, and had one son, named Adam, who died before he came to maturity. Afterwards Thomas Forster, a weaver, dwelt in this cottage. The house is now pulled down; it stood near the Parsonage House, in the yard that is now enclosed with a stone wall; and since a seat in church belongs to a house and not to land, I conceive this kneeling (although it were of right) cannot be claimed by Mr. Lloyd.

The seventh seat adjoining to the south wall of Myddle Church

belongs to vicar Gittins's tenement in Newton, to Wolph's tenement in Myddle, to Morice's tenement in Marton, and to Highway's cottage in Myddle. Mr. Gittins's tenement in Newton was formerly the land of that ancient and worthy family of the Banasters, of Hadnall. Roger Gough, who was brother to my greatgrandfather's father, had a lease of this tenement for his life and the life of Guen his wife: they had no child, and after the expiration of this lease, Mr. Gittins of Myddle, purchased it. The first tenant that Mr. Gittins had here was one Chidley, a weaver, who was married, but had no child. This Chidley, in his later days, was distracted, and would walk abroad all night, making a noise and complaining of taxes and tallages, when perhaps he had less need than is now. I can remember his widow living in a little house in Newton that had no chimney; but Mr. Gittins built a better house upon this tenement, and set it to Richard Preece, son of Griffith Ap Reece, of Newton; he after some years, removed to Broughton, and one John Bennion, a tailor, lived in it. He married Elizabeth, the daughter of John Hall, alias Dudleston, of Myddle; and soon after went for a soldier and died in the wars. After him John Trevor was tenant of it; he was son of Francis Trevor, a younger brother of the family of the Trevors of Rushley, who married the daughter of William Smith, of Acton Reynold. This Francis was a drunken, debauched person, but his wife was a quiet, modest, laborious woman, and this John Trevor imitated his mother's morals. He married a wife, whose name was Anne, but had no child by her; they were both prudent and laborious people, and lived well. After her death he married a servant of Mr. Richardson, Rector of Myddle; her name was Sarah. He died before her, and afterwards she married one John Powell, a Welshman, who pretended to have some skill in chirurgery. Mr. Gittins being informed that this Powell had some fanatical opinions, would not admit him to be his tenant, and therefore he took his wife into Wales, and now lives at a place called Treverclodd, which is two miles beside Oswestry. Afterwards Andrew Paine, son of Edward Paine, of Merrington, took this tenement and now lives in it. But yet I must say something of the tenants of the house wherein Anne Chidley lived; for after her decease Richard Clarke, of whom I have spoken at large before, built a chimney in this house, and held only the house and garden: while he was a quaker he buried several of his children, and I think one of his wives in this garden. He had one quaker's meeting at this house, but few if any of the neighbours went to hear them. When he removed to Myddle, Thomas Davis, a weaver, who now lives at the Wood Lesows by Myddle Wood, came to be tenant to it. Of him I have spoken before, but somewhat I must say of his wife: Margaret, the wife of Thomas Davis, died on the 17th day of this instant, January, 1701. She took cold in child-bearing, above twenty years before her death; she was seized thereby with pain and lameness in her limbs, and made use of several remedies for curing thereof, but all proved ineffectual. At last, as she was in an apothecary's shop buying ointments and ingredients for fomentations my uncle, Mr. Richard Baddely, an able chirurgeon, saw her and asked her how she got her lameness: she said by taking cold in child-birth. Then says he spare this charge and labour, for all the doctors and surgeons in England cannot cure it. Thou may live long, but thy strength will still decay. After this she went to little more charges, only when King James II came his progress to Shrewsbury, she was admitted by the king's doctors to go to his majesty for the touch, which did her no good. She was forced to use crutches almost 20 years ago, and I think it is now 10 years since she grew so weak that she was fain to be carried in persons' arms. About two-and-a-half years before her death, she kept her bed continually; she was bowed so together, that her knees lay close to her breast; there was nothing but the skin and bones upon her thighs and legs. About a year-and-a-half past, her two thigh bones broke as she lay in bed, and one of them burst through the skin and stood out about an inch, like a dry hollow stick, but there was no flesh to bleed or corrupt; she could stir no part of her body except her head and one of her hands a little. When she was dead they did not endeavour to draw her body straight, but made a wide coffin and put her in as she was. I heard one say that was present at laying her in her coffin, that as they laid her down one of her leg bones broke and gave a crack, like a rotten stick; and it is not to be forgotten that the Vicar Gittins, seeing that Thomas Davis had a great charge of children, and his wife lame upon his hands, did give him his house and garden rent free while he lived in it.

Another seat in this pew belongs to Wolfe's tenement in Myddle, of which tenement and the tenants thereof I have spoken before. I shall only add here, that I have not observed any tenant of that place sit in that pew since the death of Richard Wolfe; and I believe the reason was because, first, Richard Clarke lived in this tenement after Richard Wolfe and this Clarke was an anabaptist, and then a quaker, and at last a papist, but all the while I know not what but he never came to church. After that Mr. William Hollway, Rector of Myddle, took a lease of this tenement, and one Michael Braine, Jnr. was his sub-tenant, who because his father who lived in Myddle, had a better seat in church did usually sit there, and now this Michael Braine being dead, his widow (when she comes to church) sits in another pew wherein there is a kneeling belonging to this tenement.

Another seat in this pew belongs to Morrice's tenement or cottage in Marton, which formerly was the lands of Lloyd Pierce, Esq., and was purchased by Thomas Acherley, and now belongs to his son Andrew Acherley. There was one Holland who was formerly tenant to it who had a lease of it for his own life, and his wife's life, and the life of his daughter, whose name I think was Margery. This daughter was married to one Thomas Morrice, a millwright, and they had one daughter who married Arthur, the son of Andrew Davis of Marton. The house that belonged to this tenement stood a little distant from the lane or street in Marton which leads by Mr. Acherley's house, in a yard that lies between Marton Town Meadow and Mr. Acherley's barns. When the wife of Thomas Morrice died which was about three years ago, Andrew Acherley pulled down the house and set it up again by the side of the lane that leads from Marton to

Burleton, and there Arthur Davies and his wife are now living and do maintain Thomas Morrice who is very aged and blind if not deaf.

Another seat in this pew belongs to Challoner's cottage, now Highway's, in Myddle. It is the Earl of Bridgewater's land. The house stands over against the east side of Myddle churchyard; it was built for a smith's house and shop on a waste place by the side of Myddle Street; the garden and orchard adjoining to it are very small, but there are two pieces that were taken out of Myddle Wood now belonging to it; one of them is near to the Clay lake at the upper end of Myddle town, and a barn is built upon it for there is no convenient room to build a barn at the house. The first tenant of this cottage that I can give any accompt of was Allen Challoner, a blacksmith, and perhaps it was built by him. He had two sons, Richard and George and a daughter named Margery, who was married to Thomas Formeston of Marton. George was a blacksmith and succeeded his father as tenant of this cottage; Richard was a cooper of whom I hope to speak when I come to the next pew.

George Challoner married Elleanor, the sister of William Tyler, of Balderton; he had issue by her, Richard and Allen. This Richard was an untowardly liver, very idle and extravagant, endeavouring to supply his necessities rather by stealing than by his honest labour. He was bound over to appear at the assizes for stealing a cow from one of his kinsmen: the owner was bound to prosecute, but his uncle William Tyler told the prosecutor that this Challoner was his kinsman, and it would be a disgrace to him as well as to the rest of his friends to have him hanged, and that his friends would raise £5 among them to pay for the cow in case he would forbear the prosecution. To this the prosecutor agreed; he received the £5. He preferred no bill and Challoner was quit by proclamation; but soon after William Tyler threatened the prosecutor that he would ruin or hang him for taking a bribe to save a thief, and by this menacing caused the prosecutor to pay back the £5 to Tyler. This Richard Challoner, was vehemently suspected by Thomas Acherley, of Marton, concerning an attempt to rob him. This Thomas Acherley, grandfather to Andrew Acherley that now is, was a tanner and used Oswestry market constantly and brought much money thence; and as he was coming homewards in the night he found the gate at the old mill brook, near Marton, made fast, and as he stooped to open it he saw a man with a club staff arise out of the hedge and offer a blow at him, but the horse starting, Thomas Acherley escaped the blow and he rode away and escaped. He often declared it was this Challoner that offered to strike him.

Allen, the younger son of George, was a blacksmith and good workman; he married Margaret, sister of Thomas Pickerton, of Loppington, and had one daughter named Margaret, who married with Thomas Highway, who was born in or near the parish of Wroxeter; he is now tenant of this cottage and parish clerk of Myddle.

The eighth pew adjoining the south wall

in Myddle church has a post in it that bears a beam, which goes over across the church. This pew belongs to Jones' tenement in Marton, to Parker's tenement in Myddle Wood, to William Challoner's tenement in Myddle Wood, and unless I mistake there is a share in this pew belonging to John Horton's tenement in Myddle. The tenement in Marton was formerly the lands of Mr. Corbett, of Stanwardine: one Jones, a butcher, was tenant of it; he had two sons, Francis and Richard. This Richard was bred up to husbandry; he married and lived some while in this parish, and after lived at a place called the Meare Banke in Baschurch parish, and I think died there. Francis went to be a servant at Stanwardine Hall when he was but young; he continued there a menial servant above 30 years, and after he was married he belonged to the family whilst he was able to do service, but his wife lived at Marton. He was somewhat serviceable to gentlemen in anything that they could employ him in as a serving man. He was butler many years; he had skill in fishing, fowling, hawking, hunting, making of setting dogs, and was somewhile keeper of Stanwardine Park; in some he was one at everything and good or excellent at nothing. He married with Anne, the sister of one Thomas Giles of Cockeshutt, and had issue, Thomas, Elizabeth, and Letice. This Letice was married to Richard Menlove, who happened by the death of his uncle Mr. William Menlove, of Aston, near Wem, to become heir to a copyhold estate of about £60 per annum, in Aston. But he immediately upon the death of his uncle sued for the estate while the widow was living, and so brought himself in debt and sold it to Richard Corbett, of Moreton Corbett, Esq. Elizabeth was married to the son of George Higginson of Wem; she now lives in a cottage on Myddle Wood. Thomas was a butcher, and married Anne, the daughter of George Ralphs of Marton; he died about middle age and left many children behind him. After the decease of Francis Jones, Mr. Thomas Corbett sold this tenement to Richard Groome of Marton, who built a new house upon it, and now one Hugh Pritchard is tenant of it.

Parker's tenement is a house on Myddle Wood, which stands by the side of that way which goes on the south side of Myddle Wood, and leads from Myddle to Marton; it is the Earl of Bridgewater's land; and was formerly held by one John Wagge, a carpenter, who as it is thought built this house and enclosed some pieces out of Myddle Wood, and made it a small tenement. His son William Wagge who was also a carpenter, was tenant of this place after him. This William Wagge had many daughters, one of which was married to William Parker, who thereby came to be tenant of this place; he was a person that affected to be accounted somebody in this parish, and therefore procured to be made bailiff of this manor. He also had a great desire to be made churchwarden of this parish, which at last he obtained. It was said that he gave a side of bacon to Robert Moore, to the end he would persuade his brother the rector to choose him churchwarden, and afterwards he made that year the epoch of his computation of all accidents, and would usually say such a thing was done so many years before or after the year that I was churchwarden. He has a son named Thomas and a daughter named Elizabeth. She was married to one Dyas, a weaver, who came from the Long Oake in the Eleven Towns; he lived somewhile at Myddle Wood, and afterwards returned to his own neighbourhood. Thomas was a carpenter, and a very ingenious workman; he went over into Ireland in the close of the wars, temp. Car. I, and after some years returned and sold his lease of this place to one Richard Rogers and went back into Ireland. Richard Rogers is a tailor, he came when he was a young man into this parish and took a chamber with Francis Jones of Marton, and worked in this neighbourhood. He married a wife and lived in Mr. Gittins's house at the higher well in Myddle. He removed thence to Petton, and there his first wife died and he married a daughter of Michael Braine, of Myddle, who was a widow and had formerly been wife to Robert Davies, born in Hadnall Wood in this parish. She died some years after and then he married Elizabeth Astley; she was daughter of one Robert Fardoe who lived some time in Burleton, and after in Myddle. She was married first to one Thomas Jones, then to Ralph Astley, and after his death to this Richard Rogers. She is also dead and he has sold his title to one William Willetts. But here I confess I have made a mistake for I find that the seat belonging to this tenement is in the pew next above this, and because I see that I have named so many persons to have shares in the seventh pew

I doubt I am mistaken there, and I make a query whether the seat belonging to Wolfe's tenement be not in the sixth pew; but I am confident that a share in this eighth seat belongs to William Challoner's tenement in Myddle Wood. This is the Earl of Bridgewater's land, and was enclosed out of that part of Myddle Wood which lies towards Marton, and is called the Hooke of the Wood. There was one Richard Challoner of Myddle, a cooper, he was son of Allen Challoner, blacksmith, he married Katrine, daughter of Richard Wolfe of Myddle; I suppose he enclosed this tenement and built the house. He had a cottage in Myddle which Edward Baxter now lives in (of which hereafter).

Richard Challoner had a son named Allen who was tenant of this tenement. His wife's name was Jane. He had a son named William and two daughters, Joan and Elizabeth, I cannot tell whether he had more daughters. Joan was married to William Cleaton of Hollins; Elizabeth was married to Stephen Price of Burleton, a blacksmith. William married Margaret, daughter of William Formestone of Marton; he had issue, three daughters. Margaret who was married to Edward Baxter. Elizabeth and Joan are very lewd women, they were a great grief to their father; some say their ill ways broke his heart, he was very aged and dim-sighted if not blind; he died January the 18th, 1701, in which week three aged persons died in this parish. This William Challoner died on Sunday; Anne, the wife of John Groome of Houlston, died on Monday, she was very old and had been blind and deaf many years; Margaret, the wife of Thomas Davies, died on Friday, she had been lame above twenty years, but of her I have spoken before. William Challoner before his death sold his lease to Stephen Price aforesaid who is now tenant of it.

The ninth pew adjoining to the south wall

belongs to Hordley's tenement in Myddle, Edge's tenement in Marton, Ralphe's tenement in Marton, and Blacke Evan's tenement in Marton. Of Hordley's family I have spoken before.

Edge's tenement is the Earl of Bridgewater's land; it is a small thing and lies between Marton and Petton, near a place called the Rowlands. It was formerly held by the family of the Edges, and thereof got that name; but this family being extinct in this parish, Thomas Acherley, late of Marton, took a lease of it, and gave it to his youngest son Richard at marriage, and now Mr. Thomas Harwood, a grocer in Shropshire, who married the widow of this Richard Acherley, is tenant of it, but he has parted with it to one Edward Price, a miller who lives is 1706.

Ralphe's tenement is the Earl of Bridgewater's land, and has been held for several ages by the family of the Ralphes, which is very ancient in this parish. The first that I will mention is John Ralphe, who in the year 1591, married Anne, the daughter of John Wagge, of Myddle Wood, carpenter, and had issue by her, four sons John, George, Richard and Andrew. This Andrew was servant to Sir Edward Kinaston of Oatley, but he was such a proud conceited fellow that he was not beloved by his fellow-servants and was derided by other gentleman's servants. He married the daughter of one Bernard Allen, a cooper, who dwelt at Newton and Spoonhill, near Ellesmere; she was a papist and by her persuasion he became of that opinion.

Richard, the third son, was some time parish clerk of Myddle as I said before. He had two wives, and daughters by both of them; his last wife is yet living, her name is Elleanor; she can knit very well, and thereby gets her maintenance.

George, the second son, was a carpenter; he had a son, named John, who now lives in Edge's tenement of which I spoke before, and a daughter named Anne who was sometime servant to the Lord of Powes, and there she became a papist. At her return she was married to Thomas, the son of Francis Jones, of Marton; and had many children by her; one of them is set out apprentice by the parish. After the death of Thomas Jones she went to be servant to Madam Clifford of Lea Hall, and there she married Nicholas Astley an Irishman and a papist; they both now live in Marton in that tenement which we call Blacke Evan's tenement.

John, the eldest son, had issue, John who succeeded his father and is now tenant of this place; he is a peaceable man, but he has imbibed some fanatical opinions, and comes not to church.

Blacke Evan's tenement is Mr. Acherley's land; it was held by one Evan Jones who was called Blacke Evan, because there was another Evan Jones who lived in Myddle Wood, and him they called Evan Soundsey. After Blacke Evan, one Thomas Groome, a quaker, lived in this tenement many years; he was son to Thomas Groome of Fennimeare, who was brother to my grandmother and married the daughter of one Peter Trevor a wealthy farmer in Fennimeare. This Thomas Groome, the younger, married the sister of one Thomas Hole of Weston, who was a quaker; he died not many years ago, and now Nicholas Aston lives in this tenement.

The tenth pew adjoining to the south wall

belongs to Watson's tenement, in Myddle Wood, Thomas Davis' cottage in Marton, Baxter's cottage in Myddle, and Childlow's tenement or cottage in Myddle.

Watson's tenement is the Earl of Bridgewater's land, and was taken out of Myddle Wood common. One Roger Mould was formerly tenant of it. Roger Mould had three sons Thomas, John, and William, and a daughter named Sarah. Thomas was cook many years to Mr. Baker, of Sweeney. He married a wife at Weston Rin near Sweeney, and there died.

John was groom of the stable to Mr. Barker. He married the dairymaid, and went to live in Whittington and there he died.

William was a hatter but I can give no further account of him. Sarah married William Watson, a tailor, who thereby came to be tenant of this place; he had issue, William and Francis, and a daughter who is married to Thomas Shaw of Marton. Francis married Hannah, widow of Richard Guest of the township of Myddle. William is a tailor, and married a daughter of Thomas Mould, of whom I spoke before.

Thomas Davis' cottage in Marton was the lands of Lloyd Peirce, Esq. and is now Mr. Acherley's. It was held by one Thomas Clare and after by his son Roger Clare who had five or six daughters; and one Thomas Davis, a weaver, born in the parish of St. Martin, married one of Clare's daughters (I think her name was Dorothy) and thus he became tenant of this place. Of these two persons Thomas Davis and his wife hath proceeded such a numerous offspring in this parish, that I have heard some reckon up, taking in wives and husbands, no less than sixty of them and the greater part of them have been chargeable to the parish. Many great families in this parish have been extinct, but this has got so many branches that it is more likely to overspread it . . .

Baxter's cottage is the Earl of Bridgewater's, it was held by that family of the Challoners who where coopers of which I have spoken already. This Edward Baxter married Margaret, the eldest daughter of William Challoner and so came to be tenant of it. One thing I may add, that Allen Challoner the cooper, lived most part of his time at the tenement in Myddle Wood, and did set this cottage in Myddle to one Thomas Pickeren who sold ale. He had a son Richard and a daughter named Joan. Richard was a laborious man; he went to London and was servant to a refiner of silver and lived in good fashion. Joan was third wife to Francis Trevor, a younger brother of that ancient family of the Trevors of Fennimeare; he lived in Haremeare lodge and had four sons by her William, Francis, Thomas, and Richard; what became of the two first I know not. But Thomas was married and lived at Haston; he died some years since, and left a widow and a son behind him. Richard is my tenant and lives in a house by the side of the Old Field Lane. After the decease of old Francis Trevor, his widow married one Arthur Darnell, a strong man and a stout workman; he died before her.

Chidlow's tenement is in the Earl of Bridgewater's land; it is now in lease to Mr. Lloyd of Myddle. One Thomas Chidlow did live in the house, which was then a poor pitiful hut, built up to an old oak, but now it is a better house; it stands near the side of the lane called Divlin Lane formerly, and now Taylor's Lane. This Chidlow had four sons Roger, Thomas, Samuel, and James. Roger lived many years a servant to old Roger Sandford, of Newton, and had laid by some money and married Alice, the daughter of Richard Wolfe, of Acton Reynold, and soon after died. I think he had no child.

Thomas was servant to Rose Hancox, of Broughton, a widow and afterwards married her. After her decease he was husbandman to Captain Corbett of Shawbury Park; he died there, and left most part of his money to his master.

Samuel married Elizabeth Beech of Acton Reynold; she was left fatherless and motherless when she was young, and was set apprentice by the parish of Shawbury to my uncle William Wakely of Acton; she proved a good servant, and lived in that family above twenty years, and was married from thence.

Samuel Chidlow and his wife were both provident and laborious persons, and got an estate in money, and having only one son and one daughter. This Samuel by his last will left £100 to his wife, £100 to his son, and £200 to his daughter. James Chidlow continued tenant of this place after his father. He had only one daughter who was married to Thomas, the eldest son of Abraham Taylor, who is now sub-tenant of this place.

The eleventh pew adjoining to the south wall

is claimed by Daniel Hanmer for his cottage in Myddle Wood, and William Candlin for his cottage in Myddle.

This pew I believe was supernumerary at the uniforming of the seats, and that these cottages got into it and now claim a privilege in it.

This cottage of Hanmer's stands at the south side of Myddle Wood, between the end of the lane that goes from Myddle Wood to Fennimere, and the end of the Lynch Lane. There was one John Ellice, a butcher, who came from Hanmer in Flintshire, into this parish, and dwelt in a little cottage on the south side of Myddle Wood, wherein one Richard Rogers, son of Richard Rogers, a glover, now dwelleth. This John Ellice because he came from Hanmer was called Ellice of Hanmer, and I find both in the court rolls and in the parish register that he is named John Ellice, alias Hanmer. He had three sons, Richard, Thomas, and Abraham, but I know not which of them was eldest. Richard was married and lived some while in the Mearehouse at Haremeare, and afterwards removed to Sanbach forge and was there employed to oversee the coals belonging to the forge and there died. Thomas was brought up to be a good English scholar; he was some while a ploughboy at Acton Hall where my grandfather was then bailiff, but this Hanmer was so cross among the servants that he was turned off, and then kept a petty school at Shawbury; and when he grew to be a man, Mr. Wood who was then Vicar of Shawbury and parson of Cund, employed him to read service at Shawbury when he was at Cund. This Mr. Wood left me £5 by his last will; but what reason he had for it I cannot tell. I remember that I received the money at Shawbury when I was but in side coats: it was put into my hat and I had much to do to bear it. Thomas Hanmer had a son whom he brought up to be a scholar; he was sent to Oxford and was at last made doctor of divinity, and married a wife whose maiden name was Eddowes, of a good family in Cheshire. He was parson of Maurwheale, near Wrexham, a good benefit and he was a good preacher, but lived a troublesome life being always in the law with his parishioners, especially with the Lady Broughton. He died at Maurwheale.

Abraham Hanmer was a litigious person among his neighbours much given to the law. He married Katherine Emry, whose father and ancestors had for a long time been tenants of this cottage that I now speak of and by this means he became tenant of it. He had no child and therefore he took this Daniel, a bastard of his brother Thomas, and brought him up as his child.

Daniel Hanmer married the daughter of Richard Owen, of a place called Gothorns or Goddens, in Yorton township. Of this Richard Owen there is a strange and remarkable story which I will relate because I am sure that it is a certain truth: — This Richard Owen was seized with a violent fever which in a few days deprived him of his reason and understanding but not of his speech, so that he talked anything that came in his fancy and was like a man in a frenzy, so that they had much to do to keep him in bed; but afterwards his sickness brought him so weak that his speech failed and at twelve days end he died, and according to the usual manner he was laid straight upon his bed, his eyes were closed and only one linen sheet cast over him. Thus he continued one whole day whilst his wife was taking care to provide for his burial; she procured her sister Jane Tyldesley of Newton; to bear her company all night for her children were young. These two women sat by the fire all night, and about that time of night which we account cock crowing they heard something give a great sigh, Alice Owen said it was Richard, but Jane Tyldesley would not believe it. They took a candle and went into the chamber and cast the sheet from off his face and perceived no alteration in him. Jane Tyldesley said it was some beast that was on the outside of the house. They took the candle and went round the outside of the house but found nothing. They came and sat again by the fire and soon after heard the same noise again. Then they went to Richard Owen and found him all one as they left him; however they stayed by him and after some time they saw him open his mouth and give a sigh: then they warmed the bed-clothes and laid them upon him; and by that time that it was day the colour came in his face and he opened his eyes on his own accord, and by noon he recovered his speech though very weakly. He continued weak for a long time, but at last recovered his perfect health and strength and lived after this above twenty years.

This makes me remember the saying of that famous Dr. Goddard, who when I was a youth was much conversant and had great practice in this country. He gave that sovereign potion called Goddard's drops. He was used to say that he was confident that many English people were buried alive; for if they had been kept in their warm beds for forty-eight hours many of them would have recovered.

Candlin's cottage is the Earl of Bridgewater's land and was formerly held by John Mathews, a younger brother of the family of the Mathews of the House at the Higher Well in Myddle. He was a cobbler, and having full employment he followed his work constantly and so maintained himself and family. He had two children, John and Anne. She was married to some man beyond Ellesmere. John was of his father's profession; he was commonly called Little John Mathews, he had one daughter named Mary, who was somewhile a servant to Mr. Manwaring of Sleape Hall, and there she married her fellow-servant John Foden, a Cheshire man. These came to live in Mr. Lyster's chief farm in Broughton, where they kept a good stock of cows and a good team of horses with which he carried goods to London; they were in a very thriving condition and had one son named Phillip. But this John Foden died and soon after his widow's stock began to decrease, and then she came to the Redd Bull and there sold ale, and afterwards came to this cottage in Myddle and there she sold ale, and married with one Nathaniel Platt who was son of Daniel Platt, a cobbler in Wem. This Nathaniel Platt was a scholar and taught school in Myddle, and was Rector of Ford, a small benefice of about £6 per annum. Philip Foden was a draughtsman in London, and afterwards married there and became a vintner, but became broke and soon after died; yet after his mother's decease he had taken a new lease of this cottage, and before he died had sold it to a vintner in London, who sold it again to William Candlin, who married a daughter of Richard Challoner of Myddle. This house was burnt not long since.

The twelfth pew adjoining the south wall

is claimed by the tenants of Challoner's cottage, late Clarke's in Myddle Wood. This was a supernumerary pew at the uniforming of the seats, and Richard, the son of Morgan Clarke of Haremeare Hill, who when he had married a daughter of Richard Challoner of Myddle, cooper, built a house on Myddle Wood, and enclosed several pieces to it and got into this seat and so came to claim title to it. He had a son named Richard of whom I have spoken before; he had a daughter who was married to one Richard Challoner of a place called the Brown Heath which lies between Loppington and Franckton. This Challoner after the death of Richard Clark, Snr., came hither, and the son of this Challoner is tenant of it now.

The thirteenth is a small seat at the south door of Myddle Church

It was made by Evan Jones who was called Soundsey Evan, out of some waste planks and boards that were spare at the uniforming of the pews. This Evan Jones was a Welshman. He could speak neither good Welsh nor English; he was servant to Mr. Gittins of Myddle, and married with one Sarah Foulke who was born in Myddle, and built a little hut upon Myddle Wood near the clay lake, at the higher end of the town and enclosed a piece out of the common. This little hut was afterwards burnt, and having a collection made in the parish and neighbourhood he built a pretty good house. He had two sons, Richard and William, and a daughter named Mary. Richard died unmarried. William married with a daughter of one Henry Madox, who was a carpenter and a good workman; he was born in Haston but at that time lived at Myddle, in a little house off Mr. Lloyd's at the higher end of the town. This William built a cottage on Myddle Wood, and enclosed ground to it near the lower end off that which Clarke had formerly enclosed. Mary was married to one Groome and is now a widow and lives in the house that her father built.

Thus I conclude concerning the seats in Myddle church, and the year 1701 . . .

APPENDIX

CERTAIN CASES AND CONTROVERSIES WHICH HAVE HAPPENED BETWEEN THIS PARISH AND OTHER PARISHES

First Case — Myddle v Cardington

Humphrey Beddow, a lame man, was born in the parish of Cardington: he was set apprentice in the same parish to a shoemaker and there served his time; afterwards he came to work journey work in this parish, and married Mary the daughter of Thomas Davis of Haremeare Hill. Note, that at this time 40 days' continuance as an housekeeper, servant or sojourner without disturbance did create a settlement in any parish. Note also that if the parish officers did require any person to avoid out of the parish or to find sureties, this was not accounted a disturbance. But a complaint made to a justice of peace that such a person had come into a parish and was likely to become chargeable to the parish — this complaint was a legal disturbance without taking out a warrant, and the justices' clerks did commonly keep a book and enter all disturbances; but if a warrant were taken out this was a proof of the complaint and disturbance.

After Humphrey Beddow was married, a complaint was made by our parish officers to Francis Thornes, Esq., and a warrant procured which was delivered to George Cranage, who was then constable of Newton. Humphrey Beddow was then sick, but he promised to return into his own parish as soon as he was recovered. His sickness was long, and although it took not away his life yet it took away his work, for I never knew him work afterwards but was an idle beggar all his life after. Humphrey Beddow when he was recovered went to Cardington, his own parish, and was sent back by an order into this parish. We appealed to the sessions; our counsel was Mr. Barret, and theirs was Mr. Harris of Crocketon. We proved that Humphrey Beddow was born in Cardington parish, and there set apprentice and served out his time which was a good settlement. They alleged that he had procured a settlement in Myddle parish by 40 days' residence and longer time. Our warrant of disturbance was lost, and although we could prove that he was disturbed yet we could not prove that it was within the 40 days, and therefore their order was confirmed. This was the first contest that we had and thus we lost it; but thanks be to God we never lost any afterwards.

Second Case — Myddle v Shawbury

This was concerning a young child that was left in the night-time in Mr. Holloway's porch in Myddle. In the morning when the child was found, Mr. Holloway immediately sent for Richard Eaton, then churchwarden, who set the child to be nursed by the week. Mr. Holloway sent also for me and Mr. Acherley of Marton, to come to his house with what convenient speed we could. We met accordingly and Mr. Holloway acquainted us of the accident. All the intelligence that we could have from the neighbours in Myddle was that a poor woman with a young child and a boy of about two or three years old, in a whitish coat with ribbons round about his waist, did lodge in Richard Clarke's barn which we call Wolfe's in Myddle, and that she was gone before morning. Mr. Acherley and I set out immediately to enquire after her; he went towards Oswestry and I went to Shawbury. I happened to meet accidentally with my cousin Anne Newans of Greensell, who upon inquiry told me that a poor woman was delivered of a child about a fortnight ago at a house on the side of Shawbury Heath, and when she had stayed there a week she came to Greensell with her little child and a boy with her in side-coats, and had ribbons about the waist of his coat, and that the young child was baptized at Greensell by Mr. Sugar then minister there, and that some servants of the town gave the woman clothes to wrap her child in; she stayed there a week and (says she) "Yesterday she went away towards your neighbourhood." I went to Greensell and inquired there what clothes were given to this child, and one Gwen who had long time been a servant to William Kay, and was therefore called Gwen Kay, told me that she had given a piece of a green sea apron to wrap the child in. Next day Mr. Acherley and I met at Mr. Holloway's and sent for the nurse and child, and found the piece of a green sea apron about it, and so it was (as they said) when the child was found. The piece of an apron was brought and showed to Gwen, and she owned it to be that which she gave the woman. We sent for a warrant for the overseers of the poor of Shawbury parish, and it was agreed on both sides that all of us should appear at the next sessions which was then very nigh at hand; at which sessions Mr. Harris was counsel for Myddle, and Mr. Richard Whitcombe of Hardwicke (a young counsellor) was counsel for Shawbury parish. We proved that a poor woman was delivered of a child in Shawbury parish, and that she had with her a little boy of about two or three years old in a whitish-coloured coat with ribbons about the waist of the coat. We proved that the same poor woman and her young child and little boy came to Greensell, and that the woman at whose house she was delivered in Shawbury parish, came to visit her while she was at Greensell, and said that she was brought a bed at her house. We proved by Gwen Kay that she gave that woman the piece of a green sea apron which was shown in court; and we proved that the child was wrapped in it when the child was found. Mr. Whitcombe did not gainsay any of this, but began to cast some aspersions on Mr. Barnabas Holloway and his father's maids, for which he received a sharp reprimand by old Mr. Arthur Weaver, father of Mr. Arthur Weaver that now is. The judgment of the whole bench was that this child was born in Shawbury parish, and therefore made an order to remove it thither which was done accordingly. The mother of this child was found out about three years after.

Third Case — Myddle and Preston Gubballs v Thomas Williams

This was concerning Andrew Weston, who had lived some while in Marton, in a tenement of above £10 per annum, under Mr. Thomas Harwood, who married the widow of Richard Atcherley. This Weston being aged, and his wife dead, went to Merrington to Thomas Williams, who had married his daughter and gave him all his goods and cattle on condition he would maintain him during his life. Not long after Thomas Williams's wife died, and Weston became blind, and altogether helpless. Upon this Thomas Williams prevailed with the parish officers of Preston Gubballs to procure an order, and to send his father-in-law, Weston, into the parish of Myddle, being the place of his last settlement, which was done accordingly. Note, that at that time the law was that those persons that would bring an appeal, must appeal at the next quarter sessions held for that place from which the order came; but now the appeal must be made at the next quarter sessions held for the place whither any person is sent by an order. We of the parish of Myddle, appealed at the next quarter sessions held for the town and liberties of Shrewsbury. Francis Berkley of Hadnall, Esq., was our counsel, and Mr. Atkis was counsel for Thomas Williams. We fetched a witness from

Wrexham to prove the bargain between Andrew Weston and his son-in-law Williams; but Mr. Berkley insited upon the statute of the 43rd of the queen, cap. two, whereby it is enacted that the grandfathers, grandmothers, fathers, mothers and children of any poor, lame, blind, etc., being of sufficient ability, shall make such allowance for the maintenance of such poor, etc., as the justices at their quarter sessions shall allow. Here says Mr. Berkley, the grandfather-in-law, the grandmother-in-law, the father-in-law, the mother-in-law, the son-in-law, the daughter-in-law, though they be not named in the statute, yet by the equity of the statute they are obliged, and so it had been resolved in that court and in several other cases which he showed. Mr. Atkis did not gainsay any of this, but he insisted upon these words in the statute, *being of sufficient ability,* and that Thomas Williams was a poor man and not able to do it. To which Mr. Berkley answered that Thomas Williams did hold a tenement of about £16 or £18 per annum, and had a stock upon it (I think it was worth £12), that he had lands in fee simple of about £8 to £10 per annum, and that was worth but £6; that he had lately married a second wife with £100 portion (I think it was £20). Upon this the court resolved that Weston's settlement was in Myddle parish, and that Thomas Williams ought to maintain him. I insisted upon half-a-crown a week, because the parish gave so much; but the court allowed only two shillings weekly to be paid to the overseers of the poor of this parish towards the relief of Andrew Weston; I moved the court for costs, but Mr. Berkley wished me to be quiet when I was well.

Note, that at that time it was not known whether the justices had power to grant costs in such cases as this, but now by a late act it is enacted that for avoiding vexatious removals and frivolous appeals, the justices have power to award costs. When we came out of court we sent for Thomas Williams, and our parish officers threatened to sue him, and he being afraid of a suit desired a meeting at Myddle, and he would compound with us. At the meeting he offered to pay half-a-crown a week for the time that his father-in-law had been here, and he would take him away. This was accepted of and he took the blind man home with him.

Fourth Case — Myddle v Gloucestershire

The younger son of Charles Reve of Myddle Wood, had lived a year and more in Gloucestershire, came privately to his brother's house, in Myddle Wood (for he had got the French pox, and was not able to do service). His brother was not able to maintain him, and because no one else would receive him our officers were forced to give his brother 2s. 8d. a week to harbour and maintain him. Our officers brought him before Mr. Rowland Hunt, and there he declared upon oath that his last settlement was in the parish of ———, in Gloucestershire and there an order was made to bring him. Thither he was sent by water to Gloucester; Faireley of Atcham, the trowman had seven shillings to bring him thither and to maintain him by the way; but one of our parish officers went down to deliver him, and to show the order and leave a copy of it. The Gloucestershire men gave us notice of an appeal at the next sessions at Shropshire. We had intelligence that the Gloucestershire men would allege that Reve had worked by the week for a quarter of a year, and afterwards was hired for the other three-quarters, and that this did not create a settlement. Upon this we sent for a witness out of Gloucestershire, who met us at the sessions, and told us he was present when Reve was hired and that he had worked a quarter of a year by the weeks and afterwards was hired for the whole year, and his year was to begin at the time when he came thither. We had Mr. Thomas Edwards, town clerk of Shrewsbury, for our counsel in this matter, and the others had Mr. William Atkins. When the cause came to hearing, William Atkins desired that their appeal might be continued until the next sessions, and if they did then appeal they would give us new notice and pay 10s. costs. This was granted by the court and we heard no more of them. Some say that Reve died before the next sessions.

Fifth Case — Myddle v Condover

This matter came to hearing at the same sessions with that of Reve. We had the town clerk for counsel, and the officers of Condover had Mr. Wase and Mr. Atkins. The case was thus: — Elizabeth the daughter of Humphrey Beddow was an idle, wanton wench, always following after the soldiers, and at last was with child, and said she was married to one William Gittins, a soldier; she was brought a bed at her mother's on Haremeare Heath, and this Gittins came often to visit her there, and our parish officers watching an opportunity apprehended him and brought him before Mr. Hunt, and there he declared upon oath that he was born in Masbrooke, and that his last settlement was in the parish of Condover, where he had lived one whole year as an hired servant; from whence he went to be a soldier and that he was married to this Elizabeth Beddow, and

Mr. Griffiths of Ruyton was the parson that married them. Hereupon an order was made to send Gittins and his wife and child to Condover, but Gittins ran away that night and then our officers went to Mr. Berkley who made another order (reciting the first order, and that Gittins had fled out of the country) to send the wife and child to Condover. This was done and the officers of Condover appealed at the next sessions; when the cause came to hearing they produced only one witness who was a servant maid in the same house with Gittins while he lived in Condover parish, and she said she heard her master tell him when he came to be hired that he would take him on trial, but she never knew that he was hired, but she confessed that he lived there a year and then went for a soldier. The whole bench (considering the oath of Gittins and the maid's confession that he had lived there one year), agreed that he had a good settlement in Condover parish, and so our order was confirmed; and the officers of Condover took back again the woman and child.

Sixth Case — Myddle v Condover

About two years after this contest the officers of Condover brought this Elizabeth Gittins and her child unto this parish by order of two justices, and by the name of Elizabeth Beddow, for they pretended that she was not married to William Gittins. We appealed at the next quarter sessions, and now we were to prove the marriage of William Gittins and Elizabeth Beddow, and to that end we produced Mr. Griffiths, parson of Ruyton who married them; we produced several persons that were present at the wedding, and we produced the certificate made at the marriage which Mr. Griffiths owned to be his hand. Mr. Wase was our counsel and their counsel was Mr. Fones and Mr. Atkins. At the hearing our former order was read (note, that for the reading of the order our overseer of the poor, William Bickley gave the clerk of the peace a brass shilling which he showed to the court and it was ordered that it should be cut, and it was openly cut in the court. I called for the pieces to be given to Bickley which was not denied). After the reading of our order then the order sent from Condover was read, and then Mr. Arthur Weaver took it in his hand and looking over it desired their counsel to say upon what statute that order was made; but they did not and I believe they could not tell. Mr. Weaver said the order was insufficient, and the whole bench agreeing with him the order was reversed. We gave the woman a shilling to go back to Condover and take her child with her, and so she did and spared us the charge of bringing her thither.

Thus you have seen (in three contests) what great trouble and costs we have been at about this outcome drunken cobler and his family. Although I have not mentioned how we set his son twice apprentice and how he outrun both his masters, we lost our money and he was put in the house of correction; but most of the cause of all this came from the mother, who brought up her children in idleness, and favoured them in their bad courses; and it is no marvel that she was no better, for her mother Sina Davis and her children have for many years been a charge to us. She, viz. Sina Davis was a crafty, idle, dissembling woman, and did counterfeit herself to be lame, and went hopping with a staff when men saw her, but at other times could go with it under her arm, as I myself have seen her, and she had maintenance from the parish many years before she died, but the greatest charge was (and still continues), the relief of her son Andrew, who has been blind from infancy, if not from his birth. He has received from the parish £3 per annum for forty years and more, which comes to above £120, and I doubt not but if all the charges which the parish has sustained upon the account of relieving that family were reckoned up, it would amount to £150.

Seventh Case — Myddle v Wem (1700 and 1701)

This was concerning Nicholas Hampton, who was born in Wem parish, and lived there until he was able to do service as a plough boy, and then was hired as a servant in Myddle parish, for one whole year, and did perform his services during the time; and after the end of that year he went back again into Wem parish, and lived with his mother who was a poor woman, and there he fell lame and unable for service, and had maintenance from the parish eight or nine years.

In the year 1700, the officers of Wem parish procured an order from two justices, and sent Nicholas Hampton into our parish of Myddle. We appealed to the next sessions which was Easter sessions, 1701; at which time Mr. Wase was counsel for us, and Mr. Fones was counsel for Wem parish. At hearing of the cause Mr. Wase confessed the matter of fact as to the year's service, but he said that Nicholas Hampton had (after his settlement in Myddle parish) got a settlement in Wem parish by receiving maintenance for so many years in that parish. Mr. Newton and Mr. Weaver were of opinion that this was tantamount to a notice, but Mr. Clive (who was one of the justices that signed the order for sending Hampton to our parish) was of another opinion. At last Mr. Fones denied that Nicholas Hampton had received any money from the parish of Wem. But his mother was a poor woman and she had maintenance from the parish of Wem; and this they could prove by their parish book for the poor which they had not there to show, and therefore they desired the appeal might be continued until next sessions which was granted, and an order was made that Wem parish should pay twenty shillings costs to Myddle parish, and maintain Nicholas Hampton until next sessions.

At mid-summer sessions, 1701, there was a very small appearance of our parishioners to prosecute our matter, for Mr. Dale was absent and Mr. Watkins was sick, so that the whole concern lay upon me, and one of our officers who was very willing but not able to assist much: besides Mr. Newton and Mr. Weaver on whom we did much depend, were both absent and but very few justices upon the bench, so that Mr. Clive (who only differed from the rest at the former sessions), was chief speaker and sat at cushion. This made the officers and other persons of Wem there present to be more than ordinarily confident of good success. They were about thirteen in number; one of them went home before the hearing of the matter and declared that Nicholas Hampton was settled on Myddle parish. I had a friend that told me it was said among the men of Wem that the sense of the court was for them; when I had considered these things I went to our counsel and desired him to continue on appeal until the next sessions if he could. When the cause was called I saw Wem men look very cheerfully; Mr. Wase our counsel desired that an appeal might be continued until next sessions (pretending the absence of one very material witness), and hoped the worshipful bench would allow us the like kindness as had been allowed to Wem parish at last sessions. This was easily granted, and an order was made that we should maintain Nicholas Hampton till next sessions, and pay fifteen shillings costs: this made the men of Wem look under the weather to see their hopes so suddenly disappointed. At Michaelmas sessions, 1701, both parties had the same counsel and there was a full bench of justices. Mr. Wase (as formerly) pleaded that we confessed the matter of fact, but said that Nicholas Hampton had since then procured a settlement in Wem parish, by receiving money for his maintenance and wearing the parish badge in Wem for many years. Mr. Fones did not produce the parish book which in all likelihood would have proved against him, but pleaded that receiving of money could not create a settlement but paying of money might. That the money was given of charity and hoped their charity should not bring a burden upon them; and the wearing of the badge was only to save the officers harmless from the penalty in the act. Mr. Wase said that before the act was made for wearing badges, the parishioners of Wem parish had caused every one of their poor to wear a P. made of tin. And that they caused this Nicholas Hampton to wear one of them (which was then showed in court) and he said there was then at the giving of that P., no penalty to be inflicted on officers in that case. Mr. Newton said that what money was given by one, two, or a few persons might be accounted charity, but what was given out of the parish leawan, that he did not account charity; for it was what ought by law to be done, and he did not insist so much on the wearing of the badge as the payment of money out of the poor's leawan. Mr. Weaver said this person was born in Wem parish; he came into Myddle parish and there lived one year and then returned unto Wem parish and fell lame: if this person turn vagrant he must be sent to Wem not Myddle. Now when Mr. Clive had heard the sense of these two justices he went off from the bench. Then Mr. Wase desired the judgment of the bench in this matter and they all agreed, nemine contradicente, that the order for removing Nicholas Hampton into this parish shall be reversed.

SUBJECT INDEX